Pollution and the Struggle for the World Product

Pollution and the
Struggle for the World Product

Multinational Corporations, Environment,
and International Comparative Advantage

H. JEFFREY LEONARD
The Conservation Foundation

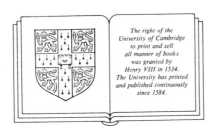

*The right of the
University of Cambridge
to print and sell
all manner of books
was granted by
Henry VIII in 1534.
The University has printed
and published continuously
since 1584.*

CAMBRIDGE UNIVERSITY PRESS

Cambridge

New York   New Rochelle   Melbourne   Sydney

Published by the Press Syndicate of the University of Cambridge
The Pitt Building, Trumpington Street, Cambridge CB2 1RP
32 East 57th Street, New York, NY 10022, USA
10 Stamford Road, Oakleigh, Melbourne 3166, Australia

First published 1988

Printed in the United States of America

Library of Congress Cataloging-in-Publication Data
Leonard, H. Jeffrey.
Pollution and the struggle for the world product: multinational
corporations, environment, and international comparative advantage
H. Jeffrey Leonard.
p.   cm.
Includes index.
ISBN 0 521 34042 X
1. Industrialization – Environmental aspects.   2. Pollution.
3. International business enterprises.   4. Comparative advantage
(Commerce)   I. Title.
HD75.6.L46   1988
338.6'042 – dc19   87–17766
CIP

British Library Cataloguing in Publication applied for

Contents

Tables

Preface

Economic historians may well look back on the last quarter of the twentieth century as marking the decline of the pattern of world trade and industrial production that had been the hallmark of the two previous centuries – the international division of labor under which a small number of core manufacturing countries accounted for an overwhelming percentage of global industrial production and a large number of periphery or developing countries provided raw materials and simple primary products to feed the industrial economies. This transition has been set in motion by a number of interactive forces, including

the ascendence of increasingly stateless multinational corporations bent on maximizing profits and minimizing production costs through the integration of global production units,

the internationalization of investment capital and financial markets,

the emergence of a new wave of rapidly industrializing nations in the periphery, and

the evolution toward "postindustrial" economies that has commenced in the United States, Japan, and a few countries of Europe.

In the midst of these forces – trying to shape, cope with, and stave off their impacts – stand the nearly two hundred individual nation-states that constitute the postcolonial political world. In general, the industrialized nations are trying to keep up the pace of innovation necessary to remain competitive in highly technological industries and at the same time to hold onto a critical mass of low-technology industries to maintain current levels of employment. Industrializing nations want to build indigenous industrial capacity and to entice industries from the industrialized world to redeploy manufacturing operations in their direction. This is what Helmut Schmidt described as the "Struggle for the World Product" (*Foreign Affairs* 52 [April 1974]:437–451) that forms the backdrop to the study presented in this book.

Most nation-states have responded to this struggle in a more or less concerted fashion by seeking to establish and maintain their special comparative advantage in industrial production. Some countries, notably the United States, still only discuss piecemeal industrial policies, such as those that promote export production, "national competitiveness," and "reindustrialization," or that seek to eliminate "unfair trade practices" of competing nations. Other countries, especially those in which national development planning is a more formalized process, have elaborated comprehensive industrial strategies that identify specific "manufacturing niches" or areas of specialization for a country and develop the appropriate mix of incentives to attract desired industries. These are the policy weapons with which nation-states have armed themselves to engage in this historical struggle.

Although recent political and economic events have accentuated that economic power is increasingly important in world politics, it is evident that many political factors will help to determine whether the struggle for the world product that continues into the twenty-first century will be carried out as a zero-sum game or as a gradual redivision of a growing pie. Will the dangers of a heated trade war among the advanced industrial nations lead to increasingly managed and negotiated flows of trade and investment? Can the industrialized nations find the "space" in their economies to keep their markets open and enable a growing number of newly industrializing nations to pull themselves up by the export "bootstrap"? Can the large economic "dropouts" from the international economic system – notably the Soviet Union, China, and Eastern Europe – be reintegrated and find their own special niches of competitiveness in international markets? These are the major issues that will help to determine whether the struggle for the world product culminates in war or in peace.

The study presented in this book forms but one tiny piece of the global economic picture. It seeks to isolate one set of contemporary factors – public concern about industrial pollution and pollution-control regulations – and to examine what incremental influence they may have had during the 1970s and 1980s on the evolution of international comparative advantage in industrial production. In the process, an effort is made to shed light on some of the macro forces shaping the world economy and the micro responses engineered by nation-states and major corporate actors that determine where in the world individual production plants are located.

This book grew out of my doctoral dissertation, presented to the Department of Politics at Princeton University in 1984. Three people at Princeton, in particular, helped to frame my conceptualization of the issues addressed. The advice and gentle channeling efforts of David Morell in the early stages were instrumental in structuring the long-term research agenda that has culminated in this book. The political-economic perspective of international trade and investment that comes through in the work has been significantly influenced by Robert Gilpin, as anyone who has read *U.S. Power and the Multinational Corporation* and his ensuing works will recognize. Finally, I am deeply indebted to Henry Bienen, who supported and encouraged my work from beginning to end, as professor, adviser, friend, and director of Princeton's Research Program in Development Studies.

In addition, I wish to acknowledge the thoughtful comments received from Laura Katz Olson, James L. Payne, and Peter Sperlich, who served as the American Political Science Association's selection committee for the 1986 Harold D. Lasswell Award. Their decision to honor my dissertation with this award for the best dissertation completed in 1984 or 1985 in the field of public policy provided strong inspiration for the process of reforming a dissertation into a book.

Much of the empirical research presented herein was conducted in conjunction with my work on the Industrial Plant Siting Project carried out by The Conservation Foundation from 1978 to 1983. A number of my colleagues from The Conservation Foundation read and commented on various drafts of the manuscript and some of the articles presenting excerpts of the research. I am indebted to Christopher Duerksen, Robert Healy, Frances Irwin, Terry Davies, and Jack Noble for their critical comments and continued encouragement.

While the research for this book was in progress, several institutions provided me with logistical and financial support, as well as comfortable environments in which to work. For the duration, facilities and support from The Conservation Foundation in Washington, D.C., were vital. Without the continued personal support of the Foundation's president, William K. Reilly, this work could not have been completed. Two institutes affiliated with Princeton University, the Research Program in Development Studies and the Center for Energy and Environmental Studies, also provided office space and clerical assistance. I am grateful to the respective directors of those centers, Henry Bienen and Rob Socolow, for their patience and for running the bureaucratic interference that permitted my unusual affiliation within the Princeton University systems.

Support for the research undertaken for this study was provided by a number of institutions. Much of the research was conducted under the auspices of The Conservation Foundation's Industrial Siting Project, supported generously by the German Marshall Fund, the Ford Foundation, and the Richard King Mellon Foundation. Supplemental support for the research in Europe was provided by the Princeton Committee for West European Studies. The research in Mexico was underwritten by the working capital fund of The Conservation Foundation and the Center for the Study of World Politics.

A number of people stand out for their assistance in researching, producing, and editing the original manuscript from which this book derives: Brad Rymph, Debbie Johnson, Bill Jones, Bernice Hudson, Marie-Claude Helman, Robin Myer, Lindsey Rodes, Michelle Krichten, and Tony Brown. Barr Hogen, Margaret Cook, Cecilia Danks, Thomas Rodes, and Jonathan Roulon assisted in updating the data and reference materials in 1986 and 1987. I also am grateful to Frank Smith, Janis Bolster, and Debra Menzell at Cambridge University Press and two anonymous readers whose collective editorial suggestions all greatly improved the manuscript as it moved through the production process.

I wish to express my deepest gratitude and love to my family for everything that they have given to me: my parents, George and Phyllis Leonard, deeply caring, selflessly devoted, and quietly proud; my in-laws, John (who died before this book could be completed) and Jane Pisano, ever supportive and nurturing; and most of all my wife, Carolyn Pisano Leonard, not only for her intellectual support and continuing love but also for the precious gifts that have arrived in the years leading up to publication of this book: our children, Michael and Anna.

Silver Spring, Maryland
January 1988

Introduction

During the 1970s the United States began to accumulate government regulations covering water effluents, air emissions, solid wastes, the manufacture and use of hazardous and toxic substances, and workplace health and safety. These new regulations forced industries in the United States to expend huge amounts of capital, and they induced fundamental changes in the domestic structure of many industries. As this collection of laws grew, it became obvious to economists that some industrial firms in the United States were spending more for pollution control than were firms in many other industrialized countries, and a great deal more than the modest expenditures necessary in countries outside Western Europe and Japan. The industries claimed not only that the costs of pollution abatement were high, but that the new regulations made it increasingly difficult for them to build and operate production facilities, even when they spent large amounts of money on environmental control.

As a consequence, many observers in the United States noted that the costs and logistics of complying with environmental regulations might prove a significant factor in determining the competitiveness and location of industries involved in world trade. Many policymakers, labor unions, business leaders, environmentalists, and academics expressed concern that strict domestic pollution-control standards might impair the ability of U.S. industry to compete with imported products and in foreign markets, although they proposed very different solutions to the problem. They feared that producers based in the United States would lose their comparative advantage in certain industrial sectors as a result. It was expected that many American firms, particularly multinational corporations with experience operating overseas, would respond by transferring facilities to countries where regulatory costs and encumbrances could be minimized.

Two related theories sought to explain how and why environmental regulations would alter the prevailing allocation of comparative advantage in industrial production. The first was that regulations would push an increasing number of industries out of the United States and other advanced industrial nations (the industrial-flight hypothesis); the second

1

was that less-developed countries would use lenient environmental regulations to attract multinational industries (the pollution-haven hypothesis). The combination of the push out of industrial countries and the pull toward less-industrialized countries was expected to exert a powerful influence on international patterns of industrial location and to strengthen the industrial-development strategies of Third World nations.

Some observers claimed that this would be a positive development, because it would reflect the increasing desire for service-sector and high-technology jobs in the advanced industrial countries and would encourage the spread of industrial development to the Third World. Still, such prospects raised two major political and economic concerns. First, the trend could have adverse effects on the U.S. economy, and national security might be threatened if many U.S. industrial facilities transferred production abroad. Second, environmental groups and some observers in developing countries feared that U.S. firms, taking advantage of the desperate desire for industry in developing countries, would set up factories that wantonly polluted the atmosphere and the water, make inadequate provisions for the health and safety of their workers, and cause other serious environmental hazards.

The debate intensified during the early 1980s for several reasons: output was low and unemployment high in many large industries hit with high regulatory costs; first industry and then the Reagan administration increased their efforts to water down or restructure environmental regulations; growing emphasis was placed on stimulating U.S. exports; and the federal government proposed policies designed to catalyze a reindustrialization of the United States. Frequently, environmental regulations have been blamed not only for increasing costs for American consumers and depressing the financial outlook of many domestic industries, but for making it more difficult for U.S. firms to compete with foreign firms and for constraining or actually reducing America's overall industrial capacity.

In addition, environmental and labor groups, contending that U.S. companies are moving to other countries to escape environmental regulations, have made an effort to follow them around the globe and examine their environmental records. These investigators have gathered evidence that American companies sometimes create pollution, neglect workplace health, and cause community-wide environmental problems in host countries.

This study attempts to assess the industrial-flight and pollution-haven hypotheses. It analyzes recent foreign-investment and import trends among U.S. firms to determine whether standards for pollution control and workplace health have pushed U.S. industries abroad and whether the U.S. industrial base and balance of trade have been negatively affected. On the basis of case-study research in four rapidly industrializing countries – Ireland, Spain, Romania, and Mexico – the study will assess whether adherence to a pollution-haven strategy has strengthened industrial development. The case studies illustrate the economic, political, and public-health dangers for governments of underindustrialized countries that follow such a strategy. They also point to the problems encountered by multinational corporations that assume that underindustrialized countries have so many more-important concerns that they will not take punitive action against polluting companies.

Theory and methodology

From a theoretical perspective, this study focuses on whether and how a relatively new set of factors – environmental and pollution-control regulations – has affected all the processes that now influence the distribution of international comparative advantage in industrial production.

The industrial-flight and pollution-haven hypotheses were derived from the work of theoretical economists who adapted classical factor-proportion explanations of trade, and least-cost approaches to industrial location, to predict the impacts that differences in national pollution-control regulations would have on the distribution of international comparative advantage. Yet, although classical theories of international comparative advantage and industrial location do provide a good starting point for analysis, they are not sufficiently dynamic or politically oriented to account for many real-world distortions and emergent conditions.

This study presents a theoretical framework that draws on several inter-related bodies of economic and political theory. This framework helps to provide a better understanding of the allocation of international comparative advantage in industrial production. In particular, five broad theoretical domains – each at a slightly different level of generality or geographic specificity – are relevant to the composite picture of international comparative advantage that forms the foundation for the research presented in later chapters. These domains are the concept of a *product cycle* in manufactured goods, which makes comparative advantage much more fluid than its classical construct; theories that explain why *foreign direct investment* takes place rather than trade or the transnational movement of other factors (for example, labor or portfolio capital); theories explaining the *industrial-location decisions* made by individual firms; the body of literature on the most advantageous *industrial-development strategies* for underindustrialized nation-states; and explanations of the *bargaining process* that determines the terms of the relationship between the international corporation and its host nation-state.

The first two chapters of this study, although they do not purport to offer a definitive or even consensual exposition, provide an overview of these theories so that the reader will be better equipped to generalize from the specific research presented in subsequent chapters. The continuous "fit" between the different levels of trade-and-investment theory noted above can be briefly summarized as follows.

Innovating firms in one country initiate production of a manufactured good; if they do so under particularly advantageous circumstances, they may also export the good to foreign markets. At some point, the economics of production and marketing shift to favor the commencement of production abroad as well. Sometimes circumstances encourage producers from the first country to set up production plants abroad; in others, foreign firms start up facilities of their own. When the individual firms in the first country react to these circumstances, several factors affect their decisions about whether, when, and where to set up production facilities abroad. Governments of foreign countries – particularly underindustrialized countries – in turn pursue a variety of strategies to attract foreign firms or to encourage domestic firms to build production facilities for manufactured goods entering the stage of internationalized production. When a country does succeed in luring a foreign firm to its soil, the country and the firm begin a continuous process of give and take, during which the relative advantage of each waxes and wanes. This bargaining process determines the ground rules of the relationship between the foreign firm and the country. Subsequent chapters will test the industrial-flight and pollution-haven hypotheses in the context of this dynamic framework.

A word about methodology is in order. To test for evidence of the validity of the industrial-flight and pollution-haven hypotheses, two types of information are necessary: statistical data that identify changes in investment patterns and trade patterns within and between the United States and industrializing nations, and information that sheds light on the reasons for the statistical trends and the motivations of the crucial actors – multinational corporations and governments of industrializing nations. Without knowledge of the internal conditions that affect the companies in so-called pollution-intensive industries and those that motivate the industrialization efforts of governments, the aggregate data cannot support the hypotheses but can only invalidate them by failing to conform to expected trends.

As it is, the data do help to eliminate some possibilities from further consideration but do not invalidate the hypotheses altogether. Thus, the methodological approach followed in this study is to narrow down to particular problem areas by establishing a series of tests whose results set the terms for the next level of inquiry. It is analogous, therefore, to peeling away the layers of an onion to reveal the core.

First, it is necessary to identify industries that have encountered extreme difficulties as a result of environmental regulations and concern about environmental problems. To do so, we shall examine capital spending on pollution controls in the last decade for all U.S. industries and for key industrial sectors. In addition, several other indicators of environmental difficulties for industry will serve as a cross-check in selecting the industries most susceptible to industrial flight.

Second, we must devise some means of assessing whether trade and investment patterns follow the expectations of the hypotheses. To do this, we shall examine aggregate figures for foreign investment and imports by key U.S. industrial sectors identified as pollution-intensive. If these industries have increased overseas investments and imports rapidly in recent years, and if a growing share of this activity involves countries outside the other heavily industrialized nations, it is possible to conclude, at a minimum, that recent trends conform to those expected.

However, the trade and investment statistics alone cannot provide the crucial information necessary to know whether the environmental factors have caused the trends, have influenced them, or have been only incidental. Thus, individual industries that show large increases in foreign investments and U.S. imports are analyzed within the whole range of political and economic factors that have affected them in recent years. This requires recourse to numerous industry reports, knowledge of the impact of particular regulations, and a general analysis of industry trends and economic factors.

Similarly, certain rapidly industrializing nations have increased their industrial production in certain industrial sectors, but we do not fully understand the reasons for this success. Thus, the industrial-development strategies of these countries are examined as a whole, in an effort to identify the importance of pollution factors in such strategies. And, because a nation can become a pollution haven unintentionally or as the result of bad negotiating, poor planning, lax enforcement of laws, and other political factors, we shall study the role of pollution in the relationships and controversies between industrializing nations and multinational corporations.

Summary of the chapters

As already noted, the first two chapters delineate the two most important sets of factors that determine the distribution of comparative advantage in industrial production: (1) the natural dynamics that account for the direction of trade and the location of industries on an international basis; and (2) the numerous interventions that are structured by particular nation-states to affect international patterns of trade and investment.

Chapter 1 contends that classical trade theory alone cannot account for the evolution of comparative advantage in industrial production because it does not adequately explain the movement of capital between countries and largely ignores the question of how firms engaged in production for international markets make locational decisions. Drawing on recent theoretical contributions, we shall show how the velocity of change in international comparative advantage has increased as a result of the mobility of capital and the cycle of technological diffusion.

Chapter 2 argues that as a result of such a process of constant evolution in international comparative advantage, the artificial factor endowments created by governments have become at least as important as natural factor endowments for countries seeking to gain comparative advantage in some industries. It provides a framework for analyzing the role of international trade in the industrial-development strategies devised by nation-states, examines many of the policy choices that governments must make in this process, and outlines the bases of the relationships that industrializing nations often form with the primary international movers of capital and technology – multinational corporations.

Chapter 3 introduces the question of whether the strong antipollution regulations recently enacted in leading industrial nations have affected the struggle for the world product. It shows how the classical trade theories based on an assessment of relative factor endowments guided the initial international discussions of the ways in which strong environmental regulations in the industrialized countries may affect trade and investment. These theories stress that countries will generally produce and export goods manufactured with factors that are abundant within the country and will import those for which factors of production are scarce. On this basis, economic theorists, policymakers from both industrialized and industrializing nations, and spokesmen for international agencies and private corporations all tended to assume that highly polluting industries would gradually move from countries with scarce environmental factor endowments to countries where such factors would be abundant.

By examining recent international trade and investment statistics for U.S. industries, Chapter 4 identifies the industrial sectors most likely to have felt the pressures for environmental redeployment and highlights some of the especially dynamic industrializing nations that may benefit from such a process. These aggregate figures indicate that no large-scale evolution of comparative advantage in industrial production seems to have begun as a result of U.S. environmental-control regulations. However, several trends indicate the possibility that there has been more selective industrial flight on the part of particular industries in the major industrial sectors examined, and that the success of some industrializing countries in a few of these industries has been boosted by their selective use of pollution-haven status.

Thus, Chapter 5 discusses the importance of pollution factors in the industrial-development strategies and experiences of four rapidly industrializing nations. This chapter shows how planners of industrial development in Ireland, Spain, Mexico, and Romania responded in the late 1970s to the possibility that they could take advantage of environmental standards in the advanced industrial nations to increase their advantage in certain industries. In each case, government officials took note of the possibilities and acted more or less in conformance with the pollution-haven hypothesis. However, evolving attitudes toward pollution and other political and economic factors have made it more difficult to call any of these countries a pollution haven today.

Chapter 6 demonstrates how the emergence of concern about industrial pollution has affected the bargaining relationship between foreign companies and the governments of host countries. In the past, multinational corporations often were perfectly willing to go along with the failure of industrializing countries to outline effective pollution-control regulations, even though from the company's perspective the pollution incentive was not a crucial variable in the bargaining process. But in recent years officials of these industrializing countries have become more sophisticated in bargaining over pollution, and this has often increased the friction between countries and companies.

Chapter 7 shows, in fact, just how politicized the issue of pollution has become in industrializing countries and how this is affecting the relationship between these countries and multinational corporations. This chatper looks at some dynamic political factors that influence the way in which pollution affects multinational corporations operating in rapidly industrializing countries. It describes how governments and important political constituencies have tended to react to increased awareness of the adverse environmental and health effects of certain industries. And it outlines some of the political and institutional barriers that have often frustrated industrializing countries, and to a lesser extent corporations, in their efforts to reduce the harmful environmental side effects of export-oriented industrial development.

The final chapter attempts to outline some of the theoretical implications that this study holds for recent explanations of international investment, industrial location, industrial-development strategy, and the relations between host countries and foreign investors. It concludes by offering a series of practical policy prescriptions for the major actors whose behavior is examined in this study: the U.S. government, the governments of rapidly industrializing nations, and officials of multinational corporations.

1

The dynamics of international trade and industrial location

The classical law of comparative advantage sought to demonstrate that productive resources in all countries could be more efficiently employed if each country, through the exchange of goods and raw materials, specialized in producing the few goods and raw materials that it could produce most proficiently.[1] A more neutral way of thinking about the concept of comparative advantage is that it describes the array of social, economic, and political forces that account for the general export and import patterns prevailing between nations. In this sense, all the other bodies of theory discussed in this and subsequent chapters contribute to an understanding of comparative advantage.

Although much of its original elegance has been muddled as a result of empirical testing, the theory of comparative advantage put forth by Eli Heckscher and Bertil Ohlin remains the highest level of generality in explaining patterns of world trade.[2] In essence, the Heckscher-Ohlin theory holds that differences in comparative advantage among countries are explained by different relative costs for the separate factors of production; these relative factor costs are determined by how well endowed each nation is with those factors. Because different goods require different factor proportions in their manufacture, countries will tend to export those goods that use large portions of their more abundant factors and import those that depend upon their scarce factors of production.[3]

In elaborating the theory of comparative advantage, economists until recently generally assumed that only commodities, not physical factors of production, moved across international borders. In large measure, this assumption reflected objective international economic circumstances. Although large firms from both the United States and Europe began to

1. David Ricardo, *Principles of Political Economy and Taxation* (1817), reissued as vol. 1 of P. Sraffa, ed., *The Works and Correspondence of David Ricardo* (Cambridge: Cambridge University Press, 1951).
2. Bertil Ohlin, *Interregional and International Trade* (Cambridge, Mass.: Harvard University Press, 1933).
3. An excellent summary of the factor-proportion approach to international trade and its limitations is found in Jan S. Hogendorn and Wilson B. Brown, *The New International Economics* (Reading, Mass.: Addison-Wesley, 1979), pp. 230–235.

establish production facilities abroad during the late 1800s, the vast majority of all private foreign investment before the Great Depression was in the form of portfolio rather than direct investment.[4] Also, much of the foreign direct investment that did take place during the first half of the twentieth century was for the exploitation of raw materials in underdeveloped areas outside the United States and Europe. Both of these types of factor movement could be reconciled within classical comparative-advantage theory because they did not substitute for trade and did not alter the relative advantage available to a country from specialization in a particular commodity for trade. An account of factor mobility, therefore, was not essential for an understanding of comparative advantage.

However, this situation was complicated when, especially after World War II, foreign direct investment in manufacturing industries became a more prominent form of international capital movement. The large-scale flow of physical capital across national borders can affect comparative advantage more directly than portfolio capital does because, like the transnational migration of labor, it can alter the relative abundance of physical production factors over a relatively short period of time, and thus it can change not only the magnitude but also the makeup of trade. A growing number of economists have viewed international factor movement as a potential substitute for trade and as a possible means by which a country can increase (or decrease) the abundance of a particular factor (in our case physical capital) so as to alter its parameters of comparative advantage.

In explaining factor movements under unrestrained conditions, the economist J. E. Meade, among others, pointed out that factors will move whenever the marginal product of the factor in one country exceeds the marginal product in another by more than the cost of movement.[5] In addition, as Robert Mundell noted, the potential interchangeability between factor movements and trade may be significantly affected by border restrictions covering international economic intercourse: any increase in trade impediments is likely to stimulate a compensatory increase in factor movements; conversely, increases in restrictions on factor movements may boost trade.[6] Thus the ability to move physical capital in addition to commodities across borders and the ability of nation-states to speed up or slow down this process significantly complicate the calculation of comparative advantage.

4. See John D. Daniels, Ernest W. Ogram, Jr., and Lee H. Rodebaugh, *International Business: Environments and Operations* (Reading, Mass.: Addison-Wesley, 1978), pp. 64–89.
5. J. E. Meade, *Trade and Welfare* (London: Oxford University Press, 1955), p. 420.
6. Robert A. Mundell, "International Trade and Factor Mobility," in Richard E. Caves and Harry G. Johnson, eds., *Readings in International Economics* (Homewood, Ill.: Richard D. Irwin, 1968), p. 101.

Widespread movements of physical capital – as well as numerous exogenous changes in international political, economic, and technological circumstances – have made it necessary to move beyond the static conception implied in the general theory of comparative advantage and to seek more dynamic expositions of how international trade and investment patterns change as factor proportions themselves evolve. In particular, even if one accepts the general validity of the Hecksher-Ohlin model, it is important to explain

1. the process and sequence by which comparative advantage in different manufacturing activities shifts as a result of changing factor inputs or factor endowments; and,
2. why the movement of physical capital through foreign direct investment (with its many inherent logistical problems and the xenophobic reactions it often provokes) is undertaken instead of commodity trade, portfolio-capital flows, or the direct sale of physical capital and expertise to would-be foreign producers.

These questions are discussed in the following expositions of the so-called product cycle and foreign-direct-investment theories, respectively.

The international product cycle

The role now played by advanced technology – and hence by research and development – in manufacturing industries has made comparative advantage a much more diffuse and artificial concept than was the case in earlier phases of the industrial revolution. That is, comparative advantage in particular manufactured products may shift from one country to another in relatively few years or decades as new technologies are introduced and mastered. In addition, the allocation of comparative advantage, when highly dependent upon levels of technological capability, may be as much a creation of competitive choice as the fulfillment of a nation-state's natural bounty.

The increased mobility of physical capital has only added momentum to the growing diffuseness and artificiality of comparative advantage, because one country need not build its own indigenous capacity before it can imitate producers in more advanced countries. A lagging country can instead find a foreign firm willing to sell technology and expertise or to take up production inside its borders.

Although rapid technological advancement and dispersion have made matters more complex than is described in simple factor-account models, this does not mean that the process by which comparative advantage evolves is entirely helter-skelter. To understand the rhythm of postwar patterns of world trade and investment, many contemporary economists view comparative advantage in terms of the stages through which manufactured products pass after their introduction. Actually, the idea of technological cycles or stages is based on earlier work by Thorstein Veblen and Alexander Gerschenkron, both of whom described a follow-the-leader syndrome in technology-based industries.[7] It is only a matter of time, they pointed out, before followers master the technology and gain a comparative advantage over the erstwhile technological leader.

This, to a great extent, is what occurred after World War II. The United States, with its industrial plant intact, its population affluent, its domestic market vast, and its technological prowess unleashed, introduced a wide variety of new manufactured products, many of which were also exported with great success. This opened the cycle, with the United States (or more precisely, American private firms) in the lead and all others (in particular, Europe and Japan) trying to close the gap.[8]

Stages of dispersion

By the mid-1960s, as the postwar cycle was running its course, international economists were able to abstract the sequence into what is formally called the *product life cycle*. In essence, this cycle consists of four stages, each stage having different implications for comparative advantage and international trade and investment patterns:

1. product introduction
2. product dispersion
3. product maturation
4. product standardization[9]

In the initial phase, the product is introduced in the United States (for example) to fill a domestic market demand or opportunity. As the product catches on, U.S. exports of the product (especially to other advanced developed countries) are strong. Although firms in other countries may seek to imitate at this stage, the technological advantages enjoyed by U.S. produc-

---

7. Thorstein Veblen, "On the Penalty of Taking the Lead," in *Imperial Germany and the Industrial Revolution*, excerpted in Max Lerner, ed., *The Portable Veblen* (New York: Penguin, 1976); and Alexander Gerschenkron, *Economic Backwardness in Historical Perspective* (Cambridge, Mass.: Harvard University Press, 1962).
8. See H. Jeffrey Leonard and Robert Gilpin, "Industrial and Technology Strategies in Western Economies," in Joseph Szyliowicz, ed., *Technology in International Affairs* (New York: Praeger, 1981), pp. 98–128.
9. Early articles describing the product cycle include Raymond Vernon, "International Investment and International Trade in the Product Cycle," *Quarterly Journal of Economics* 80 (May 1966):190–207; W. Gruba, D. Mehta, and R. Vernon, "The R&D Factor in International Trade and International Investment of the United States Industries," *Journal of Political Economy* 25, no. 1 (February 1967):20–37; and Louis T. Wells, Jr., "A Product Life Cycle for International Trade?" *Journal of Marketing* 32, no. 3 (July 1968):1–6. Although often described as a three-stage process (new product, maturing product, standardized product), the test follows the four-stage process proposed by Wells.

ers prevent foreign companies from significantly reducing worldwide sales of the U.S.-produced good.

Sooner or later, production commences in other advanced developed countries where demand for the product is high. This occurs when U.S. firms open branch plants to serve and protect their burgeoning overseas markets, when foreign companies purchase technology and licenses from U.S. firms, or when foreign companies develop their own technological capabilities to produce the good. U.S.-based firms may maintain an absolute advantage in production efficiency, but tariff barriers, transportation costs, and marketing difficulties may offset this advantage in the markets of a few imitator countries. U.S. firms, however, maintain their competitive advantage in the open markets of nonproducing countries.

As the product enters its more mature phase, foreign producers succeed in closing the technological gap to the point where they can produce the goods with high efficiency and can compete actively with U.S. firms in the markets of nonproducer countries. U.S. export surpluses of the product dwindle and eventually are eliminated.

Finally, in the standardization phase, comparative advantage in the product shifts decisively away from the United States. Increasingly, the most competitive producers are those that can minimize routine production costs, particularly for labor and raw materials. In this phase, firms in the original imitator countries find that, like their American counterparts, they have difficulty competing with firms in industrializing countries, where production costs are cheapest of all. The U.S. market is flooded with low-cost imports, and U.S.-based producers may face severe hardships if they do not receive protection or if they cannot reestablish their initial advantage by technological innovations that increase production efficiency or create a newer and better product.

The notion of a product cycle helps to integrate into comparative-advantage theory two important developments of the twentieth century: the increased role of technological innovation and the rapid diffusion of manufacturing talents and technology that follows introduction in a leading country. However, the product cycle alone does not satisfactorily explain another major phenomenon of recent decades: the veritable explosion of foreign direct investment undertaken by U.S.-based multinational corporations.

Foreign direct investment

To some extent, foreign direct investment can be viewed as one natural outcome of the product cycle. U.S. companies move production abroad to protect their markets, which they would otherwise lose to overseas imitators. But, increasingly, the foreign-direct-investment behavior of large corporations appears to be caused by more than simply a defensive effort to remain abreast of the product cycle. Indeed, there are many who feel that large multinational corporations have undertaken aggressive foreign-direct-investment campaigns that speed up the product cycle or skip some phases of the cycle altogether.[10] At the least, it is necessary to have an independent explanation of foreign-direct-investment behavior that, though affected by the product-cycle sequence, is motivated by other competitive factors as well.

The product-cycle approach, postulating a continuous and inevitable "trickling down" of technological advantage from leader to followers, neither depends upon nor necessitates foreign direct investment. In some industries that have undergone something akin to a product cycle in this century – leather goods and textiles, for example – the production dynamic has shifted from the United States to other industrialized to industrializing nations primarily through the successive buildups of domestic firms in each country. Even in more complicated industries, technology can eventually be purchased, licensed, imitated, or stolen, and portfolio capital can be imported if need be.

As Veblen, in particular, pointed out, it is extremely difficult, if not impossible, to prevent technological knowledge from spreading from one country to another. The lead of an industrial firm or an industrial nation that becomes complacent after introducing a new state-of-the-art technology is destined to be short-lived. In theory, the tendency of technological secrets to "leak" means that a would-be imitator country does not have to permit foreign firms to control technology, equity, and management in return for establishing production facilities. The same tendency should also make it harder for foreign firms to maintain an enduring advantage over domestic companies in host countries. Thus, many economists point out, under perfectly competitive international market conditions for technology, management, and capital, overseas demand for a manufactured product would tend to be served primarily by local firms as soon as the absolute advantages of the first phase of the product cycle had dissipated.[11]

The prominence of foreign direct investment in the worldwide spread

10. For a summary of the view that overseas investment has been detrimental to the U.S. economy, see Robert Gilpin, *U.S. Power and the Multinational Corporation* (New York: Basic, 1975), pp. 176–189. An extended attempt to illustrate how foreign investment by U.S. companies was speeding up the spread of technology and hence prematurely eroding U.S. comparative advantage in many industries is found in O. R. Strackbein, *American Enterprise and Foreign Trade* (Washington, D.C.: Public Affairs Press, 1965). See also Nat Goldfinger, "A Labor View of Foreign Investment and Trade Issues," in Robert E. Baldwin and J. David Richardson, eds., *International Trade and Finance* (Boston: Little, Brown, 1974).

11. See Charles Kindleberger, *American Business Abroad* (New Haven, Conn.: Yale University Press, 1969), p. 13.

of industry suggests that international market conditions are not perfectly competitive and that large international firms are well positioned to benefit from these circumstances. Otherwise, why would countries accept foreign direct investment in spite of their concerns with national sovereignty and the possibilities of obtaining technical knowledge through other channels? And why, for that matter, would international firms dispatch capital, technology, and managerial expertise abroad in spite of the innumerable obstacles and risks they face in operating outside their home countries?

Imperfect competition

There remains considerable ideological disagreement about the nature of foreign direct investment: scholars debate whether it is basically defensive or aggressive,[12] whether it increases exports and creates markets or destroys both for the home country,[13] and whether it furthers economic development or perpetuates imperialistic exploitation in host countries.[14] Yet there is surprising consensus across a broad spectrum of analysts that the advantages accruing to foreign direct investors result from political and economic circumstances that create market imperfections – that is,

12.   The concept of defensive investment was introduced by Alexander Lamfalussy, *Investment and Growth in Mature Economies* (Oxford: Basil Blackwell and Mott, 1961). It is generally endorsed by those who view overseas investment as part of a firm's strategy to preserve markets in the waning stages of the product cycle. Examples of observers who see foreign direct investment as more an aggressive process include Karl Levitt, *Silent Surrender: The American Economic Empire in Canada* (Toronto: Macmillan, 1970); David Calleo and Benjamin Rowland, *America and the World Political Economy: Atlantic Dreams and National Realities* (Bloomington: Indiana University Press, 1973); Richard Barnet and Ronald Muller, *Global Reach: The Power of the Multinational Corporations* (New York: Simon and Schuster, 1974); and J. J. Servan Schreiber, *The American Challenge* (New York: Atheneum, 1968).

13.   For empirical arguments that foreign direct investments destroy home-country exports, see Robert Gilpin, "The Multinational Corporation and the National Interest," U.S. Congress, Senate Committee on Labor and Public Welfare, 93d Cong., 1st sess., October 1973; Peggy Musgrave, "Tax Preferences to Foreign Investment," in U.S. Congress, Joint Economic Committee, *The Economics of Federal Subsidy Programs, pt. 2, International Subsidies* (Washington, D.C.: Government Printing Office, 1972); Gary Hufbauer and Michael Adler, *Overseas Manufacturing Investment and the Balance of Payments,* Tax Policy Research Study no. 1 (Washington, D.C.: U.S. Treasury Department, 1968); and W. B. Reddaway, S. J. Potter, and C. T. Taylor, *Effects of U.K. Direct Investment Overseas: An Interim Report* (Cambridge: Cambridge University Press, 1968). For the contention that the effects on exports are either neutral or positive, see Leland B. Yeager and David G. Tuerck, *Foreign Trade and U.S. Policy: The Case for Free International Trade* (New York: Praeger, 1976).

14.   This long-running argument boils down to a debate between the so-called liberal and dependency schools. Representative of the liberal view that multinational corporations can serve as an "engine of development" in host countries are Raymond Vernon, *Sovereignty at Bay* (New York: Basic, 1971); and Jack N. Behrman, *National Interests and the Multinational Enterprise* (Englewood Cliffs, N.J.: Prentice-Hall, 1970). Classical arguments that foreign investors frustrate development, exploit the host

interfere with the forces of perfect competition – in the international arena. In the vernacular of the economist, explanations of foreign direct investment increasingly fall under the rubrics of imperfect competition, oligopolistic behavior, and monopoly theory.

In this view, a multinational corporation must maintain significant monopolistic advantages over local firms in order to produce and sell in foreign markets with unfamiliar or even hostile economic, political, cultural, linguistic, legal, and social circumstances. The advantage must be perceived as less fleeting than the mere possession of one technique or formula because, as already noted, successful adaptive imitation is more or less inevitable. Moreover, the potential profit from setting up abroad not only must compensate for the increased risks and logistical complications, but must be higher than the profit potential for investing at home or the profit potential for local entrepreneurs in the foreign market.

One of the first to pinpoint some of the induplicable advantages accruing to multinational corporations as a result of imperfect competition in the international arena was Stephen Hymer. Hymer suggested that superior technology and management ability combined to give large corporations in many industries capabilities that could not be matched by local firms.[15] Although specific techniques can be licensed or imitated, the over-

country, and enlist the support of a small band of domestic compradors are found in, among many others, Paul A. Baran, *The Political Economy of Growth* (New York: Monthly Review Press, 1957); and Andre Gunder Frank, *Latin America: Underdevelopment or Revolution* (Monthly Review Press, 1969).

In recent years a more subtle and sophisticated analysis of the ways in which foreign investors warp the path of national economic development has been developed. Three examples of the dependent-development school are Fernando Enrique Cardoso, "Associated Dependent Development: Theoretical and Practical Implications," in Alfred Stepan, ed., *Authoritarian Brazil: Origins, Policies, Future* (New Haven, Conn.: Yale University Press, 1973); Peter Evans, *Dependent Development: The Alliance of Multinational, State, and Local Capital in Brazil* (Princeton, N.J.: Princeton University Press, 1979); and Colin Leys, *Underdevelopment in Kenya: The Political Economy of Neo-Colonialism* (Berkeley and Los Angeles: University of California Press, 1975).

Recent empirical studies of foreign corporate-host country relations have tended to conclude that the dependency school is right in the sense that often national economic-development goals have not been a concern of foreign investors, but wrong in that the government of the host country can take actions to cajole foreign investors into better serving its national interests. See Theodore H. Moran, *Multinational Corporations and the Politics of Dependence: Copper in Chile* (Princeton, N.J.: Princeton University Press, 1974); Thomas J. Biersteker, *Distortion or Development: Contending Perspectives on the Multinational Corporation* (Cambridge, Mass.: MIT Press, 1978); and David G. Becker, *The New Bourgeoisie and the Limits of Dependency: Mining, Class, and Power in "Revolutionary" Peru* (Princeton, N.J.: Princeton University Press, 1983).

15. Stephen Hymer, *The International Operations of National Firms: A Study of Direct Foreign Investment* (Cambridge, Mass.: MIT Press, 1976); Stephen Hymer, "The Multinational Corporation and the Law of Uneven Development," in Jagdish N. Bhagwati, ed., *Economics and World Order* (London: Macmillan, 1972); and Stephen Hymer, "The Efficiency (Contradictions) of Multinational Corporations," *American Economic Review* 60 (May 1970): 441–448.

all package of organizational skills is shared by a very small number of international competitors.

Since Hymer, numerous analysts have explored many other factors that enable multinational corporations to transfer their advantages from one country to another. Following the lead of Charles Kindleberger, we can classify into four broad categories the monopolistic advantages that induce big corporations to undertake foreign direct investment:

1. departures from perfect competition in goods markets, such as product differentiation or special marketing skills;
2. departures from perfect competition in factor markets, such as access to numerous patented processes and new technologies, or an ability to mobilize more local capital faster because of a proven track record elsewhere;
3. the potential for transnational economies of scale, by both vertical and horizontal integration of production facilities and raw-materials suppliers;
4. governmental interventions that affect the entry and exit of goods or alter the fiscal picture for a potential investor by lowering the economic risk or raising the profit potential.[16]

To explain the large-scale deployment of American corporate subsidiaries and branch plants across Europe and into the Third World after World War II, different analysts have stressed various factors from wide-ranging perspectives. Paul Baran and other Marxists point to the workings of the international capitalistic system with its inherent tendency for core areas to exploit and siphon the wealth from peripheral areas.[17] Robert Aliber has stressed the influence of imperfections in postwar world capital markets, which favored U.S. companies because the security of the dollar enabled them to borrow abroad on terms more advantageous than those available to firms from other countries.[18] Charles de Gaulle and a number of economists also focused on the role of the dollar in world economy, emphasizing that the overvalued exchange rate for the dollar artificially boosted the strength of U.S.-based firms.[19] Robert Gilpin attributes the phenomenal growth of U.S. corporations abroad to American political interest and power; the international political and economic hegemony established by the United States after the war, he says, provided the impetus to and a favorable climate for corporate expansionism.[20] U.S. labor unions and various other analysts have argued that American public pol-

16. A breakdown along these lines was suggested in Kindleberger, *American Business Abroad,* p. 14.
17. Paul A. Baran, *The Political Economy of Backwardness* (New York: Monthly Review Press, 1957).
18. Robert Z. Aliber, "A Theory of Direct Foreign Investment," in Charles P. Kindleberger, ed., *The International Corporation* (Cambridge, Mass.: MIT Press, 1970), pp. 17–34.
19. See Gilpin, *U.S. Power,* pp. 125–126.
20. Ibid., pp. 4–5.

icies fostered the movement of U.S. companies abroad by providing incentives for and reducing the risks of overseas investment.[21]

Ironically, as much as these and the many intermediate perspectives differ from one another, most fall within the bounds of the Hymer-Kindleberger theory of foreign direct investment. Almost all accounts emphasize in some way that governments and large corporations exercise political and economic power to narrow competition or give a small number of large firms an advantage in the operation of production facilities on foreign soil.

Internationalization of production

In recent years, many of the factors that conferred across-the-board advantages on foreign direct investors from the United States during the postwar years (U.S. hegemony, gunboat diplomacy, and the overvalued dollar, for example) have faded. Events in the ensuing period have underscored two important points about the nature and advantages of large multinational firms.

First, not all industries benefit equally from (or, indeed, can even create) the various oligopolistic advantages noted in the previous section. That is, some industries are much more likely than others to be dominated by multinational corporations. Second, a relatively new phenomenon in foreign direct investment has emerged that is more difficult to explain by recourse to conventional theories of product cycles and imperfect competition. Some multinational firms are building manufacturing facilities in a number of different countries; each facility performs a specialty function or is responsible for a stage of production that is part of a larger process. Rather than having each plant in each country function as a self-contained producer of finished goods, recent years have seen more attempts to apply the division of labor worldwide.

Analysts generally agree that there is one major indicator of whether an industry will be dominated by leading multinational firms or fragmented among numerous national producers, each with the natural advantage in its domestic markets: what might be called the index of imitability. The more advanced the technology, the more research-dependent the industry and the more in need of sophisticated managerial and technical skills, the more likely is it that foreign direct investors with these advantages will be able to outmaneuver domestic firms in other countries.

Stephen Magee sees the desire of high-technology firms to invest abroad as part of what he calls the "appropriability problem." Because these firms

21. Many of these arguments are stated in Gilpin, "Multinational Corporation."

must, above all else, protect their technological advantage and proprietary expertise, it is much better for them to transfer technology on an intra-corporate basis – by creating subsidiary operations abroad.[22] Other ana-lysts have come to a similar view by extending the work done by Ronald Coase in the late 1930s. From a Coasian perspective firms in technologi-cally advanced industries move abroad rather than sell their skills because the market cannot price and allocate the proper returns on technology created by long-term research-and-development expenditures.[23] At any rate, the general consensus is that multinational enterprises will have sig-nificant advantages in advanced technological sectors and "will be less evi-dent with respect to the more mature and standardized products."[24]

This formulation helps to explain why many mineral industries have become less completely dominated by foreign direct investors over the years, why simple manufactured items such as leather goods and textiles are usually reserved for domestic producers, and, conversely, why indus-tries in which technology is more complex and difficult to imitate often have been controlled by a relatively small number of multinational firms. However, it does not explain the second phenomenon noted above, the emerging tendency of large multinational firms to set up integrated inter-national production networks.

Relatively little theoretical work has been done to explain how the motivation for and ramifications of foreign direct investment as part of an international production network differ from those of the still more typ-ical branch-plant form of foreign direct investment. To a large extent, the initial work done was associated with the emergence in the late 1960s and early 1970s of the concept of the global corporation or, as George Ball dubbed it, the cosmocorp.[25]

This school rightly saw that with the relative decline of U.S. economic and political power several trends were occurring: U.S. multinationals were internationalizing their economic and political bases and looking at markets, production, capital raising, and currency dealings from a global perspective; more and more large firms from other nations, especially Japan and Western European countries, were becoming global competi-

22. Stephen P. Magee, "Information and the Multinational Corporation: An Appropriabil-ity Theory of Foreign Direct Investment," in Jagdish Bhagwati, ed., *The New Interna-tional Economic Order: The North-South Debate* (Cambridge, Mass.: MIT Press, 1977).
23. See Ronald H. Coase, "The Nature of the Firm," *Economica* 4 (November 1937): 386–405. Among those who draw on this perspective are Hogendorn and Brown, *The New International Economics*, pp. 369–373.
24. Raymond Vernon, "Future of the Multinational Corporation," in Kindleberger, ed., *The International Corporation*, p. 389.
25. George Ball, "Cosmocorps: The Importance of Being Stateless," *Columbia Journal of World Business* 2, no. 6 (November–December 1967):25–30.

tors of U.S. firms; and it was increasingly difficult for any one country – whether home country or host country – to control the activities of these giant global corporations.[26]

However, the global-corporation school, which in reality was a characterization of ongoing trends more than a cogent theory of foreign direct investment, generally did not distinguish between branch-plant and international-production-grid investments. For most analysts adopting this view, the key point was that multinational corporations were threatening to dominate global economic trends and thus to reduce the autonomy of nation-states in vital areas of interest such as currency control, taxation, employment, and border transactions.[27]

Despite the paucity of theoretical work explaining the emergence of international production networks, it appears that one of the major international trends favoring this development – in addition to the reasons advanced by the cosmocorp school – is the increased emphasis that many countries place on manufactured exports. This development is described in more detail in the next chapter. Rather than concentrating on encouraging foreign direct investors to set up "tariff factories" to produce within protected domestic markets, more countries have sought to attract firms that will use them as a platform for export.[28] This trend has enabled foreign direct investors to think more in terms of manufacturing and obtaining supplies, intermediate goods, and finished products from the most advantageous places to serve regional or global markets. It has encouraged them to break their global system of manufacturing into integrated specialty operations.[29]

26. Among many others representing such views, see Howard Perlmutter, "Super-Giant Firms in the Future," *Wharton Quarterly* 3, no. 2 (Winter 1968): 8–14; Edith Penrose, *The Large International Firm in Developing Countries* (London: Allen and Unwin, 1969); Vernon, *Sovereignty at Bay*; George W. Ball, ed., *Global Companies: The Political Economy of World Business* (Englewood Cliffs, N.J.: Prentice-Hall, 1975).

27. One of the most thorough expositions of all these potential threats to the autonomy of nation-states is found in Barnet and Muller, *Global Reach*.

28. Raymond F. Vernon, "The Economic Consequences of U.S. Foreign Direct Investment," in Baldwin and Richardson, eds., *International Trade and Finance*, pp. 292–293, offers a good description of this evolution.

29. Gilpin takes note of this evolution in his discussion of the potential ways that foreign direct investment can displace U.S. exports: "One particular type of export displacement that is destined to grow arises from so-called offshore production. Originally, this type of investment was motivated solely by cost considerations: American corporations sought out pools of skilled, cheap labor in places like Taiwan and Hong Kong to produce goods for the American market. The subsidiaries established in such enclaves, however, have increasingly been made an integral part of the global sourcing strategies of the multinationals. They now export component and finished goods throughout the world" (*U.S. Power*, pp. 177–178). Writing early in the 1970s, he pointed out: "The implications of this trend, if it were to continue, would obviously be profound for the development of the American economy" (p. 137). Vernon also alluded to this trend,

Increasingly, large firms in manufacturing industries are scouring the globe for the optimal location to produce components to supply their production facilities. In short, more manufacturing companies are applying the same criteria to locational and investment decisions on an international basis that they have long applied within countries. For the student of foreign direct investment, this development increases the importance of identifying and understanding the factors that go into the specific industrial-location decisions made by big corporations.

Industrial location

Thus far, we have examined theories that help explain aggregate international flows of trade and investment. An understanding of factor-proportions accounts, product cycles, the imperfections in international markets, and the trends favoring the internalization of production networks helps in describing the tendencies and preconditions that exist in the international economic system at any given time: why comparative advantage in steel is shifting away from the advanced industrial countries; why high-technology industries are more likely than low-technology industries to be dominated by multinational companies. What these theories do not explain is how individual firms internalize these signals and translate them into decisions that maximize their own welfare under prevailing conditions.

Theoretical economists generally have not placed emphasis on understanding the decision-making process and predicting the actual behavior of individual firms. However, economic geographers, political economists, business analysts, and political scientists have directed more attention to the processes by which microdecisions are made about the optional locations for corporate production facilities, and thereby have contributed a large volume of theoretical literature on the corporate industrial-location process.

Far more than small localized firms, large industrial corporations seek to analyze a wide variety of economic, political, and social factors before

noting that "by 1970 the product cycle was beginning to look in some ways inadequate as a way of looking at the U.S.-controlled multinational enterprise" (*Sovereignty at Bay*, pp. 107–108).

Others who have sought to make the distinction include Hollis Chenery and Helen Hughes, "The International Division of Labor: The Case of Industry" (Paper presented to the European Conference of the International Society for Development, The Hague, October 24–27, 1971); Gyorgy Adam, "Some Implications and Concomitants of Worldwide Sourcing," *Acta Oeconomica* 8, no. 2–3 (1972): 309–323; and Folker Frobel, Jurgen Heinrichs, and Otto Kreye, "The World Market for Labor and the World Market for Industrial Sites," *Journal of Economic Issues* 12, no. 4 (December 1978):843–858.

making decisions about where to locate new production facilities. This was recognized even before multinationalization of production was commonplace. Hence, the basic tenets of industrial-location theory were set down primarily to account for intranational rather than international locational decisions. Nevertheless, with certain embellishments, most industrial-location theory can be applied internationally without fundamental revision.

Although there are several different schools of thought about how industrial locations are chosen, scholars generally agree on the factors that must be aggregated in the decision-making process. These factors include raw materials, energy sources, markets, labor supply and costs, transportation availability and costs, capital availability, the potential for economies of scale, services and infrastructure (electricity, water supply, waste disposal, and so forth), governmental actions (taxes, incentives, regulations), and site costs. The various schools tend to differ over the weight assigned to each of these factors, whether the same factors guide all manufacturing industries, and the extent to which decisions ultimately result from an empirical process that adds up the pluses and minuses systematically.

Corporate costs and markets

The first modern attempt to develop a theory of location from manufacturing industries was made in Germany, by Alfred Weber. Weber assumed that the need to minimize costs, particularly the cost of transportation, was the most important consideration in the industrial-location process. To him, there were only three general factors that affected the location of all industries: transportation costs, labor costs, and certain "agglomerating" forces. Transportation costs were the primary consideration, with the other two factors acting as distortions to move the locational choice away from the point where transportation costs could be minimized.[30]

Weber viewed the location process as highly mechanistic. He believed that by calculating transportation costs and then adjusting for differentials in labor costs and the savings from economies of scale (or, conversely, the costs of operating in an overly congested location) all manufacturing industries could identify the least-cost locations for new manufacturing plants.[31]

30. Alfred Weber, *Theory of the Location of Industries,* translated by C. J. Friedrich from the 1909 German ed. (Chicago: University of Chicago Press, 1929).
31. A good summary of Weber's theory is found in R. C. Riley, *Industrial Geography* (London: Chatto and Windus, 1973), pp. 7–15. For an updated perspective drawing on Weber, see Walter Isard, *Location and Space Economy* (Cambridge, Mass.: MIT Press, 1956).

Subsequent industrial-location theorists, while adhering to Weber's least-cost maxim, have identified other factors that firms must consider in judging which location will minimize total costs. Among the most important post-Weber refinements of least-cost theory were those contributed by E. M. Hoover. Hoover considered two crucial factors that Weber had neglected. First, he sought to respond to numerous critiques of Weber's version of least-cost theory by noting the spatial implications of demand – the location and concentration of markets for a plant's output – rather than assuming, as had Weber, that all output is sold in one market and that a product produced at its least-cost location will create its own demand. Second, Hoover took into account some of the ways that governmental activities could affect the empirical calculation of a least-cost production site.

Perhaps most important, Hoover pointed out the fallacy of Weber's assumption that transportation costs were proportional to distances. Very different and fluctuating rate structures for different types of transportation and for different categories of haulage fundamentally affected the economics of various manufacturing sites in ways that were little correlated with actual transport distances, Hoover claimed.[32]

The other major school to arise in the first part of this century emphasized not the least-cost location but instead the highest-profit location. This school has been known as the market-area school, because it contends that the plant location that will maximize profits is the one from which the largest number of prospective customers can be served. This school argues that it is the potential market area – its size, the number of customers, and the demand function generated – that is the fundamental determinant of the optimal location for a manufacturing plant. Writing in the 1920s, Frank Fetter was the first to contend that the size of the market area was more important to a firm's location than its total costs.[33]

Later, shortly before the Second World War, August Losch suggested a number of modifications in market-area theory. He criticized Weber for looking only for the least-cost location but pointed out that searching only for the largest-sales location was equally absurd. To maximize profits, Losch argued, a firm should ascertain production costs at various locations and then establish the size of the market to be controlled at each location.[34]

32. Edgar M. Hoover, *Location Theory and the Shoe and Leather Industries* (Cambridge: Harvard University Press, 1937); and Edgar M. Hoover, *The Location of Economic Activity* (New York: McGraw-Hill, 1948).

33. Frank A. Fetter, "The Economic Law of Market Areas," *Quarterly Journal of Economics* 39 (1924):520–529. See Riley, *Industrial Geography*, pp. 21–22.

34. August Losch, *The Economics of Location* (New Haven, Conn.: Yale University Press, 1940).

In the last quarter century, both the least-cost and market-area approaches to industrial location have been widely criticized, not only for being one-sided and normative (rather than explanatory) but for being applicable primarily to industries of the early industrial revolution and to an era when most markets were primarily local and regional rather than national and international.[35] Curiously, the reduction in transportation costs as a proportion of total costs – which can be attributed to improved transportation efficiency and a reduced proportion of weight to product value for many modern products – has been a major factor in the antiquation of both theories.[36]

Several attempts have been made to reformulate, combine, and water down the assertions of the two classical industrial-siting schools. For example, one school of thought holds that firm managers are rarely if ever fully aware of their least-cost or maximum-profit location. But, this school contends, they do distinguish between locations where they will make profits and those where they will suffer losses, and they do have a relative sense of locations where costs will be higher and lower. Locations will fall within certain margins on both the cost and profits ledgers. But in choosing between different potential locations within the margins, firms may make their decisions on the basis of any number of extraneous factors.[37]

A more recent school, popularized by Allan Pred, carries the marginal-location school one step farther in trying to account for reality, claiming that the most nearly universal motivating factors in plant locations are the behavioral influences on the individuals who are in the position to make the decision. Industrial decision makers differ, Pred argues, not only in their abilities to aggregate information and in the access they have to relevant information, but also in their willingness to let nonbusiness circumstances (proximity to a country club or to preferred neighborhoods, for example) enter into their decisions.[38]

Pred's thesis is not that managers make highly personalistic, irrational

35. An early critique is found in Melvin L. Greenhut, *Plant Location in Theory and Practice: The Economics of Space* (Chapel Hill: University of North Carolina Press, 1956). See also Riley, *Industrial Geography;* David F. Walker, "A Behavioural Approach to Industrial Location," in Lyndhurst Collins and David F. Walker, ed., *Location Dynamics of Manufacturing Activity* (London: John Wiley and Sons, 1975); and E. Willard Miller, *A Geography of Manufacturing* (Englewood Cliffs, N.J.: Prentice-Hall, 1962).

36. See William Alonso, "Location Theory," in John Friedman and William Alonso, eds., *Regional Development and Planning: A Reader* (Cambridge, Mass.: MIT Press, 1964).

37. See, for example, D. M. Smith, "A Theoretical Framework for Geographical Studies of Industrial Location," *Economic Geography* 42 (1966):95–113; and D. M. Smith, *Industrial Location: An Economic-Geographical Analysis* (New York: John Wiley and Sons, 1971).

38. Allan R. Pred, *Behavior and Location*, 2 vols. (Lund: G. W. K. Gleerey, 1967, 1969).

decisions, because he assumes that good managers are ones who make good decisions for the firm – decisions that keep costs down, enlarge markets, and increase profits. Sometimes genuinely bad decisions are made, though, because of the individual behavioral filters of key decision makers. Or sometimes so many possibilities are available within certain ranges of profitability and production costs that it does not matter if the particular choice is based on personalistic criteria. In part, Pred's behavioral model is a response to the technological, economic, and political circumstances that have given many industries much greater flexibility in location than manufacturing industries have had in the past.[39]

The decision-making process

Weber and many who followed intended to outline a general theory for industrial location that would efficiently describe the optimal locations or explain location decisions for all manufacturing industries. Yet most contemporary analysts have focused more on the increasing complexities and unique circumstances of different industries than on the aspects shared by all. A recent survey of the distribution of manufacturing industries, for example, concluded:

> There are a number of factors that influence the location of a manufacturing plant, but the extent to which any one of these factors has a bearing on that location depends, for example, upon the nature of the industry, its degree of technical sophistication, the time period in question and upon the political and socio-economic environment. The way in which location factors interact with one another is complex, and has led to considerable differences in the models advanced by writers on industrial location.[40]

Students of industrial location tend now to devote more attention to the general process of site selection than to the ranking of the universal factors that determine location. Thus, rather than trying to develop a general theory for optimal industrial locations, industrial geographers have recently sought to devise a model of the decision-making process within which multivariate and everchanging factors are aggregated for the selection of any given industrial site.

A British geographer, John Rees, recently offered one such model, which helps to bridge the gap between the macroeconomic theories of foreign direct investment already discussed and the microeconomic the-

---

39. Pred's approach is discussed and amplified in a number of the articles contained in Collins and Walker, *Location Dynamics*.
40. Ibid., pp. 2–3.

ories of the firm that characterize most work on industrial location. Rees argues that a firm's decision to build a new plant is primarily a response to a demand problem – that is, the firm either perceives an unfulfilled demand in existing territories and in untried territories, or finds it difficult to meet current demand at the present site. Normally, the firm first considers the short-term solution of expanding output at the existing site. If expansion is not possible or if it alleviates the problem only temporarily, the firm must choose one of three long-term responses: relocation of the existing plant, acquisition of a plant from another firm, or construction of a new branch plant.[41]

If the firm decides to construct a new branch plant, it then initiates a three-stage process for choosing the location. First, the firm identifies a potential sales region in which demand is sufficient to sustain a branch plant. Next, it finds in that region a community where comparative costs are low enough to satisfy the firm's profit goals. Finally, the specific site is chosen. This last decision is frequently influenced by criteria that are not directly related to profitability – proximity to nice neighborhoods, for example.[42]

The Rees model actually combines elements of all the major schools of industrial-location theory – least-cost, market-area, marginal-location, and behavioral. But it also can be reconciled with or plugged into prevailing theories on the product cycle and foreign direct investment to help explain the decisions that U.S. firms make about overseas expansion and location. The demand problem initially perceived by a firm may well result from many of the internationalizing forces noted by analysts of the product cycle and foreign direct investment. For example, new overseas markets may be opened by the spread of an American-introduced product overseas. At the same time, production-cost differentials or other factors may make it difficult to service the overseas market from existing domestic plants, and various oligopolistic advantages may make the operation of a new overseas plant an attractive consideration.

Once this occurs, Rees's three-tier selection process operates on an international as well as a national basis. A firm may identify the European Common Market countries as its potential sales region, it may choose Scotland as an area of comparatively low total costs from which to reach

41. John Rees, "Decision-Making, the Growth of the Firm, and the Business Environment," in F. E. Ian Hamilton, ed., *Spatial Perspectives on Industrial Organization and Decision-making* (London: John Wiley and Sons, 1974).
42. John Rees, "The Industrial Corporation and Location Decision Analysis," *Area* 4 (1972):199–205; and John Rees, "Organization Theory and Corporate Decisions: Some Implications for Industrial Location Analysis," *Regional Science Perspectives* 2 (1972):126–135.

the entire market area conveniently, and it may choose a site near Edinburgh as the one that best meets its economic needs and is also close to the cultural and social amenities of a cosmopolitan area.

Industry-specific location factors

Rees's model of the industrial-location process, and a number of similar models,[43] can help to link the macroeconomic theories of aggregate trends in foreign direct investment and the microeconomic theories of a firm's behavior in selecting individual industrial locations. But, unlike previous general theories on industrial location, it does not attempt to isolate any one factor that is crucial in location decisions made by firms in all manufacturing industries. Increasingly, analysts have concluded that this is not possible, that the most crucial factors will vary by industry type. Observers have therefore sought to identify broad categories of industries that share a particular factor that overshadows others in the location process.

Although transportation costs have generally become a less important factor in industrial location, they are still a primary cause of continuing orientation to raw-material supplies in some industries. This is particularly true for processing industries, such as the copper, pulp-and-paper, and cement industries. Other industries – for example, dairy and food processing, furniture manufacturing, and soft-drink bottling – are bound to be closer to markets because of the costs or difficulties in transporting finished products. Like transportation, proximity to a source of power has declined as a major factor for many industries because of general availability of electricity and natural gas and the mobility of other fuel supplies. The textile industry no longer is bound to operate plants along rapidly flowing rivers and streams, for example. But for a few industries, notably aluminum, relative proximity to a cheap, available source of electricity remains an important factor. Other industries, such as steel and oil refining, though not strictly bound to raw-material supplies, tend to be located at transportation break points between raw materials and markets – seaports, river depots, and transportation crossroads, for example. Some industries are more "social" than others, perhaps because of the need to share raw materials or because of the logistics of co-production.[44]

43. See Howard A. Stafford, "The Anatomy of a Location Decision," in Hamilton, *Spatial Perspectives;* Michael Storper, "Toward a Structural Theory of Industrial Location," in John Rees, Geoffrey J. D. Hewings, and Howard A. Stafford, eds., *Industrial Location and Regional Systems* (New York: Bergin, 1981); and P. M. Townroe, "Locational Choice and the Individual Firm," *Regional Studies* 3 (1969):15–24. For an integrated global perspective of trade, location, and foreign investment, see Brian J. L. Berry, Edgar C. Conkling, and D. Michael Ray, *The Geography of Economic Systems* (Englewood Cliffs, N.J.: Prentice-Hall, 1976).
44. See Riley, *Industrial Geography.*

Although various factors like these loom large for several different groups of industries, many of the most important industries of the late twentieth century are increasingly flexible in locational choices. A large number of technologically advanced industries have much wider latitude in balancing many more cost- and non-cost-related factors than the typical low-value-added, high-bulk industry of yesteryear enjoyed. Still, these industries – which produce goods ranging from automobiles to chemicals and electrical equipment – are not technically footloose: they need infrastructure, appropriately skilled labor, linkages with other industries, and numerous other specific provisions.[45] The difference is that such industries depend more on the amenities offered by governments at various locations and less on natural circumstances such as raw materials and river transportation.

In addition, it is important to bear in mind that although capital-intensive industries may be flexible in selecting a new location, they cannot easily move existing production facilities from one place to another. Once in place at a particular location, physical capital in the form of big plant equipment is generally immobile for a decade or more, unless circumstances change radically. This means that frequently a plant at a location that suited a firm's needs at the time of selection may remain in operation even though the rationale for the location is no longer compelling. Industrial inertia, as this phenomenon has been labeled, introduces a significant short-term rigidity into the long-term context of flexibility for many capital-intensive industries.[46]

We can now note three general trends that fundamentally affect the industrial-location process for many modern industries. First, because of declining transportation costs and the changing nature of the industrial product, many industries enjoy more freedom in selecting locations for new industrial plants. Second, although in theory these industries thus have the opportunity to choose between many locations, the services that governments can provide at given locations are increasingly influential and essential – relative governmental provisions for energy supply, waste-disposal systems, reliable water supplies, and availability of appropriate labor may be crucial locational factors for so-called footloose industries. Third, the high costs of building advanced-technology manufacturing plants may force many of the industries that have been freed from traditional locational constraints in site selection to remain where they are over the short term.

45. James B. Cannon, "Government Impact on Industrial Location," in Collins and Walker, *Locational Dynamics*.
46. See Peter M. Townroe, "Post Move Stability and the Location Decision," and Robert B. McNee, "A Systems Approach of Understanding the Geographic Behavior of Organizations, Especially Large Corporations," in Hamilton, *Spatial Perspectives*.

These trends have operated to hasten the worldwide dispersion of industry that is inherent in the product cycle. But they have also given governments more levers with which to alter or tailor the industrial-location process than was the case when industries were more tightly bound by the dictates of nature and traditional economic factors. By providing infrastructure in one place but not another, by agreeing to train certain categories of workers, or, increasingly, by providing outright benefits (for example, tax holidays at the national level or capital grants in varying amounts at the regional level), governments have become major actors in the location process for almost all industries. Since technology-based industry tends to be relatively rigid after the initial siting decision, governments generally focus on providing maximum benefits and amenities for industries in the short term – one-time labor-training or grant-in-aid programs, ten-year tax breaks, and the like.

Conclusions

Drawing on the works of both Bertil Ohlin and Alfred Weber, Walter Isard wrote nearly three decades ago that: "location and trade are as the two sides of the same coin. The forces determining one simultaneously determine the other."[47] This is even more true today than when Isard wrote it. In a world where factors are mobile, comparative advantage in industrial production must be seen in the context of theories that explain both trade and location.

All three of the theoretical concerns addressed in this chapter – the international product cycle, the foreign-direct-investment process, and the industrial-location process – help to explain why the concept of comparative advantage has become much more tenuous in the twentieth century. Far from being fixed or changing only very gradually, advantages accruing to producers in one country may evolve over a period of decades or even years, as the product cycle runs its course. Therefore, producers from one country may seek to stay competitive by moving capital to other countries, a form of factor mobility not accounted for in classical formulations of comparative advantage. And for many industries seeking the best location for a production facility, natural factor endowments in some potential locations may be less important than the artificial factor endowments created by governments in other places.

Governments the world over are increasingly concerned with heightening overall industrial growth, assisting lagging regions, and creating jobs. They have had to respond to the dangers and the opportunities posed

47.   As cited in Berry, Conkling, and Ray, *The Geography of Economic Systems*, p. 179.

by the relative decline of static factor endowments and the rise of more dynamic elements in the determination of comparative advantage in industrial production. Industrial-development planning at the national, regional and local levels, though hardly a science, has grown dramatically more important in virtually all political and economic systems in recent decades. One consequence at the national level has been that countries have sought to take advantage of the increased importance of governmental actions and provisions in an effort to attract more industry to their shores. This effect can be observed in industrialized countries, but it has been most marked in countries that are prepared for or undergoing rapid industrial development.

Possessing the powers to manipulate factors of importance to manufacturing industries, governments in underindustrialized countries no longer passively accept the assessments of nature or high-handed economists that their comparative advantage lies in exporting primary products or simple manufactured goods. At the same time, this has meant that industrializing nations have had to depend even more on imported capital goods and technological expertise in order to build up their comparative advantage in certain lines of production. Consequently, the next chapter will analyze how governments in industrializing countries have sought to manipulate the trends described in this chapter to their advantage, and how their relationships with the owners of foreign technology and expertise are structured.

2

Industrial-development strategy and the role of multinational corporations

Like most political-economic upheavals in modern history, the industrial revolution did not originate in the plans and designs made by governments. Rather, it became the dominant force shaping world politics and economics in the nineteenth and twentieth centuries on the strength of a long series of spontaneous inventions and innovations by private entrepreneurs in Europe (especially Great Britain) and the United States. To be sure, governmental actions in Great Britain and later the United States greatly facilitated innovation, the introduction of new technology and production techniques, and the raising of capital for investment.[1] Governmental encouragement, though perhaps necessary for the industrial age to flourish, did not cause its birth. The original will to industrialize was a spark that inflamed the hearts and minds of individual entrepreneurs and subsequently molded sympathetic political constituencies within the state.

Since then, however – especially in the twentieth century – the state has become more and more directly involved in formulating the strategy, creating the spark, and even owning the capital in all countries that have sought to attain the affluence and power associated with industrialization. One reason for this, as Gerschenkron stressed, is that the advancement of several countries perforce fundamentally alters the challenge of industrial-

1. See, for example, Phyllis Deane, *The First Industrial Revolution* (Cambridge: Cambridge University Press, 1965); J. B. Condliffe, *The Commerce of Nations* (New York: Norton, 1950); E. J. Hobsbawm, *Industry and Empire* (London: Penguin, 1969); Colin Clark, *The Conditions of Economic Progress* (London: Macmillan, 1957); Veblen, *Imperial Germany;* Walt Rostow, *Politics and the Stages of Economic Development* (Cambridge, Mass.: Harvard University Press, 1965); Andrew Shonfield, *Modern Capitalism* (London: Oxford University Press, 1965); and Douglas C. North and Robert Thomas, *The Rise of the Western World: A New Economic History* (Cambridge: Cambridge University Press, 1973). For good theoretical descriptions on the role of the state in industrial development, see Bert F. Hoselitz, "Economic Growth and Development: Non-Economic Factors in Economic Development," *American Economic Review* 47 (May 1957):28–41; Edward S. Mason, "The Role of Government in Economic Development," *American Economic Review* 50 (May 1960); and Edith Penrose, "Economic Development and the State: An Objective Lesson from the Past," *Economic Development and Cultural Change* 11 (January 1963):196–202.

ization for all others. Industrialization, which in the advanced countries proceeded gradually and along a haphazard path, becomes also a process of diminishing backwardness, which demands rapid progress and strategic planning.[2]

Once advanced industrial arts have been originated and proven in one country, after perhaps decades of false starts, other countries must make a deliberate effort to catch up. Not only must technology be imitated or imported – both of which require either large investments up front or access to foreign capital markets – but all the numerous barriers that prevented the industrialization process from emerging gradually must be dismantled simultaneously. Thus, the process of industrial development for a backward country can be viewed as a series of efforts to create artificial substitutes for the factors that facilitated industrial development in the advanced countries.

It is not surprising that such efforts have required heavy involvement on the part of the state. Gerschenkron puts it eloquently:

> To break through the barriers of stagnation in a backward country, to ignite the imaginations of men, and to place their energies in the service of economic development, a stronger medicine is needed than the promise of better allocation of resources or even a lower price of bread. Under such conditions of extreme economic backwardness, even the businessman, even the classical daring and innovating entrepreneur, needs a more powerful stimulus than the prospect of high profits.[3]

The more backward a country becomes in relation to others, Gerschenkron adds, the more likely it is that industrialization will proceed under some organized direction, the form of which will depend on the degree of backwardness: the direction can come from the investment banks or industrial corporations protected by the state, or it can come directly from the state in the form of bureaucratic control of the economy and productive enterprise.[4] In either case, as Robert Gilpin states, "a seemingly necessary condition for [industrial] spread to take place at the rate desired by the periphery is the existence of some centralized political power which can counteract the economic power of existing centers and the centralizing tendency of market forces."[5]

In short, the will to industrialize has increasingly become a creation of the state rather than a serendipitous confluence of entrepreneurial activity. The natural trend toward more state orchestration of industrial develop-

2. Gerschenkron, *Economic Backwardness*.
3. Ibid., p. 24.
4. Ibid., p. 44.
5. Gilpin, *U.S. Power*, pp. 56–57.

ment has only been reinforced by observation of the common traits shared by the superindustrializers during the first two-thirds of this century. For example, although Japan and the Soviet Union have few similarities in the specifics of their economic systems, the industrialization miracles in both countries can be attributed to strong state intervention to shift surplus resources from nonindustrial sectors into industrial investment, to smash opposition to industrialization, and to accelerate the rate of industrial expansion.[6]

Hence, two points are relevant today to all countries except the most advanced industrial nations. First, the overwhelming goal of most under-developed nations has been and remains national industrialization – the creation or acquisition of an industrial and technical base in order to attain higher affluence and to escape the vicissitudes of depending upon expensive foreign manufactured products and the bounties that nature's fixed endowments can yield. Second, in order to achieve this goal it is, for all intents and purposes, an essential precondition that the state be capable of taking strong measures to plan, direct, protect, and nurture the embry-onic industrialization process.

Trade and industrial strategy

Issues of foreign trade are among the most fundamental that countries aspiring to achieve rapid industrial development must confront. The choices a country makes about trade have a profound impact on how industrialization is achieved, who pays for it, and what types of industries become leading sectors. Indeed, on the basis of empirical studies of eco-nomic development in a number of countries, Hollis Chenery concluded that "the main differences in the observed patterns of production are asso-ciated with differences in trade patterns."[7]

There are three broad approaches to international trade that nation-states can pursue in their industrialization efforts. At one extreme, they can turn entirely inward. Instead of buying and selling on international markets, they will seek to generate surplus capital internally, relying almost wholly upon indigenous technology, expertise, and innovation. *Autarky,* as this strategy is called, generally requires immense and contin-

---

6. On Japan see William W. Lockwood, ed., *The State and Economic Enterprise in Japan* (Princeton, N.J.: Princeton University Press, 1967). On the Soviet Union see Gerschenk-ron, *Economic Backwardness;* Abraham Bergson and Simon Kuznets, eds., *Economic Trends in the Soviet Union* (Cambridge, Mass.: Harvard University Press, 1963); Alec Nove, *The Soviet Economy: An Introduction* (New York: Praeger, 1969).
7. Hollis Chenery, *Structural Change and Development Policy* (London: Oxford Univer-sity Press, 1979), p. 141.

uing human deprivation and bountiful natural-resource supplies if it is to result in rapid and sustained industrial development.

Or a nation can attempt to withdraw partially and insulate itself from the international economy by pursuing policies that subsidize, reward, and protect domestic industries that replace imported manufactured goods with home-produced goods. This strategy, called *import substitution,* often means that an industrializing nation will import technology rather than finished products and will attempt to build all industries for which a domestic product demand exists rather than concentrating on a narrower range of industries for which it has obvious comparative advantage in manufacturing.

Finally, a nation-state can seek to integrate itself into the world economy by exploiting preexisting comparative advantage or finding niches within the spectrum of manufacturing industries for specialization and trade. This is called *export promotion* because policies are designed to reward industries for exporting goods, which in turn generates revenues for further domestic industrial expansion and for necessary imported manufactured goods and technology.

Embracing import substitution

In the aftermath of World War II, as many of the world's underdeveloped areas reaffirmed or attained their independence and consolidated political support for rapid industrialization, it was obvious to even the most free-market-oriented policymakers that only the government could mobilize sufficient resources to provide the social and physical infrastructure for industrial development. The phenomenal industrial push of the Soviet Union had conclusively demonstrated by then that central-government direction could impose a rapid rate of industrialization upon the populace of an underdeveloped country.

At the same time, the Soviet model was not palatable or even possible as a template for most underdeveloped nations. Few governments had the will or the strength to impose such harsh measures. Also, it became increasingly apparent, as Gerschenkron pointed out, that the long-term economic price of human suffering in the Soviet Union was to be paid in the exhaustion of the work force and later stagnation.[8] Besides, although many countries endorsed the notion of central government planning, relatively few were prepared to follow the Soviet Union in choosing to abandon private enterprise completely. Finally, the benefits, identified by

8. Gerschenkron, *Economic Backwardness,* p. 17.

Veblen, of remaining linked closely enough to the international system to borrow technology and capital (as well as to receive it in foreign assistance packages) were obvious and compelling.[9] For all these reasons, the Soviet model of draconian autarchic industrialization seemed too costly (in terms of human suffering and foregone opportunity) and not viable for most underdeveloped, small, and politically frail countries.

The rhetoric of the Soviet model, however, had a much more profound effect upon postwar industrial-development strategies. Anticolonialism, fears of the international capitalist system, and resentment of the peripheral countries' continuing dependence upon the core for manufactured goods essential for a modernizing nation – these sentiments helped push many fledgling industrial countries to puruse policies that would bring rapid industrialization through more self-sufficiency and economic independence.[10]

While arguing against a policy of ad hoc withdrawal from all intercourse with the world economy, most Third World industrial-development planners tried to avoid wholesale integration in the world economy by pursuing policies of limited autarchy. In particular, advocates of such strategies urged developing countries to reduce the import content of manufactured goods, on the assumption that imports competed with and stifled the growth of domestic producers of manufactured goods.[11] Emphasis on stimulating industrial expansion by adopting inward-looking policies designed to nurture domestic producers of manufactured goods became known as *import-substituting industrialization.*

The key postwar objective of the majority of developing countries was thus to replace as many imported goods as possible with goods manufactured within their own borders. To this end, they outlined policies to protect domestic industries from better, more efficiently produced foreign goods which, in the absence of home production or sufficient protection for domestic industries, had become entrenched in the country's markets. In many instances, if an industry targeted for import substitution was deemed too complex for domestic entrepreneurs, foreign direct investors were lured to set up "tariff factories" by the promise of monopoly access to the domestic market.

The import-substitution approach, requiring elaborate systems of tariffs and administrative controls and bolstered by extensive government subsidies for public and private enterprises, remained gospel for many devel-

---

9. See Veblen, *Imperial Germany,* chap. 2.
10. Charles K. Wilber, *The Soviet Model and the Underdeveloped Countries* (Chapel Hill: University of North Carolina Press, 1969).
11. See especially Raul Prebisch, *The Economic Development of Latin America and Its Principal Problems* (New York: United Nations Commission for Latin America, 1950).

oping countries through the 1950s and into the 1960s. Although rates of industrial expansion for developing countries varied widely during the twenty years following the war, a number of these countries managed to make major strides toward establishing a varied and scientific industrial base through import substitution.[12]

The limits of domestic demand

However, by the 1960s the limitations and drawbacks of clinging to a strategy of import substitution became more and more apparent, for a variety of reasons.[13] First, the success of the small group of countries that had spurned protectionist policies and sought to industrialize by concentrating on producing exports competitive in international markets helped belie the myth that less developed countries (LDCs) could not compete in manufactured products. Second, in a number of countries, import substitution did not even have the desired effects. While "looking inward" some countries found that they were still "paying outward":[14] their import bills actually increased because the foreign machinery and technology needed to set up certain industries cost more than it had cost to import the final products. In neglecting comparative advantage, many countries set up highly inefficient industries that wasted scarce captial resources, drained government funds, and still managed to charge consumers high prices.[15]

Finally, and most important, even the countries that had achieved some success with import-substitution policies during their first phase of industrialization were finding that this approach could not support rapid industrial growth for an extended period. In essence, many countries ran out of import-substitution possibilities – suddenly industries that had been

12. Although there is considerable historical debate about the relative progress made under postwar import substitution strategies (vis-à-vis the progress that could have been made under alternative strategies), data assembled by Alfred Maizels in the 1960s did demonstrate that the policies had been effective in achieving the primary goal of reducing manufactured imports. Between 1900 and 1959, Maizels showed, the import content of manufactured goods did fall significantly in the group of countries he called "semi-industrialized." Alfred Maizels, *Industrial Growth and World Trade* (Cambridge: Cambridge University Press, 1963). See also Albert O. Hirschman, "The Political Economy of Import-Substituting Industrialization in Latin America," *Quarterly Journal of Economics* 82 (February 1968):636–641.
13. One of the most influential and thoroughgoing critiques of import substitution is found in Ian Little, Tibor Scitovsky, and Maurice Scott, *Industry and Trade in Some Developing Countries: A Comparative Study* (London: Oxford University Press, 1970).
14. The phrases in quotes are borrowed from Micheal Todaro, *Economic Development in the Third World* (London: Longmans, 1977), p. 304.
15. Some of the early advocates of import-substitution policies later became among the harshest critics of what they considered the misguided application of these policies. See, for example, Raul Prebisch, *Towards A New Dynamic Development Policy for Latin America* (New York: United Nations, 1963).

coddled and protected by explicit policies designed to make them leading growth sectors in the domestic economy could expand no farther without exceeding domestic demand. Although the answer for further growth was exports, the entire domestic industrial structure was poorly adapted to the rigors of competing in international markets.[16]

The structural problems that make it difficult for industrializing nations to switch from import-substitution-led to export-led economic growth occur at two levels. Part of the problem lies at the level of the firm. Industrial plants built for import substitution often cannot benefit from economies of scale because they are smaller than normal factories, less specialized, and not integrated into wider supply, production, and marketing grids. They are generally accustomed to operating with subsidies and to serving protected markets with few, if any, alternate producers to prod them to improve quality, selection, availability, or pricing. In such cases, extremely vigorous, across-the-board efforts are necessary to force already entrenched producers to adapt to competitive conditions and open foreign market outlets.[17]

An even more serious problem is at the industry level. Import substitution often leads to industrial development that ignores many considerations of comparative advantage; quite simply, such a policy tends to encourage lines of industrial production that are unlikely to be competitive in an open, export-oriented economy, no matter how many adjustments are made at the firm level.[18]

The structural problems associated with the long-term pursuit of import substitution as an engine of industrial expansion have been especially marked for small countries with domestic markets that can sustain only a limited number of plants in particular industries. For them, import substitution is a strategy of limited duration, even under the best conditions. But the limits to growth from industrialization by import substitu-

16. Further elaborations of the problems encountered with import substitution are found in R. B. Sutcliffe, *Industry and Underdevelopment* (London: Addison-Wesley, 1971), pp. 260–269; Charles P. Kindleberger and Peter H. Lindert, *International Economics* (Homewood, Ill.: Richard D. Irwin, 1978), pp. 207–213; W. M. Corden, "Trade Policies," in John Cody, Helen Hughes, and David Wall, eds., *Policies for Industrial Progress in Developing Countries* (New York: Oxford University Press, 1980), pp. 39–92; and G. K. Helleiner, *International Trade and Economic Development* (London: Penguin, 1972).

17. This problem applies both to domestically owned firms, which often do not have the capital, technology, or knowledge to produce on larger scale, and to foreign-owned firms, many of which have purposely built scaled-down operations in import-substituting countries because of the relatively small domestic market. See Little, Scitovsky, and Scott, *Industry and Trade*, pp. 57–58; and Corden, "Trade Policies," pp. 67–69.

18. See, in addition to others already cited, Bela Belassa et al., *The Structure of Protection in Developing Countries* (Baltimore: Johns Hopkins Press, 1971).

tion have plagued larger industrializing nations with the market potential to sustain a varied industrial base and multiple plants in the same industries. Many of these nations – Mexico, Spain, and India are good examples – still pursue policies of selective import substitutions, but most have taken significant steps to identify industrial sectors for active export promotion.[19]

Outward-looking industrial growth

The results of the emphasis on outward-looking industrial growth have been significant. The last two decades witnessed dramatic industrial progress in a number of countries outside the most advanced industrial nations. The list includes countries commonly known as newly industrializing countries (Hong Kong, South Korea, Taiwan, Singapore, Brazil, Mexico, Spain, Turkey, Greece, and Portugal), as well as Ireland, the socialist countries of Eastern Europe, and several other countries in South America, Africa, and Asia.

Much of the strong industrial growth taking place in many newly industrializing nations is attributable to large increases in manufactured exports.[20] The number of less-developed countries exporting significant amounts of manufactured goods increased more than sevenfold (from four to thirty) between 1960 and 1968.[21] While the output of manufactured goods in less-developed countries expanded at an annual rate of 7 percent between 1960 and 1975, the output of manufactures for export grew more than twice as fast – 15 percent per year. And this rate of expansion for manufactured exports was also twice as fast as the annual growth regis-

19. In effect, many industrializing countries, particularly those with large domestic markets, have sought to pursue policies which are simultaneously inward- and outward-looking. Often this occurs in the same industry – an excellent example being found in the Mexican automobile industry. Mexico continues to maintain very high tariff barriers on imports of completed automobiles; domestic producers (all of whom are large foreign companies) remain highly protected and operate small-scale plants that could not be competitive in world markets. At the same time, the Mexican government has actively encouraged the buildup of an export-oriented automobile-parts sector that is dependent on integration into worked production systems. See Jerry Brady, "Automotive Industry," in Brady, ed., *Mexican Industrial Development Plans: Implications for United States Policy* (Washington, D.C.: Ventana Associates, 1981).

20. Among recent studies that draw a clear link between export expansion and industrial growth as well as overall economic growth are Maizels, *Industrial Growth and World Trade;* Michael Michaely, "Exports and Growth: An Empirical Investigation," *Journal of Development Economics* 4 (1977):49–53; Bela Belassa, "Export Incentives and Export Performance in Developing Countries: A Comparative Analysis," World Bank Staff Working Paper no. 248 (January 1977).

21. Chenery and Hughes, "International Division of Labor."

Table 2.1. *Share of developing-country exports in the consumption of selected manufactured goods in industrial countries, 1970–80*

Manufactured goods	Share in estimated consumption (%)		Import penetration (average annual % change)	
	1970	1980	1970–77	1977–78
Food	3.5	3.7	3.4	−5.0
Clothing, textiles, & footwear	3.1	10.5	15.5	9.0
Clothing	4.0	16.3	18.6	9.0
Textiles	2.3	5.4	9.1	9.0
Footwear	2.6	16.3	24.3	8.0
Leather products	6.2	17.3	12.6	8.0
Wood products	1.9	3.6	6.6	8.0
Paper	0.2	0.5	11.2	20.0
Chemicals	2.0	3.8	7.8	11.0
Nonmetallic minerals	0.3	1.1	13.7	15.0
Base metals	3.5	4.1	−0.6	14.0
Machinery	0.4	2.1	20.6	15.0
Cutlery and handtools	0.8	3.3	16.2	13.0
Metal furniture	0.6	1.6	12.2	5.0
Radios, televisions, etc.	1.1	6.7	23.5	13.0
Other	4.0	8.0	7.2	10.0
Total	1.7	3.4	8.4	7.0

Source: World Bank, *World Development Report 1983* (New York: Oxford University Press, 1983), p. 14, table 2.7.

tered for total exports by less-developed countries.[22] The rapid expansion of manufactured exports has meant that developing countries have greatly increased their penetration of markets in developed countries, as shown in Table 2.1.

This record of success has profoundly altered the prevailing dogma about industrial development. The industrial-development strategies of industrializing nations have placed increasingly heavy emphasis on the need to encourage the buildup of export-oriented industries as a means of generating economic growth, providing large numbers of jobs, and improving the balance-of-payments outlook. In short, much of the recent progress in industrialization outside the highly industrialized countries

22.   Heien Hughes, "Achievements and Objectives of Industrialization," in Cody, Hughes, and Wall, *Policies for Industrial Progress*, p. 12; and Hollis B. Chenery and Donald B. Keesing, "The Changing Composition of Developing Country Exports," World Bank Staff Working Paper no. 314 (January 1979).

has come as a result of expanded integration of underindustrialized countries into the world industrial production system.

International specialization

If import substitution leads governments to attempt to break away from the classical dictates of comparative advantage by ignoring them, the embracing of the export-promotion approach leads governments to make vigorous efforts to create a whole new definition of comparative advantage for an underindustrialized nation. This often sets a nation on an intense search for a new niche in the international production function to replace its traditional role as a supplier of raw materials or a seller of simple, labor-intensive manufactures. Producing parts, assembling of finished goods, manufacturing particular intermediate or semifinished chemical products, and supplying various exotic materials associated with downstream processing of domestic (or even imported) raw materials are some of the possible specialty areas for export promotion. In most instances, especially in the case of small and medium-sized countries in this category, countries have found particular manufacturing specializations to exploit as their comparative advantage; a combination of labor costs, geographical location, workforce skills, availability of raw materials, and other factors determine what goods they can produce most competitively. In addition, transfers of technology from the developed countries – whether in the form of wholly owned subsidiaries of multinational corporations, joint venture projects, licensing agreements, or outright sale of equipment – have figured strategically in the industrial development of most of these countries, including the socialist countries of Eastern Europe.

Stages of comparative advantage

With many industrializing countries achieving growing success in breaking into world export markets, analysts have focused more attention on identifying which industries are candidates for redeployment in response to the shifting of comparative advantage from industrialized to industrializing countries. Recent empirical work by economists has yielded some broad guidelines.[23] In general, the economists postulate a stages approach

23. See, for example, G. Fels, "The Choice of Industry Mix in the Division of Labor between Developed and Developing Countries," *Weltwirtschaftliches Archiv* 108, no. 1 (1972):71–121; Robert M. Stern, "Testing Trade Theories," in Peter B. Kenen, ed., *International Trade and Finance* (Cambridge: Cambridge University Press, 1975), pp. 3–50; P. S. Heller, "Factor Endowment Change and Comparative Advantage," *Review of Economics and Statistics* 58 (February 1976):283–288; Gerald K. Helleiner, "Industry Characteristics and the Competitiveness of Manufactures from Less-Developed Countries," *Weltwirtschaftliches Archiv* 112, no. 3 (1976):507–524.

to "revealed" comparative advantage[24] in goods. This approach comports well with the Heckscher-Ohlin and product-cycle theories.

According to the stages approach, the structure of developing countries' exports will evolve with the gradual accumulation of physical and human capital – beginning, naturally, with goods that require low amounts of capital and high amounts of unskilled labor. For example, newly industrializing countries can specialize in electronics components, apparel and textiles, stone clay and glass, and footwear and other leather products – all highly labor intensive. On the other end of the spectrum, industries such as petroleum refining, pulp and paper, and organic and inorganic chemicals are highly capital intensive and thus generally seen as being reserved for export specialization by already-industrialized countries and by industrializing countries that have reached advanced stages.[25] A rule of thumb, then, is that developing countries should concentrate on exporting "light" manufactures at an early stage of industrial development and gradually move up the ladder toward heavier manufactures. Japan is generally cited as the archetypal example of a country that has evolved through these stages. The general validity of the rule is demonstrated by the record of market penetration by less-developed countries in select manufactured goods, as shown in Table 2.1.

Nevertheless, the targeting of industries ripe for redeployment to developing countries is not as clear-cut as the broad theoretical work of economists might suggest. First, there is considerable variation within particular industry groupings. For example, as Bela Belassa points out, although apparel items are considered labor intensive, fur goods may be quite capital intensive, and explosives are labor intensive even though they are chemical products.[26] Many products also can be made with varying amounts of capital and labor intensity, depending on which is most abundant in a country. Of even greater importance, most developing countries desire to build productive capacity in a broad range of industrial sectors to meet domestic needs for such products as steel, fertilizers, and paper goods. This may lead them to distort the system of incentives for industry in favor of products in which they do not yet have a comparative advan-

24. The term *revealed comparative advantage* is borrowed from Bela Belassa, who uses it to emphasize that he and others use relative export performance as a proxy for overall comparative advantage, on the assumption that the pattern of imports is fundamentally influenced by systems of tariffs and other protectionist devices. See Bela Belassa, "A 'Stages Approach' to Comparative Advantage," in Irma Adelman, ed., *Economic Growth and Resources,* Proceedings of the Fifth Congress of the International Economic Association, Tokyo, Japan, 1977, vol. 4 (London: Macmillan, 1979), and reprinted in the World Bank Reprint Series as no. 136, p. 129.
25. Ibid.
26. Ibid., p. 139.

tage, for reasons that go beyond the desire to optimize economic efficiency.

Another variable may have profound implications in determining the success industrializing nations have with various categories of manufactured exports: the degree to which markets in the most important advanced industrial countries remain open and unimpeded by tariff and nontariff barriers. In recent years many analysts have become concerned that increased protectionist sentiments in the advanced countries are posing a threat to continuing progress in many newly industrializing nations.[27] The trade barriers erected against manufactured exports are likely to vary widely among different industries, depending on factors well beyond the control of the industrial planners in developing countries – for example, the political influence of various regional and interest-group constituencies in the advanced countries. Here again, political factors may significantly alter the *ceteris paribus* conditions imposed by economists; they may even deprive a thriving manufacturing industry of its major markets almost overnight.

Policy choices for industry

Partly because of these uncertainties and partly because of differing factor endowments, it remains difficult to target industries for export promotion. Despite widespread endorsement of export promotion as a means of unshackling industrial growth from its dependence on domestic market expansion, the strategies pursued by different industrializing nations have been by no means uniform. There is no set formula for following a "stages" approach to comparative advantage in manufactured goods, and many developing countries, for a wide variety of reasons, are eager to hurry the evolution or even to skip a few stages altogether.

Still, from a policy perspective there are several overarching questions that each country must answer in making its choices of industrial specialization. In particular, a country that decides to make a concerted effort to break into world markets for manufactured goods must address four broad concerns.

Type of industry. As the discussion above indicates, one of the most important yet least obvious choices is that of manufacturing specialties. In which industries does a country have a solid chance of breaking into

27. Discussions of the potential deleterious impacts of protectionism in the industrialized nations can be found in Chenery and Keesing, "Changing Composition," pp. 41–44; and World Bank, *The World Development Report 1983* (New York: Oxford University Press, 1983), pp. 27–39.

world markets? This is most important because the initial costs of entry into most manufacturing industries are high, and the risks of selecting declining, no-growth, slow-growth, or flash-in-the-pan industries are quite high. A five- to ten-year commitment to expend massive resources to build up an industry in which international demand turns out to be limited could be a major disaster for a capital-short, industrializing nation.

The problem is that there are often no easy guidelines for assessing comparative advantage for specialty in one or another manufacturing industry. In some cases industrializing nations may seek to develop industries on the basis of the availability of raw materials. For example, a country with vast reserves of phosphate rock would be expected to specialize in the manufacture of detergents and phosphate chemicals. But in many cases the choices are not so obvious. Comparative advantage is hard to define and requires very sophisticated analysis of international industrial trends – at the very least, ability to predict future growth sectors in manufacturing, to target areas of unfilled international demand, and to anticipate the potential for increased protectionism in various industries in the industrialized nations.

In the end, the choice of industry or specialty is bound to be somewhat arbitrary. Luck, timing of investments, marketing ability, and other domestic factors have more to do with whether a country succeeds as an exporter of one or another esoteric product than does the inherent rightness or wrongness of the initial specialization choice. This is one consequence of a fact noted in Chapter 1, that comparative advantage in technologically based manufacturing industries is increasingly a government creation – the criteria for selection are more and more vague.

Control of equity and technology. In whom should ownership of the means of production be vested? Of particular concern is the role of foreigners. Should foreign investors be brought in to establish wholly owned subsidiaries of multinational corporations or joint ventures with domestic companies? Or should industry be domestically owned and contract for whatever external technology and assistance is needed? Applying the postulates discussed in the first chapter, we can generally assume that the more sophisticated the technology used by the industry, the more likely it is that the country will need to permit foreign equity control or joint control in order to achieve success.

But choice of ownership is often settled as much by political as by economic concerns. Some countries may try to develop their own technology in relatively advanced industries, even if that reduces the chances of success. In other countries the government may be so pro-foreign investment that it permits high-foreign-equity ownership even in industrial sectors where idigenous capacity is available.

In many respects this choice is not nearly as black and white as it was once perceived to be, and its significance may not be as great as it seemed in the 1970s climate of heated rhetoric about imperialism, dependency, and the supposed evil machinations associated with multinational corporations. As the next section in this chapter indicates, countries now choose among a broader range of shared equity and nonequity arrangements for building industrial capacity with the assistance of external technology. In the end, few industrializing countries today have foregone technology imported from foreign firms,[28] and technology purchase, turnkey plant construction, and limited-equity arrangements may create their own built-in dependencies that are almost or equally as difficult to live with as are the problems associated with foreign-owned companies that directly operate production plants.

Range of government subsidies. Governments must also choose what kinds of investments they will make to support industrial expansion generally and what incentives they will offer specific firms for building new industrial facilities. These choices are, of course, influenced by the types of industry targeted for specialization and the decisions made about control over equity and technology.

At least four broad categories of subsidies or promotional devices can be identified:

1. the provision of services, including roads and other transportation modes, electricity, raw materials, water, waste disposal, and other infrastructure to support the industries;
2. manipulations of the terms of trade with the outside world, including domestic price supports, tariffs or licensing protection from import competition, and export-subsidization schemes;
3. use of fiscal policies and public finance institutions such as industrial-development banks and promotional agencies in order to reduce taxes, ensure access to adequate amounts of capital, and provide direct-subsidy grants to encourage capital investments;
4. institution of programs, such as job-training schemes, to enhance the quality and quantity of the industrial labor force, and educational investments to enhance technical, scientific, and managerial skills.

Choices about the last three types of promotional policies tend to be determined primarily by the depth of the government's commitment to its industrialization scheme and by the workings of the domestic economic and political systems.[29] Guided by these external constraints, different

28. See G. K. Helleiner, "Manufactured Exports from Less Developed Countries and Multinational Firms," *Economic Journal* 83 (March 1973):21–47.
29. Sutcliffe, *Industry and Underdevelopment*, p. 285.

countries may find a wide range of institutional arrangements to provide the best means of promoting industrial expansion.

Of more speculative interest, however, is the question of the most efficient timing and quantity of investments in public services, or what economists call *social-overhead capital*. Are there levels of public investment in social-overhead capital above which or below which industrialization can be impaired? Is large-scale public investment in infrastructure a prerequisite for rapid industrial expansion or a secondary need created by industrial progress?

Many economists agree that there is an optimal level of public investment in social-overhead capital. They see that the absence of basic infrastructure and certain basic industries not directly productive of final goods may severely inhibit the establishment and retard the growth of many manufacturing industries, and that only the government can make these investments. In this case, large, indivisible, up-front investments are necessary to create future investment opportunities in other industries.[30]

But it is quite possible to overinvest in social-overhead capital. In this case, rather than stimulating expansion of directly productive activities, the money and skills that go into the "excess capacity" of infrastructure siphon factors that could be put into wealth-creating investments.[31] The problem for an industrializing country is to identify this public analogue of Pareto optimality, and the challenge is to prevent the political process from exceeding it and creating infrastructural white elephants.[32]

The question of the proper timing of infrastructural investment is more contentious. The notion of large-scale infrastructural investment as a precursor to rapid industrial expansion was integral in the "big-push" thesis advanced by Rosenstein-Rodan.[33] Similarly, Rostow included infrastructure investment among the crucial external economies created in the second stage of economic development, which he called "the preconditions for take-off."[34]

30. See Mrinal Datta-Chaudhuri, "Infrastructure and Location," in Cody, Hughes, and Wall, *Policies for Industrial Progress*, pp. 235–237.
31. Gerschenkron contended that overly large public investments in railroad construction "kept down the rate of industrial growth in Italy during the big growth spurt of 1896–1908" (*Economic Backwardness*, p. 113). He also asserted that the government's creation and indulgence of "the expensive and inefficient steel industry retarded the rise of the Italian machinery industry" (p. 116).
32. Datta-Chaudhuri concludes: "For an economy in early stages of development . . . careful programming of social overhead capital is extremely important, so that productive investments are not inhibited for lack of overhead facilities, and excessive amounts of scarce resources do not become locked up in unproductive infrastructural facilities" ("Infrastructure and Location," p. 240).
33. Paul N. Rosenstein-Rodan, "Problems of Industrialization of Eastern and South-Eastern Europe," *Economic Journal* 53 (June–September 1943):202–211.
34. Walt W. Rostow, *The Stages of Economic Growth* (Cambridge: Cambridge University Press, 1960), pp. 24–26.

However, others have questioned whether large infrastructural expenditures are more a necessity created by an initial spurt of industrial growth than a precondition for creating it.[35] One observer notes that as each industry begins to expand, it will "demand a particular quantity and type of infrastructure. Infrastructural investment may be, therefore, as much a consequence as a cause of industrial expansion."[36]

The practical implication of this "chicken-or-the-egg" debate is that it is difficult for industrializing countries to know whether to attract industry first and then meet infrastructural demands on an incremental basis or to concentrate on providing the infrastructure on the theory that its existence will help create a "demand" for the industry. As with the question of total amounts of resources devoted to infrastructural investments, it is obvious that there is some fine median line for optimizing industrial growth. In reality, though, any number of countries have erred on both sides: they have made major infrastructural investments only to find that conditions in the world market have turned against the industry for which the investments were intended; and they have also attracted industry with the promise of subsequent public services that were never completed.

Structural and locational considerations. Often government investments and incentives have significant structural impacts in the industrial sector. For example, they may accelerate investment in a particular industry far beyond what would have taken place under natural conditions. This obviously is of major importance for industries in which there is a high threshold of investment and productive capacity to achieve adequate economies of scale and a competitive status in world markets. By the same token, it is possible to push induced government acceleration of investment to the point of creating excess capacity, beyond the level of existing domestic and international demand. Government choices for providing subsidies and services can also have a profound impact on the number and size of domestic producers that enter a particular industry.

The pattern of government incentives and overhead investment also has major implications for the distribution of industrial activities in industrializing countries. Such spatial impacts, however, are usually temporary,

---

35. Gerschenkron says that many so-called prerequisites to industrialization are "rather something that developed in the course of industrial development" (*Economic Backwardness*, p. 33). In his review of Rosario Romeo's works on preindustrial capital accumulation in Italy, he strongly questions the notion that a period of investment in social overhead capital occurs before substantial industrial progress: "In the industrial history of those European countries whose degree of backwardness was considerable, preparation for industrialization and industrialization itself tended to be much more closely interwoven." He goes on to suggest the possibility that "in a backward country a period of preparation that is consummated before the industrial upsurge takes place makes it impossible for the latter to materialize" (p. 113).
36. Sutcliffe, *Industry and Underdevelopment*, p. 102.

changing with the advancement of industrialization. In the early period of industrialization, the spatial impacts of governmental policies are most often unintentional, because the government's main objective is to increase industrial development in the aggregate. This generally means that prevailing spatial trends dictated by political and market forces are reinforced. Thus, core urban regions that already possess political clout, some natural comparative advantage, and a higher level of infrastructure tend to become even more dominant as a result of early governmental industrial policies.[37] Even if government planners care to try to counteract these forces, it is difficult at this stage to consider optimal long-term patterns of industrial location, since this would often increase short-term governmental expenditures and entail a sacrifice in the creation of productive capacity.[38]

However, at some point governments of industrializing countries generally begin to be concerned about the heavy spatial concentration of industry that has resulted from initial industrialization efforts. Gradually, they begin trying to reduce the market forces favoring industrial agglomeration and, conversely, to induce industries to locate in underindustrialized regions of the country.

Often the first efforts to develop regional industrial policies and new industrial growth poles are not overly successful. Congestion, pollution, and numerous other diseconomies may be accumulating in core industrial areas. But the combination of political power, market centralization, and numerous infrastructural and social bottlenecks in areas designated for industrial growth makes it difficult to induce industrial decentralization without a very heavy show of governmental force. Only when the diseconomies in core areas far exceed the costs associated with movement, and when the whole range of governmental subsidies and investments for industrial development is arranged to support regional industrial development goals do decentralizing efforts begin to show significant results. Most rapidly industrializing countries today are still caught between the rhetorical-planning phase and the working-policy phase of their regional industrial-decentralization efforts.

Bargaining for technology

For industrializing nations seeking to build domestic industrial capacity by attracting foreign direct investment or by purchasing foreign technology, the terms of their relationship with multinational corporations are

37. Cannon, "Government Impact on Industrial Location," p. 109.
38. Datta-Chaudhuri, "Infrastructure and Location," p. 243.

often a source of great consternation. The particular deals negotiated with individual foreign companies ultimately influence the kinds and amounts of technology imported; the allocation of ownership, control, and profits in the domestic industry; and the percentage of the net benefits that accrue to the government or foreign private investor.

Framework for negotiations

Analysts of the process by which host countries simultaneously attract and negotiate with foreign investors have tended to construct models that emphasize the relative bargaining strength of each party. They characterize this bargaining relationship as one in which multinational corporations, trying to find the optimal location for a new production facility or a customer for their technology packages, and nation-states, eager to attract foreign capital and technology for economic and employment purposes, each seek to maximize their interests. Companies rely on their technological, capital, and managerial resources and on their job-creating potential to win tax concessions, grants, and other forms of fiscal assistance; frequently they play different countries against each other to ensure the best possible deal. Countries, to offset somewhat the bargaining strengths of corporations, try as much as possible to conduct negotiations with a number of companies from a variety of countries. The terms under which a foreign enterprise may do business in a host country and the distribution of benefits derived from that business are the result of this process.[39]

Most studies of the bargaining relationship between countries and companies conclude that in the preinvestment phase, before a company actually builds a plant in one or another country, the upper hand tends to belong to the corporation. In order to initiate activities in the country, foreign firms demand assurances that government interference in business decisions will be minimized and that they will receive ample compensation for the risks they incur. Thus the initial terms negotiated between host countries and multinational corporations frequently require the governments of host countries to give up more control and profits to foreigners than they would like.

However, after a deal has been struck and physical capital successfully deployed by the foreign investor, the balance of power may shift in favor of the host country. At this time the risks of investment are lessened, and it is more difficult for a company abruptly to remove its physical capital.

---

39. See Raymond Mikesell, ed., *Foreign Investment in the Petroleum and Mineral Industries: Case Studies in Investor-Host Country Relations* (Baltimore: Johns Hopkins University Press, 1971).

Observers of the bargaining process have noted that quite frequently host-country governments press foreign companies to renegotiate concessionary agreements at this stage of the investment cycle.[40]

This shifting of bargaining strength between host country and foreign investor is repeated each time the foreign investor contemplates a new investment, reinvestment, or production expansion. Because the investor will undertake the additional investment only if the terms are suitable, and because the host country may not have many alternatives and may be eager for the additional employment and foreign-exchange earnings, the balance of power at the moment of investment is again weighted in favor of the investor. Once more, however, when the additional operation is on line and successful, the host government is in a position of strength from which it can seek to redirect more benefits to the country.

Several trends in recent decades have forced analysts to inject a more dynamic element into this classic bargaining model of foreign investor-host country relations. This framework has had to account for three evolutionary trends in particular:

1. the diversification of types of industries undertaking foreign investment;
2. the increasing nationalism and sophistication that host countries display in negotiating with foreign investors, and their greater understanding of the complex nature of international finance and intracorporate transactions;
3. increased competition among foreign investors from various nations (Japan and European countries in particular), which has broadened the options available to host countries and especially increased the potential for countries to secure technology transfers without necessarily giving up equity control.

New factors in bargaining

The original analyses of bargaining between host countries and corporations focused primarily on the extractive industries. This reflected the fact that outside the countries belonging to the Organization for Economic Co-operation and Development (OECD), a large portion of all foreign direct investment was made by mining and petroleum companies in search of natural resources to send back to their home countries as raw materials.[41]

The postulated cycle – that bargaining power resides with the foreign company up to the point of investment and shifts thereafter toward the

---

40. In addition to the studies in Mikesell, *Foreign Investment,* see *Multinational Corporations,* esp. pp. 153–172; Penrose, *Large International Firm;* and Franklin Tugwell, *The Politics of Oil in Venezuela* (Stanford, Calif.: Stanford University Press, 1975).

41. See Gilpin, *U.S. Power,* pp. 113–115; Isaiah Frank, *Foreign Enterprise in Developing Countries* (Baltimore: Johns Hopkins University Press, 1980), pp. 17–20.

host country – suits these extractive industries quite well. Investors in typical natural-resource projects must make large up-front investments in circumstances of high uncertainty and risk (the size and quality of ore and mineral reserves are usually a matter of speculation). However, once the reserves are proven and the operation is successful, the operation is much more routinized. Natural-resource investments are among the best examples of what has been called the "obsolescing bargain."[42]

The spread of more and more manufacturing industries around the globe has forced analysts to realize that the stages of the bargaining cycle are not so easily identifiable for other industries as for the extractive industries. At the very least, the unique contribution of the foreign investor may not dissipate or become obsolescent as rapidly or as uniformly after the point of investment as it does with the extractive industries. In addition, while extractive industries are often separate even if highly important enclaves in the economy, manufacturing industries often are much more directly enmeshed in the entire economy and certainly more visible to the general population.[43] This also may make the bargaining cycle less applicable to manufacturing industries than to the extractive industries. Analysts have generally considered the bargaining strength of foreign manufacturing corporations to be more enduring than that of petroleum and mining firms, because manufacturing firms have many locational choices; depend on continuing inflows of expertise, technology, and patents from parent companies; and are not as dependent upon the raw material resources of the particular country.[44]

Although fewer studies have been undertaken to outline all aspects of conflict and resolution within a bargaining framework for manufacturing industries, two general assumptions are widely accepted. First, the leverage of the foreign firm is thought to be increased if the manufactured product is intended primarily for export instead of for the domestic market. Such involvement presumably gives the firm crucial leverage in affecting overall manufacturing employment and export earnings.[45] Second, it is widely believed that the more sophisticated the manufacturing technology and production processes, the more the balance of negotiating

---

42. Frank, *Foreign Enterprise in Developing Countries*, p. 28.
43. See David Apter and Louis Wolf Goodman, eds., *The Multinational Corporation and Social Change* (New York: Praeger, 1976), pp. 21–27.
44. For a discussion of some of the added difficulties of regulating multinationals in the manufacturing sector, see Raymond Vernon, *Storm over the Multinationals: The Real Issues* (Cambridge, Mass.: Harvard University Press, 1977), pp. 71–72, 394–396; C. Fred Bergsten, Theodore H. Moran, and Thomas Horst, *American Multinationals and American Interests* (Washington, D.C.: Brookings Institution, 1978), pp. 130–140, 377–380.
45. Frank, *Foreign Enterprise in Developing Countries*, pp. 35–36.

strength will rest with the foreign corporation. If the technology is more standardized and available on a nonproprietary basis, the ability of the foreign company to extract what amounts to high rents is obviously lessened, while high-technology operations may demand higher compensation.[46]

Thus the ascendance of manufacturing industries as foreign direct investors has changed the bargaining picture, making it more difficult to pinpoint a shift in the balance of power from foreign investor to host country. Suffice it to say that, all other things being equal, analysts agree that the more sophisticated and export-oriented manufacturing industries present a tougher challenge for host countries than do the extractive industries.

However, the other two trends noted above – more awareness on the part of host countries and more international competition among firms – have tended to work in the other direction, increasing the bargaining strength of host-country governments. Since at least the 1960s, virtually all countries that accept foreign direct investors have displayed increasing vigilance and increasing technical abilities. Host-country nationalism prompted a growing will among domestic groups in most host countries to extract more from foreign investors. This process has been partly ideological: host countries, especially in the Third World, have reacted against past exploitation and have endorsed the dependency analysis of corporate-host country relations. But this has been a universal trend as well. Even domestic groups supportive of free enterprise and foreign investors have pushed increasingly to get foreign companies to contribute more to the host country's national welfare and economic development.[47]

The concept of a "host-country learning curve" has been introduced to account for increased capabilities in most host countries to master more and more of the previously mysterious contributions of foreign enterprise (managerial capability, marketing knowhow, and the like).[48] In addition, regulators in host countries are more knowledgable about corporate operations and the complex financial arrangements often existing between firms, parent companies, foreign marketers, creditors, and others. It is harder for companies to manipulate, launder, or disguise the benefits they extract from doing business in a particular country.[49]

46. See notes 43 and 44.
47. See H. Jeffrey Leonard, "Multinational Corporations and Politics in Developing Countries," *World Politics* 32, no. 3 (April 1980):454–483, and the books reviewed in that article.
48. Moran, *Multinational Corporations*, pp. 163–167.
49. Leonard, "Multinational Corporations and Politics," pp. 457–458; Barnet and Muller, *Global Reach*, pp. 185–210.

Finally, host countries have benefited from the fact that in the last two decades their options for doing business with foreign firms have become both broader and deeper. In recent years, more firms from a growing number of home countries – including the Western European nations, Japan, and now such countries as South Korea, India, and Brazil – have become multinational investors. This contrasts sharply with the situation in the late 1950s and 1960s, when multinational business was dominated by U.S. firms. As a result, host countries can offset the advantages for foreign investors to a certain extent by trying to play firms from different parent countries against one another.[50]

Of even greater importance, some foreign investors have shown a growing willingness to break the foreign-direct-investment package into pieces, which has significantly increased the depth of possibilities open to host countries. Through much of the postwar era, U.S. corporations were the major overseas investors in the world. Typically, they sought as much as possible to maintain equity control whenever they transferred technology and supplied organizational expertise abroad. They were wary of sharing or selling their technology on nonequity terms because they feared that this would more quickly erode their competitive advantage by speeding up the product cycle and reducing the aura of technological mystique that kept many countries dependent on foreign direct investors in certain industries.[51]

Three factors, in particular, have been responsible for increasing the range of options for technology transfers considered by U.S. corporations. First, several countries proved that if they were shrewd enough and resisted equity arrangement long enough, they could find ways to get hold of U.S. technology without having to accept foreign-enterprise ownership as the price. The Japanese were the first to have success in strategically "unbundling" the foreign-direct-investment package – by borrowing capital, hiring or shanghaiing technology and management expertise, and spurning foreign direct investors. Later, in the 1970s, several Eastern European countries became proficient at this approach. This made it increasingly difficult to sell the all-or-nothing package in other industrializing countries. Or, as one observer noted, more countries started to ask, "If you went into Hungary with a management contract and no equity ownership, why can't you come here on the same basis?"[52]

50. Barnet and Muller, *Global Reach*, pp. 185–210; Frank, *Foreign Enterprise in Developing Countries*, pp. 20–24.
51. Jack Baronson, *Technology and the Multinationals* (Lexington, Mass.: Lexington, 1978).
52. Peter Gabriel, as quoted in Barnet and Muller, *Global Reach*, p. 201.

Another trend that has undermined the ability of U.S. companies to keep technology wholly within their control has been the rise of multi-national engineering, construction, and consulting firms (many from the United States) that sell technology, expertise, and even whole production plants in a wide range of industries. By offering an alternative to foreign direct investment, these firms became, in a sense, competitors of U.S. manufacturing companies in some industries. Often such firms have been contracted to build industrial capacity and provide expertise in conjunction with major lending packages assembled for developing countries by development-assistance agencies such as the World Bank.[53]

A final related trend has been the willingness of industrial corporations from emergent competitors of U.S. companies – notably the Japanese – to break up the foreign-direct-investment package and to sell or license technology without demanding control. This has been especially prominent in the mineral-extraction industries.[54] Despite these trends, firms in some industries are still reluctant to unbundle the direct-investment package. Once again, observers tend to agree that the high-technology manufacturers are more reluctant to share on nonequity terms (and are more able to protect their proprietary interests). On the other hand, developing countries' efforts to unbundle foreign investment in the extractive industries have been so successful that this has "become the rule not the exception."[55]

Conclusions

Two clear trends characterize the efforts of virtually every country that has sought to stimulate rapid industrial development during the second half of the twentieth century. First, the role of the state, whether as owner of capital or facilitator for quasi-public or private enterprises, continues to be more and more pivotal in the success of such efforts. Industrial-development planners increasingly try to decide ahead of time what industries to favor, what facilities and infrastructures to supply, and where they would like to see industries concentrate.

Second, more and more countries are stressing an increase in manufactured exports as a crucial element of their industrial-development strategies. Reflecting an understanding of the international product cycle reviewed in Chapter 1, industrial-development planners tend to target a stages approach to the evolution of their comparative advantage in man-

53. See Baronson, *Technology and the Multinationals.*
54. See Raymond F. Mikesell, *The World Copper Industry: Structure and Economic Analysis* (Baltimore: Johns Hopkins University Press, 1979).
55. See Frank, *Foreign Enterprise in Developing Countries,* pp. 56–60.

ufacturing industries: they seek to upgrade gradually from low-technology, labor-intensive industries to more capital-intensive industries.

With the levels of state involvement and planning expanding in almost all countries, and with so many industrializing countries simultaneously seeking to stimulate manufactured exports, competition in the international marketplace has intensified. This places more and more importance on the numerous decisions about industrial development that must be made by the state: forms of ownership, relationship with foreign enterprises, types of incentives for industries, timing of infrastructural investments, when to intervene to offset structural imbalances and adverse externalities resulting from industrialization. In the end, all these choices, coupled with the general economic and political climate created in a country, tend to have as much or more to do with establishing a country's comparative advantage in industrial production and determining its success in international markets than its natural factor endowments do.

On balance, the basic nature of the bargaining relationships between multinational corporations and developing countries has been changing rapidly. Many governments have gained the knowledge and technical expertise to assess the economic issues involved in dealing with foreign business. New forms of relationships – such as service contracts, turnkey arrangements, and joint ownerships – have in many instances replaced wholly owned and controlled subsidiaries. In short, developing countries have learned to assert themselves more and are trying to calculate the economic benefits they can derive from foreign investors and to devise better ways to contain or minimize economic costs. Numerous technical and economic challenges remain, particularly in areas such as technology and transfer pricing, for any Third World country whose development strategy relies upon multinational corporations. These problems are usually more complex for manufacturing industries than for those dealing in raw materials, and are still more complex in the industries that rely on advanced technology.

3

Pollution and comparative advantage in industrial production

Taken together, the theories and concepts discussed in the preceding chapters make up a picture of comparative advantage in industrial production in a dynamic world of competitive nation-states and increasingly multinational firms. The most advanced industrialized countries (notably the United States) sit atop the global ladder of comparative advantage, faced with prospects that the ever-increasing velocity of the product cycle will prevent them from remaining overwhelmingly dominant in any particular arena of industrial production for very long. They – or, more accurately, firms operating on their soil – must consistently develop new products, more efficient technologies, and new methods of production to ensure that the work of the product cycle does not undermine their overall industrial advantage.

For their part, large firms from the most advanced nations, more and more multinational in outlook, have designed international strategies to respond to and take advantage of geographical evolutions of comparative advantage. Until recently, owing to the tariff policies set by host countries and the continuing home-country orientations of big corporations, most manufacturing firms made foreign direct investments for the construction of relatively small branch plants to serve relatively small domestic markets. However, with the growing focus among many nations on stimulating manufactured exports, the liberalization of international trade rules, and the internationalization of the marketing and production strategies of many big corporations, more foreign direct investment has been coordinated to fit into broad international production networks that apply the division-of-labor concept across national borders. The adoption of such foreign-investment strategies by large multinational firms has made it more difficult for the advanced developed countries to hang on to their advantage in many areas of industrial production.

But these same strategies have offered substantial opportunities for semiindustrialized nations among the middle-income countries of the world and, increasingly, for newly industrializing nations among the so-called less-developed countries. Many of these second- and third-tier industrializers have focused intensively on identifying industries that might be entering the internationalization phase of production and on designing packages of incentives, subsidies, and supporting services that will enhance their attractiveness as a venue for multinational producers. In some cases, too, countries have sought to find nonequity means of obtaining technology without sacrificing national control.

After nearly three decades of relatively continuous economic growth and industrial expansion, global events of the early 1970s underscored some of the problems posed by the evolution of international comparative advantage. Observers began to note that the growth curves of many industries that had fueled the immense progress of the postwar decades – for example, automobiles, manmade fibers and other chemical products, electronics, aluminum, and steel – appeared to be flattening out, much like those of leading sectors from previous eras, such as cotton, coal, and iron.[1] With the perceived slowing of innovation in these industries, the closing of the technology gap between industrialized and industrializing countries, and the tremendous shocks of external economic events, economic competition among nation-states and hence the potential for political and economic conflict increased.

In short, in the 1970s it began to appear that a major bottleneck was forming on the rungs of the world industrial ladder, and that the bottleneck threatened to make it more difficult for all nations to prosper from the stages approach to comparative advantage as they bunched up closer behind the advanced industrial countries. Some observers spoke of the impending "struggle for the world product"[2] and the "coming investment wars."[3]

This tension helped to provoke debate in the United States and other advanced industrial countries about whether the actions of domestic corporations and governmental policies were speeding up the dispersion of technology and the internationalization of industrial production to the detriment of the mother country.[4] At the same time, the threat of protectionism in the advanced countries merely prompted industrializing

1. See Peter Drucker, *The Age of Discontinuity* (New York: Harper and Row, 1969); Robert Gilpin, *U.S. Power*, pp. 258–262; and James R. Kurth, "The Political Consequences of the Product Cycle: Industrial History and Political Outcomes," *International Organization* 33, no. 1 (Winter 1979):1–34.
2. Helmut Schmidt, "Struggle for the World Product," *Foreign Affairs* 52 (April 1974):437–451.
3. C. Fred Bergsten, "Coming Investment Wars?" *Foreign Affairs* 53 (October 1974):132–152.
4. See Gilpin, *U.S. Power*.

nations to redouble their efforts to identify factors that might help them secure a "redeployment" of industries in their direction.[5]

This general state of affairs sets the stage for consideration of a relatively new factor with the potential for influencing all the previously discussed aspects of international comparative advantage in industrial production: the introduction in the United States and other advanced industrial nations of a wide range of new government regulations to control pollution, improve workplace health and safety, and limit the adverse environmental impacts of industrial facilities. This bundle of regulations was meant not to subsidize or protect industrial producers but, in one way or another, to assign the real or social costs of production to industrial firms and consumers of industrial products. Such regulations obviously did not affect all industries equally, because some industrial activities create more environmental hazards than others. Of even greater importance, the range of regulations that emerged varied in type and level of stringency among countries; the farther down the industrial ladder one looked, the fewer regulations were apparent and the less invasive those regulations seemed to be.

The point of departure, then, is the question whether, in an atmosphere of growing international industrial competition, the emergence of stringent environmental regulations in the advanced countries has affected the international distribution of comparative advantage in industrial production. This chapter looks at some of the theories formulated to explain the potential effects of environmental regulations on comparative advantage and reviews the considerable literature recently generated in the United States on this question.

Environment as a natural factor endowment

The multitude of new federal regulations enacted in the late 1960s and early 1970s forced many industries to make fundamental changes in the ways they operated in the United States. Manufacturers had to make huge capital investments as they adapted to new laws controlling water effluents, air emissions, disposal of solid wastes, use of hazardous and toxic substances, and exposure to dangerous chemicals in the workplace. In many instances, products were withdrawn from the marketplace, production processes were changed, and new raw materials were necessary. Moreover, the labyrinth of new regulations at the federal, state, and local levels, coupled with mounting public opposition, made it difficult for some

---

5. See Herbert Giersch, *The International Division of Labour: Problems and Prospects* (Tubingen: Mohr, 1974); and Herbert Giersch, *Reshaping the World Economic Order* (Tubingen: Mohr, 1977).

industries to receive permission to build new production facilities or expand existing ones.

Although frequently guided by a different regulatory philosophy from the one prevailing in the United States, pollution-control requirements expanded in Japan, Great Britain, Germany, Sweden, France, and other Western European nations as well. The United States was generally thought to have issued the most stringent and most complex set of regulations. Each of the other advanced industrial nations, however, established particularly tight antipollution standards in response to its most acute problems.[6]

During the early phase of this era of rapidly changing environmental regulations in Europe and the United States, many observers tried to develop an international response under the auspices of the United Nations. Three motivations appear to have been behind the supranational focus. First, there was a genuine belief that the environmental crisis manifested most clearly in the advanced industrial nations had reached such menacing proportions that only a global approach could prove effective.[7] Second, some countries expressed strong concern that unless all countries agreed to take actions together to reduce pollution, those that did act decisively would be paying for free riders and would also suffer a competitive disadvantage in many areas of trade. Finally, the hope that the U.N. could step into the role of arbiter and regulator of an international environmental program was also motivated by the feeling that the pollution challenge at last provided an apolitical issue around which the U.N. could build consensus for increased global cooperation. Two political scientists, for example, noted that if the U.N. could demonstrate its ability to deal effectively with the environmental issues requiring international action, it could make an important contribution "to revitalizing the entire United Nations system, particularly in the eyes of the major powers which have shown growing disenchantment with the organization in recent years."[8]

Nevertheless, any illusions that the world of nation-states would decide upon communal resolutions to guide their effort to reduce pollution were dispelled by the time of the 1972 Stockholm Conference on the Human Environment. Representatives of less-developed countries argued vocifer-

---

6. See Richard L. Siegel and Leonard B. Weinberg, *Comparing Public Policies: United States, Soviet Union, and Europe* (Homewood, Ill.: Dorsey Press, 1977); Cynthia Enloe, *The Politics of Pollution in a Comparative Perspective* (New York: McKay, 1975); and Charles Pearson and Anthony Pryor, *Environment: North and South* (New York: Wiley Interscience, 1978).

7. George F. Kennan, "To Prevent a World Wasteland," *Foreign Affairs* 48, no. 3 (April 1970):401–413.

8. David A. Kay and Eugene B. Skolnikoff, "International Institutions and the Environmental Crisis: A Look Ahead," *International Organization* 26, no. 2 (Spring 1972):487.

ously against any efforts to harmonize pollution-control regulations, on the grounds that they were still industrializing and "pollution control is a response of post-industrial societies to a lingering and intensifying problem of industrialization."[9]

Realizing that many environmental regulations would not be duplicated outside the most industrialized nations, economic theorists began to consider the potential trade effects of differential pollution-control regulations among countries. A great deal of new theoretical work was devoted to reconciling or integrating environmental factors with classical models of international trade.[10] The starting point for most theorists was the

9. Quote is from Siegel and Weinberg, *Comparing Public Policies*, p. 411. See also p. 381; and Enloe, *Politics of Pollution*, pp. 111–141. The definitive statement by a spokesman from the Third World is Jauo Augusto de Araujo Castro, "Environment and Development: The Case of the Less Developed Countries," *International Organization* 26, no. 2 (Spring 1972):401–465.

10. Some of the initial attempts by economic theoreticians to integrate environmental factors into international trade theory include: Ralph C. d'Arge, "International Trade, Domestic Income, and Environmental Controls: Some Empirical Estimates," in Allen V. Kneese, Sidney E. Rolfe, and Joseph W. Harned, eds., *Managing the Environment: International Economic Cooperation for Pollution Control* (New York: Praeger, 1971), pp. 289–315; Ralph C. d'Arge and K. D. Kogiker, "Economic Growth and the Environment," *Review of Economic Studies* 40 (1973):61–78; Ralph C. d'Arge, "Trade, Environmental Controls and the Developing Economics," in *Problems of Environmental Economics* (Paris: Organization for Economic Cooperation and Development, 1971), pp. 1–79; Ralph C. d'Arge and Allen V. Kneese, "Environmental Quality and International Trade," *International Organization* 26, no. 2 (Spring, 1972):419–465; William J. Baumol, *Environmental Protection, International Spillovers and Trade* (Stockholm: Almquist and Wiksell, 1971); Richard Blackhurst, "International Trade and the Environment: A Review of the Literature and a Suggested Approach," *Economic Notes* 42, no. 7–8 (May–August 1974):5; Bruce A. Forster, "A Note on Economic Growth and Environmental Quality," *Swedish Journal of Economics* 74, no. 2 (June 1972):281–285; Herbert G. Grubel, "Some Effects of Environmental Controls on International Trade: The Hecksher-Ohlin Model," in Ingo Walter, ed., *Studies in International Environmental Economics* (New York: Wiley, 1976), pp. 253–290; Allen V. Kneese, "Background for the Economic Analysis of Environmental Pollution," *Swedish Journal of Economics* 73 (1971):3–50; Allen V. Kneese, "Environmental Pollution: Economics and Policy," *American Economic Review* 61, no. 2 (May 1971):153–166; Anthony Y. C. Koo, "Environmental Repercussions and Trade Theory," *Review of Economics and Statistics* 56, no. 2 (May 1974):235–244; Wassily Leontief, "Environmental Repercussions and the Economic Structure: An Input-Output Approach," *Review of Economics and Statistics* 52, no. 3 (August 1970):262–271; Stephen P. Magee and William F. Ford, "Environmental Pollution, the Terms of Trade and Balance of Payments of the United States," *Kyklos* 25 (1972):101–118; R. Pethig, "Pollution, Welfare and Environmental Policy in the Theory of Comparative Advantage," *Journal of Environmental Economics and Management* 2 no. 3 (February 1976):160–169; Horst Siebert, "Trade and Environment," in Giersch, *International Division of Labour;* Horst Siebert, "Environmental Protection and International Specialization"; Horst Siebert, "Environmental Quality and Gains from Trade," *Kyklos* 30 (1977):657–673; Horst Siebert, "Comparative Advantage and Environmental Policy: A Note," *Zeitschrift für Nationalökonomie* 34 (1974):397–402; and Horst Siebert, "Environmental Control, Economic Structure and International Trade, in Walter, *Studies in International Environmental Economics*.

Heckscher-Ohlin theorem, that a country will export goods whose production depends upon high inputs of factors that are abundant in the country and will import goods produced with factors that are scarce in the country.

In essence, economic theorists contended, the quality of the environment and its assimilative capacity can be viewed as a natural factor endowment. A country richly endowed with environmental inputs in production will generally produce and export those goods whose production is environment-intensive.[11] Under circumstances in which other factors are internationally identical, comparative advantage can be defined in terms of environmental abundance or scarcity. A country richly endowed in environmental quality or environmental assimilative capacity will have a trade advantage over countries not so well endowed.

Measuring assimilative capacity

Despite the simplicity of this formulation, the concept of an environmental factor endowment is complex and difficult to operationalize – it cannot be easily defined or measured and is not static. Theorists identified at least four different determinants:[12]

1. the natural assimilative capacity of the land, water, and atmosphere, as determined by such factors as climate, rainfall, wind patterns, and geographical location;
2. the value that government officials and the population place on environmental quality, a value generally thought to accord with the country's level of affluence, education, and urbanization, and assumed to be transmitted via government regulations concerning pollution;
3. the current demands on the natural assimilative capacity of the environment, as broadly reflected in the levels of industrialization and urbanization and the types of pollutants generated by industrial and urban activities;
4. the amount of public and private investments undertaken either to increase the

11. One theoretical analysis noted: "A counterpart of the balance of payments is the balance of pollution. Importing/exporting goods that cause pollution during the production process is equivalent to exporting/importing pollution. This adds a further dimension in international resource allocation. Those countries where pollution causes much damage should specialize in clean production, and those where it causes little damage should specialize in pollution generating production ... The adaptive capacity of a country with respect to pollution is a resource just like technological know-how or mineral deposits." D. E. James, H. M. A. Jansen, and J. B. Opschoor, *Economic Approaches to Environmental Problems: Techniques and Results of Empirical Analysis* (Amsterdam: Elsevier Scientific, 1978), pp. 231–232.

12. An excellent summary of the different interpretations of the concept of environmental factor endowment is found in Horst Siebert and Ariane Berthoin Antal, *The Political Economy of Environmental Protection* (Greenwich, Conn.: JAI Press, 1979), pp. 171–181.

natural assimilative capacity of the environment (liming lakes, digging canals, and so forth) or to decrease the demands placed upon it (waste-treatment plants and pollution-control technology, for example).

In this view, a country's environmental endowment is a function of the natural and social assimilative capacity to deal with industrial waste. Obviously, there is room for great variation along these dimensions. Some countries may have a large available environmental endowment because of their highly resilient and self-cleansing natural systems; others may benefit from a high social tolerance to pollution; still others may simply have such a low level of industrial development that much natural and social assimilative capacity is unclaimed.

The important "bottom line" from a theoretical point of view is whether available assimilative capacity is underutilized or overutilized. Thus the concept of environmental endowment is really relative: if a country has unused assimilative capacity, its environmental factor endowment is said to be abundant; on the other hand, if its assimilative capacity is overutilized or fully subscribed, its environmental factor endowment is scarce.[13] Of course, given its complex attributes, applying the concept of environmental assimilative capacity by assigning relative measures and weights is not easy in the real world. Moreover, the relative nature of the environmental factor endowment points up the fact that the environmental scarcity or abundance may evolve over time, depending especially on such factors as rate of industrialization and urbanization, mobilization of antipollution constituencies, and changing legal codes.[14]

The theoretical significance of environmental endowment

To determine the potential importance of the concept of environmental endowment for different countries and for the allocation of comparative-advantage trade, several other variables must be assessed. In addition to distinguishing between environmentally rich and environmentally poor countries, the more sophisticated analyses note that it is equally important to distinguish between pollution-intensive and nonpollution-intensive goods in postulating the effects of environmental factors on trade.[15] As with the concept of environmental assimilative capacity, the notion of a pollution-intensive good is amorphous, because it is subject to a wide vari-

13. See the discussion in Charles Pearson and Anthony Pryor, *Environment*, pp. 159–167.
14. Most of the theoretical works cited above did not introduce this dynamic element.
15. See Martin McGuire, "The Effect of Environmental Regulation on Production and Trade in a Hecksher-Ohlin World," Working Paper 79-22 (College Park: University of Maryland, Department of Economics and Bureau of Business and Economic Research, 1979).

ety of interpretations and measures. Economists have tended to use the term in its broad theoretical sense to imply that production of the good requires significant inputs of the environmental factor endowment: either it causes pollution or costs must be incurred to ensure that pollution does not occur.

For production of many goods, the environmental factor is more or less unutilized and thus has a neutral effect on trade. Obviously, little advantage accrues to a country from its rich environmental factor endowment if the good it is producing does not utilize this factor because production generates low levels of pollution – that is, if the good is not pollution-intensive. In the case of a pollution-intensive good, however, producers in a country that is overutilizing its environmental endowment may be penalized (in the form of pollution-control costs, for example). Conversely, producers in countries where the environmental endowment is underutilized may receive an advantage in production of pollution-intensive goods.

Another variable is whether the pollution generated by production of a good is local (that is, whether it creates disutility only within the producer country) or global (impinging on the environmental endowment beyond the borders of the producer country).[16] If pollution is global, the apparent advantage for an environmentally rich country in producing a pollution-intensive good may not be as large as it initially appears. The consumption of scarce environmental assimilative capacity can effectively be reduced by international transport of pollution, offsetting the disadvantages to countries in which environment is already overutilized.

A related variable is whether regulatory actions to control pollution are undertaken unilaterally by one country, in coordination among a block of countries, or by international agreement of all countries. Some theorists assume that national regulations will reflect the natural and social differences in environmental endowments among countries. In reality, however, a comparison of national pollution-control regulations shows a bandwagon effect that disproves the assumption that environmental policies reflect environmental demand functions. On the other hand, the argument that international agreements neutralize the trade effects of differential national environmental endowments is also flawed. In different countries a given level of environmental control or environmental quality may be achieved at a very different cost in resources. Thus some international effects on international comparative advantage must be anticipated even if countries agree on uniform international standards.[17]

16. Ibid.
17. See Ingo Walter, "International Trade and Resource Diversion: A Case of Environmental Management," *Weltwirtschaftliches Archiv* 110, no. 3 (1974):482–493.

A final variable that is important over time is the international mobility of factors of production in pollution-intensive industries. The nature of some industries circumscribes the international mobility of capital: many products are difficult to transfer across borders (electricity generation is a case in point), and nation-states consider certain industries (weapons manufacturing, for example) to have a vital role in maintaining national security. The effects of differential factor endowments would not realistically be expected to alter international comparative advantages in producing such goods, no matter how pollution-intensive.

Armed with all these definitions and distinctions, scholars were able to consider the theoretical significance of introducing environment as a natural factor endowment. Starting from a standard Heckscher-Ohlin model, economists postulated a world made up of two countries, each with similar endowments of labor and capital, and two goods with similar requirements for inputs of labor and capital. Under circumstances of perfect competition and infinite mobility of factors, the model can then be modified to assume that industry X is pollution-intensive but industry Y is not, and that country A has an abundant environmental endowment (by virtue of low industrialization, low regulation, or high natural assimilative capacity) but this factor is scarce in country B.

The combined effect of differences in environmental endowments between the countries and differences in environmental-input requirements among the industries is to give country A an absolute advantage in industry X. Country B will be completely driven out of production in industry X. On the other hand, the impact of differential environmental endowment on comparative advantage for industry Y should be neutral. In such circumstances, country B would tend to specialize in and seek to increase exports by industry Y to offset the absolute disadvantage caused by the scarcity of the environmental factors needed in the production of X.[18]

Redeployment of industry predicted

Drawing on these broad theoretical postulates, observers attempted to integrate environmental factor endowments into prevailing explanations of comparative advantage in a world of nation-states, imperfect competition, and "lumpy" investment cycles. The concept of differential national environmental factor endowments fits conveniently with the thinking of

18. Excellent overviews of this general theoretical model, with mathematical notes, are found in McGuire, "Effect of Environmental Regulation"; Pearson and Pryor, *Environment*, pp. 159–167; and Siebert and Antal, *Political Economy of Environmental Protection*, pp. 171–181.

international economic theorists on "real-world" comparative advantage. The fact that the relative abundance of environmental factors was expected to vary significantly among nations was thought to reinforce already-identified trends in the evolution of comparative advantage. This variation would further speed up the product cycle, increase foreign direct investment by firms from industrialized nations, enhance the industrial development of underindustrialized nations, and provide potential host countries with one more bargaining chip with which to attract foreign investors.

One international economist summarized the potential impacts, predicting a gradual shift of pollution-intensive forms of economic activity from higher-income to lower-income countries. Furthermore, he noted that "there may indeed be instances where the export of pollution through capital investments abroad becomes national policy in certain economic sectors, to the benefit of both capital exporting and capital importing countries."[19]

By taking advantage of differing preferences for environmental quality and a large, as yet unutilized environmental assimilative capacity, under-industrialized countries could build capacity in certain highly polluting industries and "thereby achieve a trade position superior to industrialized states with assumed high emission or environmental quality standards."[20] In this view that environment would become a new factor in comparative advantage, an important assumption was, of course, that the multinational firms that controlled a large percentage of world productive capacity in high-technology, high-pollution industries (for example, chemical manufacturing and petroleum refining) would be sensitive to environmental-control costs in their worldwide location decisions.

A widely used textbook on international political economy concluded, for example, that multinational corporations would be very sensitive to disparities among various states' pollution-control standards, and that such disparities would "have a substantial impact on investment decisions by corporations and on the trade position of various states."[21] Similarly, a report to the U.S. Department of Commerce noted that "as an element affecting both sides of the economic equation, therefore, environmental policy is likely to have an influence on the behavior of multinationals and

19. Ingo Walter, "Environmental Management and the International Economic Order," in C. Fred Bergsten, ed., *The Future of the International Economic Order: An Agenda for Research* (Lexington, Mass.: Heath, 1973), pp. 313–314.
20. Marion Clawson, "Economic Development and Environmental Impact: International Aspects," in *Political Economy of Environment* (Paper presented at the United Nations Symposium at the Maison des Sciences de l'Homme, Paris, July 5–8, 1971).
21. David H. Blake and Robert S. Walters, *The Politics of Global Economic Relations* (Englewood Cliffs, N.J.: Prentice-Hall, 1976), p. 159.

this, in turn, will tend to magnify and accelerate its impact on international economic relationships."[22]

In short, it was widely predicted that differential national environmental factor endowments would become more prominent in determining comparative advantage in industrial production and would reduce the locational advantage of the highly industrialized nations (where environmental factors would become increasingly scarce) and accelerating the industrial development of underindustrialized countries (which possessed abundant environmental factor endowments). Two mutually reinforcing hypotheses sought to explain the specific actions of governments and firms that would actually bring about these changes. The industrial-flight hypothesis outlined the factors that were expected to combine to reduce the abundance of environmental endowment in already-industrialized countries, and that would thereby tend to drive away pollution-intensive industries. The so-called pollution-haven hypothesis, on the other hand, showed how underindustrialized countries could use their abundant environmental factor endowments to lure such industries to their shores.

The industrial-flight hypothesis

Predictions that a diminishment of the environmental factor endowment would push pollution-intensive industries out of the United States and other advanced industrial countries have actually been based upon at least three distinct though not mutually exclusive observations. The first is that pollution regulations drive up total capital and production costs for heavily polluting industries. The second is that environmental regulations coupled with growing public alarm about pollution also frequently have the result of decreasing the availability of sites for industrial location. And, finally, some regulations have the effect of directly limiting the range of products that can be manufactured and the types of inputs and production processes that can be used in a country.

Pollution-control costs. Industrial firms do not make locational decisions on the basis of theoretical speculations about the relative abundance of factors in one place or another. Rather, as Chapter 1 emphasized, they act on proximate measures of factor endowments that can be quantified: the cost of labor and transportation, the size of the potential market to be served from a location, the cost and availability of raw materials, and so forth. The same is true of environmental factor endowments. For indus-

---

22. Ingo Walter, "Economic Reasons of Multinational Companies to Environmental Policy," Report to the U.S. Department of Commerce, August 1976.

tries that integrate environment into the location calculus, the most important question is costs: How much will the regulatory requirements or the general scarcity of environmental assimilative capacity increase capital spending and production costs?

Consequently, the most obvious basis for the industrial-flight hypothesis is that by driving up the costs of producing a particular good in one country, environmental factors have clear impacts on comparative advantage when firms in that country compete in international trade. Sooner or later, firms with the capability to move capital investments across national boundaries would be forced to do so to regain their cost competitiveness in producing the good. If other cost factors remained equal, capital would migrate from countries in which firms had high environmental costs to countries with low environmental costs of production.[23]

But rising pollution-control costs were not the only basis for the industrial-flight hypothesis. The potential effects of a widening international gap in pollution-control costs were compounded in the late 1970s by the observation that environmental regulations and public concern might also push industry abroad by reducing the availability of particular industrial sites or by making it too difficult or complicated for certain industries to continue operating. It was thought that these capacity-restraining or capacity-reducing impacts would affect two types of industries in particular: those requiring very large, often multiprocess production facilities or complexes (petroleum refining and many types of chemical manufacturing are good examples) and those that produce chemicals, products, or by-products that pose occupational and community hazards not easily alleviated by technologies that reduce or prevent exposure.

Social blockage of new plants. Observers noted that even where total costs were not substantially increased, environmental regulations and public concern could push industry out of advanced industrial countries by effectively decreasing the ease and speed with which industries build new plants or expand old ones. If site choices are too restricted, or if the legal procedures required for permission to develop new sites are slowed too much, industries may simply give up hope and move abroad.

In the United States, certain federal environmental regulations – such as requirements that new or expanded plants in nonattainment areas obtain air-pollution offsets, and standards for the prevention of significant

23. Ingo Walter, "Pollution and Protection: U.S. Environmental Controls as Competitive Distortions," *Weltwirtschaftliches Archiv* (Review of World Economics) 110, no. 1 (1974):104–113; and Ingo Walter, "Environmental Control and Patterns of International Trade and Investment," *Banca Nazionale del Lavoro, Quarterly Review* 25 (1972):382–383.

deterioration in areas with good air quality – have, according to industry spokesmen, delayed or blocked new industrial proposals at particular locations in recent years. Moreover, state and local controls (often made stricter in response to local opposition to particular siting proposals) and the delays caused by hostile local governments, public protests, and lengthy court proceedings have apparently had an even more significant impact than any federal environmental regulations. A 1979 study concluded that "a major factor in industrial location in the United States is local blockage of new plants, often through land use zoning controls or local referenda." Thus, although an industry may not refuse to consider locating a new plant in a jurisdiction or region with a reputation for strong environmental awareness, the industry will go elsewhere when it becomes apparent that the plant will never receive final approval because of local resistance.[24]

This problem of rising "blockage" of industrial sites actually has caused some companies to cancel planned industrial projects altogether or to begin anew their search for a viable location.[25] Some observers contend that this phenomenon may have become widespread enough in the 1970s to increase the number of U.S. firms that decided to locate abroad. In fact, some business analysts have contended that social activists' pressure to keep industrial plants from locating "in their backyard" is an indicator of and causal element in an impending transition of the United States to a postindustrial economy.[26]

In a 1980 study that documented increased social protest over new industrial-siting proposals during the 1970s, Thomas Gladwin concluded that the United States "may be entering an even more difficult era in which growing demands and diminishing resources will increase the frequency and intensity of the 'social' breed of environmental conflict."[27] In another article, Gladwin and Ingo Walter noted that blockage resulting from social opposition to new plants was becoming a dominant element in the

24. Christopher J. Duerksen, "Remodeling the U.S. Environmental and Land-Use Regulatory Process" (Paper presented at a Conference on the Role of Environmental and Land-Use Regulation in Industrial Siting, sponsored by the Conservation Foundation, Washington, D.C., June 21, 1979), p. 3.

25. Some of the celebrated incidents in the United States are reviewed in Christopher J. Duerksen, *Environmental Regulation of Industrial Plant Siting: How To Make It Work Better* (Washington, D.C.: Conservation Foundation, 1983).

26. Michael O'Hare, "Not on My Block You Don't: Facility Siting and the Strategic Importance of Compensation," *Public Policy* 25 (Fall 1977):17–23; and Thomas N. Gladwin, "The Management of Environmental Conflict: A Survey of Research Approaches and Priorities" (Working Paper no. 78-09s, New York University Graduate School of Business, January 1978).

27. Thomas N. Gladwin, "Patterns of Environmental Conflict Over Industrial Facilities in the United States, 1970–78," *Natural Resources Journal* 20 (April 1980):274.

"locational calculus" of multinational corporations: "The most critical factor in the entire equation," they said, "is environmental opposition to new plant siting in the developed countries."[28]

Environmental opposition leading to "blockage" is assumed to be speeding up two trends that relate to worldwide industrial development: the increased service orientation of developed countries and the movement of "dirty" industries to developing countries. Gladwin and Walter stated that "increasing environmental opposition to new manufacturing investment in many developed countries is merely reinforcing shifts toward a greater service orientation and is a major factor in favoring increased relocation of industrial production to developing countries."[29]

Constraints on hazardous production. In addition to the burdens imposed by the costs of controlling air, water, and solid-waste pollution and the rise of social blockage, some observers expressed the view that standards to reduce public and worker exposure to numerous chemical compounds would force U.S. industries to move abroad. Not only were the costs of meeting expanded workplace-health regulations great, these observers noted, but in many cases the regulations were so stringent that the manufacture of certain products would simply be forced to come to a halt in the United States and other industrial nations.

A report issued in 1978 by a private consultant, Barry Castleman, highlighted some of the industries where this phenomenon was already occurring or appeared to be imminent. Castleman's report attributed plant closings in the United States and new plant openings abroad in the asbestos-products, zinc-smelting, arsenic, benzidine-dye, and pesticide industries to stringent standards for workplace health, which had made these products difficult to produce in the United States. Of even greater significance, however, the report – entitled "The Exportation of Hazardous Factories to Developing Nations" – said that "the economy of hazard export is emerging as a driving force in new plant investment in many hazardous and polluting industries."[30]

Inevitably, Castleman predicted, "in the next decade, the export of hazards from the U.S. to Third World Countries is likely to increase," and "may soon lead to wholesale exodus in major industries."[31] The report, which was read into the *Congressional Record* and publicized as a result

28. Thomas N. Gladwin and Ingo Walter, "Environmental Conflict and Multinational Enterprise" (Working Paper no. 79-36, New York University Graduate School of Business, March 1979), p. 866.
29. Ibid., pp. 914–915.
30. Barry I. Castleman, "The Exportation of Hazardous Factories to Developing Nations" (Mimeographed paper, Independent Report, Washington, D.C., March 1978).
31. Ibid., p. 3.

of congressional hearings, went on to cite the numerous international problems that these trends might cause. It expressed particular concern about the implications for worker health in countries receiving these industries.[32]

Subsequently, a number of other studies and journalistic inquiries have sought to corroborate Castleman's findings and have identified numerous individual cases where factories producing substances harmful to workers have moved from the United States to countries where governmental workplace-health standards are less onerous.[33]

The pollution-haven hypothesis

Underlying the view that underindustrialized countries would willingly seek to become pollution havens in order to attract more foreign direct investment was the assumption that their social tolerance for pollution would remain quite high. Pollution was regarded as a rich man's disease, and developing countries were not expected to institute comprehensive environmental standards and clean-up programs until they had attained mugh higher levels of affluence. In short, it was assumed that the level of concern for environmental control would remain a function of per-capita income.[34]

32. Ibid., pp. 1–2. The report was entered into the June 29, 1978, *Congressional Record*. In addition to appearing in the Congressional Record, various versions of Castleman's original report have also appeared as "How We Export Dangerous Industries," *Business and Society Review*, Fall 1978, pp. 17–23; "Industries Export Hazards: U.S. Companies Locate in Non-Regulating Havens in Third World," *Multinational Monitor* 1, no. 1 (Winter 1978–79):26–32; and "The Export of Hazardous Factories to Developing Nations," *International Journal of Health Services* 9, no. 4 (1979):41–53.
33. Among these inquiries are: David C. Williams, "Hazardous Jobs Have Become One of America's Major Exports," *Los Angeles Times*, September 23, 1979, p. 17; P. Sweeney, "Juarez Plant a 'Runaway' Firm?" *El Paso Times*, April 4, 1978, pp. 9–10; Barry I. Castleman and Manuel J. Vera Vera, "Impending Proliferation of Asbestos," *International Journal of Health Services* 10, no. 3 (1980):389–403; Edward Flattau, "U.S. Firms Seek Refuge from Regulations,"*Chicago Tribune*, June 16, 1979, p. 4; Kathleen Agena, "Hazards International: No Easy Solution Is Possible," *New York Times*, April 27, 1980, p. 22; Barry I. Castleman, "Double Standards: Asbestos in India," *New Scientist*, February 26, 1981, pp. 522–523; David Weir and Mark Schapiro, *Circle of Poison: Pesticides and People in a Hungry World* (San Francisco: Institute for Food and Development Policy, 1981); Deborah Baldwin, "The Untouchables: Global Corporations Are Proving That National Boundaries Can't Stop Pollution," *Environmental Action*, July 24, 1978, pp. 8–10; Robert Lamb, "Third World Used as Multinationals' Dustbin," *Earthscan Bulletin* 3, no. 2 (March 1980):3–4; and Herman Rebhan, "Labor Battle Hazard Export," *Multinational Monitor* 1, no. 2 (March 1980):18–19.
34. See especially *Development and Environment* (Report and Working Papers of a Panel of Experts Convened by the Secretary-General of the United Nations Conference on the Human Environment, Founex, Switzerland, June 4–12, 1971), referred to as the Founex Report.

Many less-industrialized countries, in light of their desire for rapid growth and their lingering poverty and squalor, were unlikely to be overly concerned with pollution control in the foreseeable future. Developing countries, the Brazilian delegate to a 1972 United Nations conference asserted, prayed for the day when they would share in the developed world's industrial pollution and would welcome multinational investors willing to help them pollute.[35] And many less-developed countries viewed the issue of environmental quality with open suspicion, seeing it as a threat to their growth and fearing that developed countries would attempt to export their preferences for pollution control or to place "environmental" tariffs on imports from countries with lower standards.[36]

For all these reasons, the emerging disparities between environmental regulations in industrialized and underindustrialized countries were expected to continue to widen for several decades beyond the 1970s. As the chasm widened between countries that regulated industrial pollution and those that did not, it was assumed that underindustrialized countries would increasingly compete with each other for foreign investment on this basis. The common assumption was that industrial-development planners would use permission to pollute – or guarantees of "grandfather-clause" protection from future governmental regulation of pollution – much as they did tax holidays and other tax incentives.[37]

In other words, the absence of costly environmental controls was seen as an important complement to the industrial-development strategy of a country seeking to establish its position as an export platform for manufactured goods. But some analysts went farther, making the point that developing countries could use their pollution-haven status as a means of skipping over certain stages in the evolution of their comparative advantage. They could attract more sophisticated industries that might be less

35. See Castro, "Environment and Development."
36. Ibid. Such a possibility was raised in the Founex Report, which stated: "The real danger is if the environmental standards enforced by the developed countries are unrealistic and unilateral and are arbitrarily invoked by them to keep some of the exports of the developing countries out of their markets"(p. 31). Although the General Agreement on Tariffs and Trade permits the imposition of measures "necessary to protect human, animal, plant life, or health," it limits this exception to ensure that such measures do not constitute "a disguised restriction on international trade." See "Industrial Pollution Control and International Trade," GATT Studies in International Trade, no. 1 (1971). Also, the Stockholm Declaration issued at the UN Conference on the Human Environment in 1972 warned that environmental standards should not be "directed towards gaining trade advantages," and urged that the UN monitor and report "the emergence of tariff and nontariff barriers to trade as a result of environmental policies." See the United Nations Conference on the Human Environment, Recommendation 71, UN Doc. A/Conf. 48/14 (1972).
37. Harold Malmgren, "Environmental Management and the International Economy," in Kneese, Rolfe, and Harned, eds., *Managing the Environment.*

inclined than labor-intensive or low-technology industries to be searching for export platforms with low wages.[38] By offering the right to pollute, less-developed countries could provide for capital-intensive industries a cost-saving incentive that might induce them to take advantage of the shrinking of the globe brought about by air freight, containerization, and other technological advances.

Some concern was raised that pollution havens might encounter many of the same problems of tax havens. Like countries that offered tax holidays for specific periods of time, countries that formally declared a moratorium on pollution control for foreign investors might find that the action had caused resentment among domestic interests. Worse yet, a certain percentage of industries might close shop as soon as the exemption expired.[39] The fear of secondary industrial flight at a later date might therefore prevent countries from responding with environmental regulations as their natural environmental assimilative capacity was being diminished.

However, as has generally been the case with tax havens, the prevailing attitude was that underindustrialized countries should focus on attracting the industries they desired and deal with the subsequent challenges when they arose. In addition, some observers pointed out that the alternative – to focus primarily on labor-intensive industries – was probably even more risky from the standpoint of potential secondary industrial flight, because labor-intensive industries can often move quite easily. Citing the industrial-inertia phenomenon discussed in Chapter 1, some felt that because the pollution-haven incentive would be more valuable to capital-intensive industry, less secondary industrial flight would occur as a country's social and natural environmental assimilative capacity was depleted.[40]

Political and economic perspectives

At least in theory, many international economists have considered a gradual shift of whole industrial sectors caused by differential pollution-con-

38. United Nations Conference on Trade and Development, "Implications for the Trade and Investment of Developing Countries of United States Environmental Controls," TD/B/C2/150/Add. i/Rev.1 (1976).
39. These possibilities are noted in V. Ranganathan, "Environmental Policies and Their Implications for Trade and Development: A Case Study of India," UNCTAD/ST/MD/ 10 (November 10, 1977), p. 50.
40. A good overview of the different arguments for and against the redeployment of industries on the basis of environmental considerations is found in Rahmatullah Khan, "Redeployment of Industries to Developing Countries: Environmental Considerations," in *Trends in Environmental Policy and Law* (Gland, Switzerland: International Union for Conservation of Nature and Natural Resources, 1980), pp. 1–23.

trol costs or other environmental factors as a positive development for both developing and developed countries. They argue that such a shift would contribute to overall global economic efficiency, stimulate more rapid industrial development in the Third World, and lead to a more efficient international division of labor. On the other hand, they think that any efforts to stifle this process run counter to the principles of an open world economy and are likely to drive up consumer prices, frustrate the economic-development aspirations of developing countries, and reduce overall productive investments by corporations worldwide.[41]

In line with the general tendency to view environment as one of many natural factor endowments that help determine patterns of trade and industrial specialization, international economists have contended that any international disturbances resulting from differential environmental regulations should be viewed as a function of the natural process of evolution of comparative advantages.[42] These economists have opposed proposals to prevent corporations from moving from one country to another to reduce the costs of regulatory control, as well as proposals to enforce uniform international environmental standards on corporations and developing countries. These economists expect that U.S. producers will demand protection from imports produced in countries where environmental-control costs are lower than in the United States, and they argue that the government ought to resist these demands. Noting that policy makers are under pressure to establish countervailing duties or other special import tariffs to offset competitive advantages gained by manufacturers with plants in countries with less stringent environmental standards, Ingo Walter points out that to "countervail competitive advantages attributable to environmental measures is . . . no more justified than similar protection designed to offset differences in capital or labor costs."[43]

Blackmail, unfair trade, and imperialism

Some observers consider environmentally induced shifts to be less benign in practice than in theory. Analysts who adopt a political perspective of economic events usually view the possible consequences of differential pollution-control costs from a different vantage than their more purely theoretical colleagues. Moreover, the persistence of economic hard times, coupled with international political reaction against multinational cor-

41. See, in addition to the theoretical articles already cited, the articles in Kneese, Rolfe, and Harned, eds., *Managing the Environment*.
42. See "Industrial Pollution Control" for a more detailed argument against intervention to equalize the environmental factor by imposing tariff and nontariff barriers.
43. Walter, "Pollution and Protection," pp. 11–12.

porations, has prompted calls for the U.S. government and various international organizations to intervene in this process.

From the beginning, industry groups and business groups argued that the cost and logistics of complying with all the new environmental regulations might undermine the competitiveness of American firms in world trade and might induce U.S. companies to locate new production facilities abroad. For example, in 1975 an economic-impact study commissioned by the Manufacturing Chemists Association (now the Chemical Manufacturers Association) warned that passage of pending toxic substances control legislation would lead to "considerable emphasis toward the redirection and growth of chemical process industries abroad. Multinational firms would seriously reconsider their positions with a strong emphasis on foreign investment."[44] Such prospects raised concern in the United States that the U.S. economy and overall industrial base would be adversely affected. It was feared that employment, the balance of trade, and even national security would be threatened if substantial numbers of U.S. industrial facilities transferred production out of the United States in response to high environmental costs.[45]

But environmental groups also worried that U.S. firms would take advantage of developing countries' intense desire for industry and set up factories that polluted the atmosphere and the water, ignored considerations of workers' health and safety, and caused other serious environmental hazards in the Third World. Others were concerned that U.S. corporations could use relocation abroad as a threat in their efforts to roll back U.S. regulations, as a means of undermining the intent of regulations, and as a weapon for extracting concessions from developing countries. A group of prominent environmentalists wrote that both environmentalists and U.S. labor leaders should be alarmed over the emergence of "foreign pollution havens," adding that especially for the less-developed countries, desperately in need of development and capital, this shift amounted to what might be termed a subtle form of blackmail.[46] And two political

---

44. Foster D. Snell, Inc., "Economic Impact on Toxic Substances Control Legislation" (Report presented to the U.S. House, Committee on Interstate and Foreign Commerce, July 1975), reprinted in Alexander McRae, Leslie Whelchel, and Howard Rowland, eds., *Toxic Substances Control Sourcebook* (Germantown, Md.: Aspen Systems, 1978), p. 145.

45. See for example, Council on Environmental Quality, Department of Commerce, and Environmental Protection Agency, *The Economic Impact of Pollution Control: A Summary of Recent Studies* (Washington, D.C.: U.S. Government Printing Office, March 1972), for an overview of early concerns.

46. Eugene V. Coan, Julia N. Hillis, and Michael McCloskey, "Strategies for International Environmental Action: The Case for an Environmentally Oriented Foreign Policy," *Natural Resources Journal* 14, no. 1 (January 1974):94. See also the testimony of Ralph Nader, in U.S. Senate, Committee on Public Works, Subcommittee on Air and Water Pollution, *Hearings on Economic Dislocations Resulting from Environmental Controls*, 92d Cong., 1st sess., 1971.

economists pointed out that in a climate in which states could be expected to compete with one another to attract investment and increase export earnings by maintaining relatively lenient pollution-control standards, "the combined effect of this behavior . . . is to give every state interested in environmental improvement the incentive to work just a little less vigorously than its neighbors to control pollution."[47]

Others worried about the leverage that the emergence of industrial flight and pollution havens might give to developing countries. For example, C. Fred Bergsten, former assistant secretary of treasury, speculating on ways in which developing countries might seek to harm the U.S. economy, noted that "some major LDCs (Brazil, for example) are in fact already inviting those industries most heavily restricted by new antipollution standards in the U.S. to come to their countries with a promise that they will be free from the antipollution measures that are raising production costs in the U.S."[48]

In the Third World, some Marxists and dependency analysts view the supposed impending transfer of highly polluting industries as one more means of continuing "imperialist" exploitation of developing countries. Samir Amin, one of the most renowned Third World economists, wrote that "to acquiesce in the transfer of industrial pollution is also to accept the transfer of its eventual costs from capital to the peoples of the Third World." This would imply, he added, acceptance of "a new unequal international division of labor, continued unequal relations between a dominant center and dominated periphery, and a growing gap between standards of living."[49]

But the reaction in the Third World to the prospects of environmentally induced relocation has not been uniformly negative. In many instances, governments and industrial-development planners have tried to determine whether they could use such a trend to their advantage. Indeed, over the years the notion that lax pollution standards could become a major factor in speeding Third World industrial development has continued to receive heavy credence in the United Nations Industrial Development Organization (UNIDO). One recent UNIDO study of mineral-processing potential in developing countries advised developing countries that "environmental subsidies" could be "a relatively advantageous form of incentives" for attracting industries to make investments.[50]

47. Blake and Walters, *Politics of Economic Relations,* p. 159.
48. C. Fred Bergsten, "The Threat from the Third World," in Richard N. Cooper, ed., *A Reordered World: Emerging International Economic Problems* (Washington, D.C.: Potomac Associates, 1973), p. 114.
49. Samir Amin, *Imperialism and Unequal Development* (New York: Monthly Review Press, 1975), p. 35.
50. United Nations, Industrial Development Organization, *Mineral Processing in Developing Countries* (New York: United Nations, 1980), p. 94.

The politics of industrial redeployment

Reactions in the United States

Two domestic political coalitions, in particular, have expressed alarm about what might happen if the industries most affected by pollution control costs, social blockage, and hazard controls migrated in large numbers to other countries. One coalition – an amalgamation of labor unions, environmental groups, and consumer advocates – essentially argues that (1) in the absence of international agreements equalizing environmental controls, the U.S. government should find some means of protecting U.S. firms from offshore competition by unregulated industries; (2) steps should also be taken to prevent firms from fleeing the U.S. to escape regulations; and (3) U.S. companies operating abroad should be required to abide by the same regulations and standards as in the United States.

The other political coalition, composed primarily of business and conservative groups, believes that many of America's economic woes are attributable to overregulation of industry. These groups argue that environmental regulations have forced U.S. companies to move abroad and therefore have contributed to national unemployment, decreased industrial production, and balance-of-trade woes. They contend that this is one reason why the United States should ease, or in some cases altogether eliminate, its environmental regulations.

Attempting to halt "runaway shops." In reaction to the expected export of highly polluting American factories, labor unions, groups associated with organized labor, and various environmental organizations began to monitor U.S. companies and to lobby for legislative or executive intervention. Some observers assumed that some means of controlling runaway shops ought to be imposed by the United States, both to protect U.S. workers from unemployment and to protect foreign workers from industrial hazards. The Castleman Report, for example, contended that "poverty and ignorance make communities in many parts of the world quite vulnerable to the exploitation implicit in hazard export." As a consequence, it said, the efforts of recipient countries "to implement environmental controls for hazardous industries may have to be complemented by measures that prevent the mere displacement of killer industries to 'export platforms' in nonregulating countries."[51]

Although several proposals to reduce corporate mobility were discussed during the 1970s, no legislation of this nature was passed in the United

51. Castleman, "Exportation of Hazardous Factories," p. 3.

States.[52] However, a number of organizations took it upon themselves to monitor plant closings in the United States and the overseas activities of the affiliates of multinational corporations.[53] These information-gathering efforts helped to strengthen the efforts of an alliance of U.S. environmental groups who, through intense lobbying and court actions, sought to influence U.S. governmental agencies to apply the provisions of the 1969 National Environmental Policy Act to activities undertaken abroad by U.S. government agencies, either directly or in support of private groups and individuals.[54]

Inevitably, however, these efforts also contributed to the arguments of those who contended that U.S. environmental standards must be weakened because they were too burdensome and forced industry abroad. Therefore, as an alternative to weakening regulations, the coalition of environmental and labor groups proposed that the U.S. should act unilaterally to halt the importation of goods produced under conditions not tolerated in the United States. For example, the AFL-CIO called in 1980 for a program of "national stewardship" over the health consequences of exported hazardous goods, exported capital equipment, and imported goods whose production or use at home would be subject to restrictions to safeguard human health. While acknowledging that long-term solutions would require multilateral action because equally dangerous products or equipment could be bought elsewhere, the AFL-CIO report contended that the U.S. could take unilateral action to control "worker exposures in countries from which we import by ending our imports of toxic commodities (or goods produced with exposure to toxic substances) manufactured under circumstances manifestly more hazardous than established by domestic requirements."[55] Walter Cronkite, in a letter to the *New York Times,* made essentially the same suggestion, arguing that the United States should act unilaterally to "protect both American industry and the environment by barring products from any country that does not enforce pollution standards as strict as our own."[56]

52. See Richard B. McKenzie, *Restrictions on Business Mobility: A Study in Political Rhetoric and Economic Reality* (Washington, D.C.: American Enterprise Institute, 1979).
53. One effort to monitor U.S. plant closings yielded several publications. See Data Center, *Plant Shutdowns: Good Business, Bad News,* Press Profiles, no. 3 (Oakland: Data Center, June 1980); and Data Center, *Understanding and Combatting Plant Closures* (Oakland: Data Center, 1981). One of the most extensive efforts to track the overseas environmental record of U.S. companies was reported in a ten-part series: Bob Wyrick, "Hazards for Export," *Newsday,* December 13–31, 1981, pp.1–43.
54. The strategy was outlined in Coan, Hillis, and McCloskey, "Strategies for Environmental Action."
55. Sheldon W. Samuels, "National Stewardship: Unilateral International Regulation of Occupational and Environmental Hazards" (Position paper, Industrial Union Department, AFL-CIO, September 29, 1980), pp. 62–63.
56. Walter Cronkite, "To Save Our Industry and the Environment," *New York Times,* October 8, 1980.

An argument for weakening U.S. regulations. As part of their overall concern about the impacts of government regulation on business activity in the United States, many conservatives expressed alarm about effects of U.S. environmental regulations on international competitiveness.[57] Thus, Murray L. Weidenbaum, the first chairman of the Council of Economic Advisers under President Reagan, contended that the pressures for production processes to meet government environmental and safety requirements "are resulting in a smaller productive capacity in the American economy than is generally realized."[58] Moreover, Weidenbaum wrote, because American business does not operate in a closed society, "it finds itself more and more handicapped in competing at home and abroad with foreign companies that do not bear similarly heavy regulatory burdens." The ultimate costs of excessive government involvement in the economy, he concluded, "can be seen in the factories that are not built, the jobs that are not created, the goods and services that are not produced, and the incomes that are not generated."[59]

The reaction of industry groups has not always been uniform, however. Some have also complained that a few unscrupulous companies have put competitive pressure on others by actively searching for countries with lax environmental regulations. They have called for government action to prevent "underdeveloped countries [from] being used as pollution havens by corporations seeking to evade the antipollution laws of the U.S. and other industrialized nations."[60]

The U.S. government's conflicting response. U.S. government policymakers have tended since the mid-1970s to operate on the assumption that environmental regulations are indeed responsible for significant declines in the competitiveness and productive capacity of U.S.-based firms, for increases in imports of manufactured products, and for increasing the number of U.S. industries locating abroad. For example, in a published interview in 1977, a high-ranking official of the Occupational Safety and Health Administration (OSHA), Dr. Joseph Wagoner, said that the need to adhere to U.S. standards "has in some cases already had the conse-

57. See Susan J. Tolchin and Martin Tolchin, *Dismantling America: The Rush to Deregulate* (Boston: Houghton Mifflin, 1983). See also Michael Gordon, "Reaganites, with OMB List in Hand, Take Dead Aim at EPA's Regulations," *National Journal* 13, no. 7 (February 14, 1981):256–259; and S. Scheible, "Regulatory Relief," *Barron's*, June 8, 1981.
58. Murray L. Weidenbaum, "Government Power and Business Performance," in Peter Duignan and Alvin Rabushka, eds., *The United States in the 1980s* (Palo Alto, Calif.: Hoover Institution, 1980), p. 203.
59. Ibid, pp. 209–210.
60. D. H. Dawson, Chemical Manufacturers Association, July 23, 1975, cited in Samuels, "National Stewardship," p. 63.

quence of removing the dirty operations to Latin America and keeping the cleaner part of the production process here."[61]

As a result, calls mounted in the late 1970s and early 1980s for the federal government to intervene either by regulating U.S. companies more closely to keep them from running away from U.S. regulations or by easing the burdens of U.S. environmental regulations so that U.S. companies are not impelled to migrate abroad.

Since 1972 the U.S. government has gone through three distinct phases in responding to these various concerns. Up to about 1977, government analysts attempted to assess whether any aspect of the industrial-flight hypothesis was in fact valid. Then the Carter administration took steps to secure international agreements on pollution control and hold U.S. interests operating abroad to more stringent environmental standards. During the Reagan administration the emphasis shifted decidedly toward reducing the regulatory burden on U.S. industries.

The U.S. Congress first expressed its anxiety about pollution-control costs in the Federal Water Pollution Control Act Amendments of 1972, which directed the Department of Commerce to study and report annually on the competitive impact of environmental regulations on U.S. companies. The amendments also required the president, as a means of heading off any competitive disadvantages, to "undertake to enter into international agreements to apply uniform standards of performance for the control of the discharge and emission of pollutants from new sources" through multilateral treaties, the United Nations, and other international forums.[62]

Several legislative proposals during the decade also were designed to offset any competitive disadvantages accruing to American-based producers as a result of pollution-control costs. In 1977 and 1979, Morris Udall (D-Arizona) introduced the Copper Environmental Equalization Act (H.R. 9697 and H.R. 3267) which would have increased prices on imported copper to account for the difference in the cost of complying with environmental regulations in the U.S. and in importing countries. Neither bill gathered enough support to pass.

U.S. negotiators explicitly addressed the effect of environmental and workplace-health regulations on American industry in 1979 at the Tokyo Round talks on the General Agreement on Tariffs and Trade (GATT). President Carter's chief trade negotiator, Robert Strauss, urged represen-

61. Joseph Wagoner, interview with the North American Congress on Latin America, December 1977, quoted in "Dying for Work: Occupational Health and Asbestos," *NACLA Report* 12, no. 2 (March–April 1978), p. 21.
62. Public Law 92-500 (October 18, 1972); 86 Stat. 879-98. See also U.S. Senate, *Hearings on Economic Dislocations.*

tatives at the trade talks to consider international environmental and workplace-health standards in light of a "pattern of flight" by industry to countries with low standards. While cautioning against a new protectionism, Strauss said: "American standards in these areas are among the highest in the world, and we do not want this U.S. willingness to protect the environment and our workers to disadvantage the various U.S. producers willing to pay such costs."[63]

The Trade Act of 1974 had directed the president to seek the adoption of international fair-labor standards and had increased the power of the federal government to compensate for or reverse the damage that occurred to U.S. trade because environmental control costs were lower abroad.[64] In 1978 U.S. Labor Secretary Ray Marshall indicated that environmental-control costs included the costs of meeting standards for workplace health and safety and proposed that this issue also be addressed at the GATT meetings.[65]

In 1979 Assistant Secretary of State Lucy Benson, following up on the congressional mandate for the executive branch to seek international accords, proposed an international treaty on the environment. Although intended to apply primarily to large projects with transnational environmental impacts, this treaty was seen by some officials of the Carter administration as a step toward reducing international disparities in environmental regulations.[66] The treaty was never enacted.

During this time the Carter administration also issued guidelines requiring U.S. government agencies to perform some form of environmental assessment of activities they undertook or supported abroad. Private ventures of U.S. corporations were included in this requirement if they were supported by the U.S. Agency for International Development, the Export-Import Bank, or the Overseas Private Investment Corporation. However, these guidelines had numerous exceptions and were later substantially watered down by the Reagan administration.[67]

63. As quoted in *Environment Reporter* 9, no. 10 (July 1, 1978):451. See also "Increased Export of Hazardous Jobs Could Be Brought Up at GATT Meeting," *International Environment Reporter* 1, no. 11 (November 10, 1978):356.
64. See Sanford E. Gaines, "The Extraterritorial Reach of U.S. Environmental Legislation and Regulations," in Seymour J. Rubin and Thomas R. Graham, eds., *Environment and Trade: The Relation of International Trade and Environmental Policy* (Totowa, N.J.: Allanheld, Osmun, 1982), pp. 102–135.
65. Helen Deward, "Labor Standards Urged as Lever in Trade Talks," *Washington Post*, January 11, 1978, p. A6.
66. Margot Hornblower, "U.S. Proposes Treaty on Environment," *Washington Post*, April 24, 1979, p. A15.
67. See Gaines, "Extraterritorial Reach"; and Mary Patricia Azevedo, "Trade in Hazardous Substances: An Examination of U.S. Regulation," in Rubin and Graham, *Environment and Trade*, pp. 135–154.

In contrast to the Carter administration, the Reagan administration approached the problem of industrial relocation by seeking to roll back regulations that industry targeted as burdensome, rather than by trying to bring the rest of the world up to U.S. standards.[68] One of the first steps taken by President Reagan after assuming office in January 1981 was to establish the Task Force on Regulatory Relief, a cabinet-level committee chaired by Vice President George Bush. In the testimony provided to the task force by hundreds of industry groups, environmental and workplace health regulations were among those most often identified as overly burdensome. Frequently, industry groups cited the loss of competitiveness by domestic production facilities as a major justification for regulatory relief and noted that the alternative was for U.S. manufacturers to build more plants abroad.[69]

Efforts by international organizations

Although many felt that the only solution to the impending problem of relocation was international environmental standards administered by the United Nations, efforts along these lines never really got off the ground. Most of the actions taken by international bodies to address the issue of environmentally induced relocation have centered around the designation of codes of behavior for multinational corporations and on assisting developing countries to decide which polluting industries to accept and on what basis.

A number of organizations that have issued guidelines and international codes for multinational corporations have noted the need for corporate concern about environmental pollution. The Commission on Transnational Corporations of the U.N. Economic and Social Council includes environmental factors in its code of conduct for multinational corporations. The draft code calls on corporations to disclose to the authorities of the countries in which they operate all relevant information concerning features of their products or processes which may harm the environment and the measures and costs required to avoid harmful effects; and prohibitions, restrictions, warnings, and other regulatory measures that other countries have imposed, on grounds of protection of the environment, on

68. For an overview of the underlying assumptions that guided this approach, see Louis J. Cordia, "Environmental Protection Agency," in Charles L. Heatherly, ed., *Mandate for Leadership: Policy Management in a Conservative Administration* (Washington, D.C.: Heritage Foundation, 1981), pp. 967–1038.

69. See especially Chemical Manufacturers Association, "Response to the Vice President and Recommendations for Regulatory Reform," summary and 2 vols. (Submissions to the Task Force on Regulatory Relief, May 1, 1981).

products and processes that the firms have introduced or intend to introduce in the countries concerned.[70]

The 1976 OECD guidelines on multinational corporations contain a general statement that corporations must give due consideration to the host country's aims and priorities, including the protection of the environment.[71]

The International Chamber of Commerce, in 1981, also enacted its own set of environmental guidelines for world industry, calling on all members to take independent actions to improve the environment even in the absence of legislation in host countries. The guidelines also expressed industry support for negotiating international conventions and harmonizing environmental legislation.[72]

Developing countries asked the United Nations Conference on Trade and Investment (UNCTAD) to investigate concerns that the environmental regulations of some countries have been employed as covert trade barriers. As a result of that investigation, UNCTAD established an "early warning system" to alert exporters to impending changes in environmental regulations in importing countries.[73]

In 1972 OECD members agreed to adopt the "polluter pays" principle to ensure that the cost of pollution abatement would be borne by producing firms (and their consumers) and to help reduce trade distortions that arise from disparate financing arrangements among trading partners.[74] The "Guiding Principles concerning Trade and Environment" obligates adjustments to equalize environmental costs.[75] Over the years, OECD members have shown considerable concern about whether industrial flight is occurring and pollution havens are emerging. They have discussed charges that poorer countries of Europe may have sought an advantage by not enforcing pollution controls; Belgium, Ireland, Italy, Spain, and Greece have been among the countries discussed. Another question raised was whether the ability of some Eastern European countries to undersell Western European chemical producers was in part due to an absence of

70. Commission on Transnational Corporations, "Transnational Corporations: Code of Conduct; Formulations by the Chairman," I/C.10/AC.2/8 (December 13, 1978), pp. 9–10.
71. See Charles Pearson, "An Environmental Code of Conduct for Multinational Companies?" in Rubin and Graham, *Environment and Trade*, p. 156.
72. International Chamber of Commerce, "Environmental Guidelines for World Industry," revised text of the first draft revised guidelines, Document no. 210-22/2, 1981.
73. See UNCTAD Report, "UNCTAD/UNEP Informal Meeting of Experts on Trade Aspects of Environmental Policies and Measures," UNCTAD/MD/92, GE.
74. See Organization for Economic Co-operation and Development (OECD), *The Polluter Pays Principle-Definition, Analysis, Implementation* (Paris: OECD, 1975).
75. See OECD reg. C(74)55, cited in OECD, *Legal Aspects of Transfrontier Pollution* (Paris: OECD, 1978).

pollution-control costs. However, most of these discussions have been highly speculative and preliminary. Internal politics prevented the OECD from investigating formally.[76]

Conclusions

The emergence of differential environmental regulations between nations was expected, in a Heckscher-Ohlin world, to lead to an evolution of comparative advantage in trade and production in industries that depended upon the services of the natural environment as a factor in production. The quality of a country's environment, the absolute size of the natural capacity to assimilate pollution, the extent to which this capacity is undersubscribed or oversubscribed, and the attitudes of the country's people and government toward pollution were all expected to accumulate into an environmental factor endowment that would influence patterns of international trade and investment. Countries with an abundant environmental factor endowment would produce and export "environment-intensive" industrial goods in order to exploit their comparative advantage.

These broad theoretical postulates about the impacts of differential environmental-control regulations on international comparative advantage filtered down to guide the assumptions made by policymakers in the United States, developing countries, and international organizations. Whether environmental redeployment was viewed as a positive development that would enhance industrialization efforts outside the First World or as one more example of the advanced countries' exploiting the periphery to their advantage, national and international discussions of the subject almost invariably were founded on an acceptance of the basic premise.

Public and private actors at all levels tried to secure policies based upon their outlooks of environmental redeployment. Industry spokesmen in the United States argued for reduced regulation; they warned that strict controls would force them to act according to self-interest and leave for countries with less stringent environmental regulations. Environmental groups in the United States sought legislation to prevent industrial flight by applying U.S. environmental regulations to U.S. interests operating abroad. For a time the U.S. government attempted to secure international agreements to equalize environmental standards; later it focused on reducing and simplifying U.S. regulatory requirements. Officials of developing countries encouraged industries to take advantage of their abundant environmental factor endowments. In cooperation with UNIDO and other international

---

76. Interview with Michael Potier, head of the Environment and Industry Division, Environment Directorate, OECD, Paris, July 12, 1980.

groups, they sought to identify high-pollution industries they might welcome. To prevent extreme environmental hazards in industrializing nations, various international bodies promulgated environmental codes of conduct for multinational corporations. At the same time, Third World Countries and international organizations manifested an underlying suspicion of environmental redeployment. Some urged underindustrialized countries to reject the role of dumping ground for the industrialized world.

The following chapters turn to the question of whether the industrial-flight and pollution-haven hypotheses that have stirred so much theoretical posturing and policy debate within and between nation-states are, in fact, significant contributors to the evolution of comparative advantage in industrial production.

4

Environmental regulations and the industrial-flight hypothesis

It is difficult from a methodological standpoint to assess whether environmental factors actually have, in the aggregate, induced U.S. manufacturing firms to select more foreign sites for branch plants and have increased the rate of industrialization in countries whose environmental factor endowment is still abundant. The logic of comparative advantage says that if all other things are equal and if environmental regulations significantly affect industry cost calculations, divergent national standards will promote a reshuffling of international industrial-location patterns. But pollution-control costs and other environmental concerns affecting industries cannot be examined in a vacuum. A number of factors make up total costs of production, and costs in turn may be only one of a number of tangible and intangible factors that determine where a company sets up productive facilities.

Consequently, this chapter seeks to establish some recent trends in foreign investment by U.S. industries that might coincide with those to be expected following the introduction of differential national environmental regulations in a Heckscher-Ohlin world. After outlining some of the factors that make it difficult to single out the effects of environmental regulations on comparative advantage in the real world, we shall employ a variety of methods to ascertain whether industries with high pollution-control costs in the United States have recently increased investments in countries with low environmental standards.

Isolating environmental factors

The direct macroeconomic effects of environmental regulations on gross national product, inflation, unemployment, and productivity have generated considerable political debate in the United States. Most empirical studies have concluded that environmental regulations have contributed incrementally but not fundamentally to high unemployment in certain industries, to general inflation rates, and to the slowdown in productivity growth in a number of industries.[1] Although some critics still insist that environmental regulations have made a major contribution to America's recent economic and industrial woes, the evidence is to the contrary. Even Christopher DeMuth, the former executive director of President Reagan's Task Force on Regulatory Relief, said that the available empirical evidence "fails to convict the newer regulatory programs of being major culprits in diminishing U.S. competitiveness. . . . [U.S.] experience with costly environmental and workplace controls is not radically different from that of our major competitors. Nor do available statistics suggest that regulation has been a dominant cause of our declining productivity growth."[2]

Some attempts have also been made to examine the less direct effects of environmental regulations – especially whether and how they have altered rates of capital formation in major industrial sectors.[3] This second type of inquiry has proven more problematic, because no macroeconomic model or set of indicators can measure foregone investment, much less whether environmental regulations might be responsible. It may be true, as Brookings Institution economist Robert W. Crandall contends, that the maze of environmental regulations does not encourage new investment.[4] Yet it is

1. For results of recent empirical analyses, see Gregory Christianson, Frank Gollop, and Robert Haveman, *Environmental and Health/Safety Regulations, Productivity Growth and Economic Performance* (Washington, D.C.: Office of Technology Assessment, 1980); *Cost of Government Regulation Study* (New York: Business Roundtable, 1979); Robert W. Crandall, "Pollution Controls and Productivity Growth in Basic Industries," in T. Cowing and R. Stevenson, eds., *Productivity Measurement in Regulated Industries* (New York: Academic Press, 1981), pp. 348–368; Edward Denison, "Pollution Abatement Programs: Estimates of Their Effect upon Output per Unit," *Survey of Current Business 59*, no. 8 (August 1979):58–64. A number of statistical studies have estimated the macroeffects of environmental regulation on the economy: Chase Econometrics issued a study in 1976 estimating that pollution control increased the Consumer Price Index (CPI) marginally – about 0.03 percent per year; a 1979 Data Resources estimate put this figure at 0.02 percent; and the Council on Wage and Price Stability concluded in 1979 that all government regulations (for example, economic and social) added 0.075 percent to the CPI annually.
2. Christopher DeMuth, "Domestic Regulation and International Competitiveness" (Paper presented at conference on U.S. productivity, Brown University, February 27–28, 1981).
3. Peter K. Clark, *Issues in the Analysis of Capital Formation and Productivity Growth*, Brookings Papers on Economic Activity (Washington, D.C.: Brookings Institution, 1979); *Federal Regulation of New Industrial Plants* (Washington, D.C.: American Bar Association, 1980); Robert H. Haveman and V. Kerry Smith, "Investment, Inflation, Unemployment and the Environment," in Paul R. Portnoy, ed., *Current Issues in U.S. Environmental Policy* (Baltimore: Johns Hopkins University Press, 1979), pp. 164–200; Henry M. Peskin, Paul R. Portnoy, and Allan V. Kneese, eds., *Environmental Regulation and the U.S. Economy* (Baltimore: Johns Hopkins University Press, 1981); and *Workshop on Effects of Environmental Regulation on Industrial Compliance Costs and Technological Innovation*, PRA Reports 83-9 and 83-10 (Washington, D.C.: National Science Foundation, 1983).
4. Crandall, "Pollution Controls," p. 368.

not clear how much more major capital investment would have taken place during the past decade if there had been no regulatory encumbrances.[5] Do the regulatory expenses and difficulties only slow and deflect new plant investments in the short run, or do they reduce the total amount of investments made in the long run? Ultimately, the question is nearly impossible to answer unequivocally. Thus, John Quarles, former deputy administrator of the U.S. Environmental Protection Agency, recently pointed out that the basic question is clear: Do these regulatory impacts – both the delays and uncertainties of permit processing and the actual increases in construction costs – significantly inhibit the reindustrialization of America? Yet, he added, the question is not so easy to answer: "One yearns for data, but no data exist."[6]

Linking cause and effect

Obviously, because it is difficult to determine whether investments are being permanently foregone in the United States because of environmental regulations, we cannot easily say whether environmental factors have caused industries to locate abroad rather than in the United States. The latter question is complicated by the fact that foreign investments by U.S. companies are undertaken for many reasons unrelated to regulations. Although figures on overseas investments made by U.S. corporations are readily available, they offer no clues to the reasons for making the investments. Comparative costs for environmental regulations are available for the United States and many other countries, but these cannot be presumed to have affected flows of capital investment unless they are examined alongside all other factors that determine industrial location. Moreover, indices of the number of canceled or delayed plants in the United States or of the number of older plants shut down as a result of stricter environmental regulations do not necessarily tell whether greater overseas investment has ensued.

Another problem, of course, is that regulations have not affected all industries or groups of industries in the same way and to the same degree. Some U.S. industries have clearly borne a disproportionate share of the burden of pollution-control costs, public opposition to new plants, and workplace-safety requirements. Examining aggregate statistics for all

5. Crandall himself, in another article, makes this point, saying: "It is very difficult to measure opportunities foregone." Robert W. Crandall, "Regulation and Productivity Growth," in *The Decline in Productivity Growth* (Proceedings of a conference held in June 1970), Federal Reserve Bank of Boston Conference Series, no. 22.
6. John Quarles, "Environmental Regulation and Economic Growth: Another View" (Remarks delivered to a conference on siting new industry, sponsored by the Conservation Foundation, San Francisco, May 23–24, 1983).

manufacturing industries may fail to reveal problems in particular manufacturing sectors. Furthermore, the potential influences of environmental standards on industrial location patterns are only one aspect of the complex, interrelated social and economic trends encouraging the spread of industry and technology around the globe. The worldwide redistribution of industry began long before environmental issues were major public-policy issues, a fact that must be kept in mind when looking for a cause-and-effect relationship between environmental controls and the movement of industry from the most advanced countries to countries that are seeking to attain higher levels of industrialization (a category that includes both the so-called developing countries and the second-level developed countries). The most important question may be not whether environmental regulations are causing industrial flight, but whether they are intensifying or skewing locational and investment trends in general and whether they have a particularly significant impact on specific industries.

Another important aspect of the larger world picture is the desire of developing countries to increase and diversify their percentage of total world industrial output by the turn of the century. In many cases these countries have adopted a strategy of rapid industrialization based upon a range of incentives designed to attract multinational corporations. In countries like India and Brazil, the right to produce and sell in a heavily protected domestic market is often ample inducement to lure multinational companies. In other cases, countries compete actively for multinational facilities, offering tax holidays, low labor costs, infrastructure provisions, special treatment of capital expenditures, and numerous other direct fiscal incentives.

The strategy of building industrial capacity by encouraging foreign companies to locate domestically has been followed by Ireland, Malaysia, South Korea, Brazil, and even Canada, to name countries at very different levels of economic development. The fact that all of these countries have consciously encouraged pollution-intensive industries to relocate within their borders does not in itself indicate that they are international pollution havens. The building up of heavy industrial capacity is an integral part of the economic development and diversification plans of most countries – few nations are content to permit their economies to remain completely dependent upon external producers for heavy industrial needs or to compete only in labor-intensive, light industrial exports over the long term.

All these factors emphasize a fundamental point: when U.S. companies, even those facing extreme pressures because of pollution problems at home, decide to build a plant abroad instead of in the United States, they do not necessarily do so because of differentials in pollution control costs or because governmental and public concern for the environment may cause delays in construction. Conversely, an industrializing country may have no intention of becoming a pollution haven, but other forces may induce it to attract certain high-pollution industries just the same. Thus, a major methodological problem is that it is difficult to single out the effects of any one factor in assessing either international comparative advantage or individual industrial-location decisions.

There is no question that most industries spend more on pollution control in the United States than they do anywhere else except in Japan and a few European countries. But this does not necessarily mean that these cost differentials have been substantial enough (as a portion of total capital investment and operating costs) to have provoked large-scale flows of investments from countries with high costs of compliance to countries with low costs of compliance with environmental regulations. Even where environmental costs form a large portion of total costs, many foreign-direct-investment decisions are made on the basis of criteria other than costs – availability of skilled labor, raw materials and energy; access to markets; and political stability are among the most important. And, while environmental-control costs can be minimized overseas, the total costs of plant construction and operation are often much greater in foreign countries than in the United States. In short, merely showing that environmental control costs are sharply higher in the United States than in other countries does not prove that industries have moved or will move abroad to minimize these costs. The real-world environment in which firms make long-term trade and investment decisions is not a Heckscher-Ohlin world, and all other things are never equal.

Given wide ranges in both the amount of pollution generated by various industries and the impacts of new regulations on different industries, most analysts now tend to agree that it is not likely that "environmental dislocation" has altered the *overall* patterns of investment for U.S. industry. One study, for example, concluded: "Although the volume of foreign investments by American corporate affiliates has continued to grow during the 1970's, overall investment patterns do not appear to have been different than they would have been if the United States had not undergone a revolution in its environmental standards."[7]

A number of other studies in recent years have drawn this same conclusion. However, many have gone on to point out the need for more focused

7. H. Jeffrey Leonard and Christopher J. Duerksen, "Environmental Regulations and the Location of Industry: An International Perspective," *Columbia Journal of World Business* 15, no. 2 (Summer 1980):56. An earlier version of this paper was presented at the Conference on the Role of Environmental and Land Use Regulation in Industrial Siting, sponsored by the Conservation Foundation, Washington, D.C., June 21, 1979.

examination to isolate the effects on particular high-pollution industries in which production and related cost factors have been substantially altered by more stringent pollution-control requirements.[8] In an attempt to determine which industries have been most susceptible to possible international dislocations caused by environmental regulations, the next section identifies those broad industrial sectors that have been hardest hit by environmental regulations in the United States, are sufficiently foot-loose to invest abroad in response to changing short- and medium-term circumstances, and have not had their recent locational decisions governed by a specific set of overwhelming factors unrelated to environmental concerns.

Pollution-intensive industrial sectors

Identifying the particular industrial groupings most susceptible to relocation abroad because of environmental factors is fairly easy, because the same industries have generally been hardest hit by pollution-compliance costs, social blockage, and workplace hazards. Including, for the moment, petroleum producers among manufacturing industries, Table 4.1 shows that four broad industry groups – mineral processing, chemicals, paper, and petroleum – paid between two-thirds and three-fourths of all annual

---

8. See Thomas N. Gladwin and John G. Welles, "Environmental Policy and Multinational Corporate Strategy," in Walter, *Studies in International Environmental Economics;* Pearson and Pryor, *Environment,* pp. 170ff.; "Corporate Investment and Production Decisions: Does Environmental Legislation Play a Role?" *Economist Intelligence Report,* November 1978; and "Environmental Factors Seen Rarely Decisive in Site Selection," *International Environment Reporter* 1, no. 5 (May 19, 1978):142. The Gladwin and Wells study, after reviewing behavioral characteristics of several firms, the factors that generally weigh heavily in foreign-direct-investment (FDI) decisions, and the current empirical evidence, concluded: "Flows of foreign direct investment do not appear, as yet, to differ substantially from what would be expected in the absence of environmentally-induced shifts except in a few instances. More importantly, we do not expect a flow of environment-induced FDI of any real significance to materialise in the future.... A slight shift at the margin has, indeed, been introduced into the locational calculus of FDI, but for most MNCs (multinational corporations) the shift will not be significant enough to counterbalance the higher costs and risks involved in seeking out a developing national "pollution haven" for major new facilities. MNCs will of course try to locate in areas in which all costs ... are minimized. FDI will, of course, continue to flow to developing nations, especially those with stable governments and indigenous natural resources, but for intrinsic reasons largely unrelated to low environmental costs" (p. 202).
    In addition, interview studies with corporate officials in the United States and Europe have demonstrated that environmental factors are almost never predominant in selecting locations at home or abroad. See Howard Stafford, *The Effects of Environmental Regulations on Industrial Location,* Report on National Science Foundation Grant no. SES-8024562 (Cincinnati, June 1983); and Gabrielle Knodgen, "Environmental Regulations and the Location of Industry in Europe" (Paper presented at a conference on siting new industry, sponsored by the Conservation Foundation, San Francisco, May 23–24, 1983).

Table 4.1. *New plant and equipment expenditures for pollution abatement, 1973–84 (in billions of dollars)*

	1973	1974	1975	1976	1977	1978	1979	1980	1981	1982	1983	1984
All manufacturing	3.17	3.62	4.66	4.49	4.32	4.30	4.77	5.35	5.36	4.78	4.26	4.53
Total high-pollution sectors	1.97	2.45	3.49	3.38	3.13	2.87	3.25	3.70	3.75	3.40	3.00	3.14
Mineral processing	0.70	0.78	1.05	0.97	0.90	0.79	0.94	1.01	0.83	0.80	0.56	0.74
Chemicals	0.42	0.54	0.76	0.88	0.82	0.62	0.62	0.69	0.79	0.68	0.61	0.58
Pulp and paper	0.31	0.38	0.47	0.43	0.37	0.33	0.43	0.46	0.45	0.35	0.37	0.54
Petroleum	0.54	0.75	1.21	1.10	1.04	1.13	1.26	1.54	1.68	1.57	1.46	1.28
High-pollution-sector expenditures as percentage of all manufacturing	62.1	67.7	74.9	75.3	72.5	66.7	68.1	69.2	70.0	71.1	70.4	69.3

Note: All figures are revised on the basis of the latest benchmark study. 1984 figures are preliminary.
Source: Environmental Economics Division, "Plant and Equipment Expenditures by Business for Pollution Abatement," *Survey of Current Business* 66, no. 2 (February 1986):39–45.

Table 4.2. Pollution-abatement expenditures as a percentage of total new plant and capital expenditures, 1973–84: all manufacturing and select industries (%)

	1973	1974	1975	1976	1977	1978	1979	1980	1981	1982	1983	1984
Mineral processing	14.7	12.6	14.2	12.9	12.1	9.8	10.1	10.0	7.5	8.0	6.3	7.0
Chemicals	10.1	8.7	10.7	11.9	11.2	8.0	6.3	5.9	6.0	5.4	4.7	3.8
Pulp and paper	15.6	13.2	16.0	14.4	10.6	8.7	8.2	7.1	7.4	6.3	6.3	7.5
Petroleum	11.7	10.7	13.3	11.0	8.8	8.6	8.3	7.9	6.5	5.9	6.3	5.0
All manufacturing	4.5	6.9	8.7	7.7	6.4	5.5	5.0	4.8	4.2	4.0	3.7	3.3

Note: All figures are revised on the basis of the latest benchmark study. 1984 figures are preliminary.
Source: Environmental Economics Division, "Plant and Equipment Expenditures by Business for Pollution Abatement," Survey of Current Business 66, no. 2 (February 1986):39–45.

Table 4.3. *Sampling of conflicts over industrial facilities in the United States, 1970–78*

Type of facility	Number of cases	Percentage of total sample
Inorganic chemical	62	17
Organic chemical	40	11
Nuclear power	40	11
Mineral mining	40	11
Transport & storage	33	9
Oil refining	29	8
Ferrous metal	26	7
Nonferrous metal	22	6
Pulp & paper	22	6
Petrochemical	18	5
Electrical utility	11	3
All others	23	6
Total sample	366	100

Source: Thomas N. Gladwin, "Patterns of Environmental Conflict over Industrial Facilities in the United States, 1970–78," *Natural Resources Journal* 20 (April 1980):249.

capital expenditures for pollution control made by manufacturing industries in recent years. Table 4.2 illustrates that all four industry groups have tended to incur higher pollution expenditures in proportion to total new plant and capital expenditures than have all manufacturing industries. No other grouping of manufacturing industries has been above or even close to the average.

These four manufacturing-industry sectors – along with the nonmanufacturing sectors of mineral mining, electric utilities, and nuclear power plants – also turned up frequently in a major study by Thomas Gladwin of 366 industry-related environmental conflicts during the 1970s. In fact, 60 percent of all the conflicts were over facilities in the mineral-processing, chemicals, petroleum, or pulp-and-paper sectors. No other manufacturing industry registered a significant percentage in Gladwin's survey, as illustrated by Table 4.3. Furthermore, all of the industries cited by the Castleman Report as experiencing locational problems because of workplace hazards fall within either the mineral-processing sector or chemicals sector.

Which of the four sectors has been most highly susceptible to industrial flight in response to environmental regulations and restrictions? First, from all indicators noted above, it appears that the chemical and related industries could be susceptible to locational changes owing to environmental factors and thus deserve further attention. The chemicals sector also makes an excellent case study because many chemical products are still at an early stage of the product cycle, where comparative advantage in production would be expected still to be in the original producer country – the United States.

Petroleum industries (including refinery, storage, and transport facilities) have also experienced high pollution-control costs, difficulties in building new plants, and problems with industrial hazards; and those industries appear more footloose than most. However, a potential problem is that the dynamics of location for these industries have been heavily influenced by extraordinary circumstances affecting the world distribution and availability of crude oil during the past decade and a half. Thus this section does not examine further the impact of environmental regulations on international locational trends in the basic petroleum-refining industry. Nevertheless, once converted into petrochemical feedstocks, petroleum products are frequently shipped to nonpetroleum-producing countries for further manufacturing activity. These petrochemical manufacturing activities are subsumed under chemical and allied products in the tables in the rest of this section.

For several reasons, the mineral-processing industries also appear to be one of the most likely industrial sectors to have undertaken international locational shift as a result of environmental factors. First, they have been the hardest hit of all manufacturing groupings in terms of capital expenditures for pollution abatement, as Tables 4.1 and 4.2 show. Second, most of the industries that Castleman examined for extreme industrial-hazard-related problems fall within this grouping. Third, while traditionally depending on domestic ores for raw material, recent changes in transportation economics and the decreased availability of high-grade U.S. ores have made most mineral-processing industries more mobile than in the past.

By contrast, it is less likely that U.S. pulp and paper industries have been pushed abroad, for at least two reasons. First, pulp and paper industries have not traditionally operated on as global a scale as have chemical, petroleum, and mineral-processing firms, although operations in Canada account for over four-fifths of foreign investments made by U.S. companies. Second, the paper and allied industries do not appear to have been as severely affected by blockage and the problems of workplace hazards as chemicals, mineral-processing and petroleum-related industries have been. Capital expenditures for pollution-abatement equipment seem to have been the single biggest environmental challenge for paper-related industries, and, judging by the downward trend shown in Table 4.2, many paper companies were able to reduce their expenditures for pollution equipment as a proportion of total costs after an initial spurt of investment in the mid-1970s.

The two broad industrial sectors that do appear to have been most susceptible to international redeployment in response to environmental regulations – chemicals (including petrochemicals) and mineral processing – are examined more closely in the rest of this chapter. In particular, the following sections seek to determine if foreign-investment and trade figures for the past decade reflect trends that might substantiate the industrial-flight and pollution-haven hypotheses.

Identifying significant trends

A large number of factors affect the choices of location by specific industries and individual firms. Short of an in-depth study of the numerous locational factors weighed in countless decisions by individual firms, it is virtually impossible to identify precisely how important environmental concerns have become in the chemical and mineral-processing industries. By themselves, statistics on foreign investments and imports do not necessarily indicate how important environmental factors have become to high-pollution manufacturing industries making those decisions. However, for the purposes of this study, analyzing foreign-investment and import trends for the high-pollution sectors is a good starting point. At the least, such an analysis can indicate whether trends are moving in the direction that would be expected if national environmental factor endowments were gaining the prominence in the real world that they would be expected to hold under *ceteris paribus* conditions.

If environmental regulations are causing an exodus of high-pollution industries from the United States, as some claim, several trends should be quite pronounced. Although the existence of these trends would not prove that they are caused by environmental factors, the absence of the trends would provide strong evidence that environmental factors have not gained the prominence in locational decisions that many analysts predicted. If significant flight from U.S. environmental regulations is occurring, we should be able to identify four trends in foreign-investment and import figures:

1. the high-pollution manufacturing sectors should be increasing their foreign direct investment more rapidly than other manufacturing industries;
2. U.S. imports of chemical and processed mineral products should be expanding faster than overall manufactured imports;
3. less-developed countries (LDCs) should be receiving an increasing share of the total foreign direct investments made by U.S. firms in the high-pollution sectors; and

4. an increasing share of U.S. imports of goods produced by high-pollution industries should be coming from the LDCs.

The extent to which trade and investment patterns over the past decade have conformed to these trends can be seen by examining three sets of data that are generally available, consistent, and broken down by broad industry groupings: the total value of foreign direct investments abroad by U.S. companies; annual capital expenditures abroad by U.S. companies; and U.S. imports of manufactured products. By using these figures to compare the two key pollution-intensive manufacturing sectors with other manufacturing industries, it can be seen whether U.S. imports and direct investments by U.S. companies in foreign countries are growing faster for the chemicals and mineral-processing sectors than for other industries.

These figures can also indicate whether LDCs that have significantly weaker environmental regulations than the United States are grabbing larger shares of overseas investments made by U.S. firms in pollution-intensive sectors and larger shares of U.S. import markets for goods manufactured by these sectors. Of particular interest is whether LDCs have made substantial progress in attracting investments and exporting products from chemical industries, because this might imply that the product cycle was being speeded up and that some LDCs were moving rapidly through the "stages" of comparative advantage into more sophisticated industries.

Direct investments abroad

If pollution-control costs and other environmental factors did become much more important in determining international comparative advantage during the last decade, this trend should be reflected in several changes in the patterns of foreign investments made by U.S.-based companies. First, the rate of overseas expansion should have increased as more U.S. firms felt the pressures of regulatory initiatives in the United States. While it is difficult to assess whether the total amount of direct investment abroad would have been lower between 1970 and 1980 if no new environmental regulations had been passed, we can determine whether total direct investments made abroad by those manufacturing industries hit hardest by the regulations have increased faster than those made by other manufacturing industries. In fact, as Table 4.4 shows, the chemical and mineral-processing industries' share of total foreign direct investment by manufacturing industries did creep upward by several percentage points during this decade.

Many factors could be responsible for this slight increase. If it were caused primarily by environmental regulation and concern, we should be

Table 4.4. Direct investment abroad by U.S. companies, 1973–85: all manufacturing, chemicals, and mineral processing (in millions of dollars)

	1973	1974	1975	1976	1977	1978	1979	1980	1981	1982	1983	1984	1985
Total of all manufacturing industries	44,370	51,172	56,039	61,161	65,604	74,080	78,640	89,160	92,386	83,452	82,907	85,253	95,586
Chemicals	8,415	10,172	11,172	12,183	13,374	16,026	16,878	18,888	20,176	18,274	18,788	19,032	19,847
Mineral processing	2,971	3,411	3,649	3,785	4,022	4,167	5,506	6,322	6,521	5,463	4,974	5,079	5,458
Total of two industries	11,386	13,583	14,821	15,968	17,396	20,193	22,284	25,210	26,697	23,737	23,762	24,111	25,305
Chemicals and mineral processing as % of all manufacturing	25.7	26.5	26.4	26.1	26.5	27.3	28.5	28.3	28.9	28.4	28.7	28.3	26.5

Source: "U.S. Direct Investment Abroad," Survey of Current Business 54–66, no. 8 (August 1974–August 1986). Mineral processing includes both primary and fabricated metals.

able to detect two other trends. First, manufacturing firms should have shifted their direct investments from other developed to developing countries, and this shift would have been accentuated for chemical and mineral-processing industries. Table 4.5 indicates that among manufacturing industries in general, there was a marginally higher percentage of direct investment in developing countries by the end of the decade. Yet the long-term distributional trends of U.S. direct investment abroad showed no abrupt changes during the past decade.

The trends in the combined figures for chemicals and mineral-processing industries did not differ much from those of all manufacturing industries, even though it would be expected that they would have expanded faster than other industries if environmental factor endowments had become an important aspect of comparative advantage. For chemicals, which have traditionally had nearly one-fourth of all direct foreign investment in the Third World, the percentage share actually shrank slightly during the past decade. On the other hand, the mineral-processing industries did make an increasing proportion of their investments in the Third World in recent years. Although total mineral-processing investments in developing countries are only about one-third of those made by chemical producers, this shift could be significant if the trend continues in the future. Though not large, it certainly parallels the trends to be expected if environmental factors were affecting comparative advantage for U.S.-based mineral processors. Thus the shift at the margin noted for the mineral-processing industries merits further investigation later in this study.

Finally, if environmental regulations were now a major determinant of the destination of U.S. direct investment abroad, significant changes should be detected in the individual countries favored by U.S. corporations in the chemicals and mineral processing industries. Slower growth for investments in the advanced industrial countries and faster growth among the developing countries should be noted for chemicals (Table 4.6) and mineral processing (Table 4.7). In both cases, investments by U.S. companies in several countries, especially Mexico and Brazil, did grow quite rapidly. Yet, particularly in the case of chemical industries, the growth of U.S. investment in European countries has matched or exceeded investment in these rapidly industrializing countries. Comparing, for example, Germany with Brazil and France with Mexico (Table 4.6) it is difficult to hypothesize that environmental factors were decisive.

In fact, as the tables illustrate, a very small number of countries account for the vast majority of U.S. chemical and mineral-processing investments outside Canada, Japan, and the highly industrialized countries of Europe. Two countries, Ireland and Spain, held over 85 percent of the total 1980 U.S. direct investment in the peripheral, underindustrialized nations of

Table 4.5. Percentage of U.S. direct investment abroad in less-developed countries, 1973–85: all manufacturing, chemicals, and mineral processing

	1973	1974	1975	1976	1977	1978	1979	1980	1981	1982	1983	1984	1985
All manufacturing industries	17.6	18.0	18.6	18.6	18.7	19.2	19.2	19.9	21.0	23.1	21.2	22.1	20.6
Chemical industries	22.9	23.1	23.8	23.7	24.2	22.8	22.8	23.5	22.9	24.5	21.6	22.5	21.4
Mineral-processing industries	22.8	23.1	23.7	24.4	23.7	25.4	25.5.	26.1	28.4	29.3	24.6	27.4	24.4

Source: Calculated from figures in "U.S. Direct Investment Abroad," Survey of Current Business 54–66, no. 8 (August 1974–August 1986). Mineral processing includes both primary and fabricated metals.

Table 4.6. Direct investment by U.S. companies in individual countries, 1973–85: chemical industries (in millions of dollars)

	1973	1974	1975	1976	1977	1978	1979	1980	1981	1982	1983	1984	1985
Canada	1,767	2,049	2,268	2,462	2,373	2,875	2,996	3,402	3,719	4,178	4,546	4,642	4,581
United Kingdom	1,042	1,221	1,262	1,327	1,578	1,982	2,010	2,139	2,189	1,791	1,798	1,876	2,067
Germany	578	691	770	915	1,005	1,341	1,394	1,500	1,633	1,092	1,137	1,143	1,351
Brazil	343	450	528	676	822	1,153	992	1,036	1,048	1,384	1,276	1,275	1,274
Netherlands	402	546	564	616	762	840	1,171	1,183	1,294	1,098	1,164	1,054	1,114
Belgium	467	672	693	761	896	820	1,248	1,288	1,320	1,114	1,042	1,085	1,202
Mexico	503	652	720	654	699	787	870	1,061	1,144	687	658	746	779
France	453	543	592	638	699	776	919	1,049	1,042	797	745	679	785
Australia	498	545	540	587	609	678	499	511	599	1,150	1,277	1,416	1,296
Italy	350	383	402	450	479	561	614	712	728	514	569	512	572
Japan	301	327	360	374	406	497	670	700	767	778	1,148	1,175	1,244
Ireland	173	245	339	442	568	—	590	833	1,121	278	298	291	490
Spain	124	159	191	288	275	305	368	431	448	305	330	330	368
Argentina	171	198	180	207	222	243	299	416	362	347	252	244	280
Venezuela	130	145	168	189	235	280	309	346	398	368	220	220	188

Note: Dash means figures not available.

Source: "U.S. Direct Investment Abroad," *Survey of Current Business* 54–66, no. 8 (August 1974–August 1986). Mineral processing includes both primary and fabricated metals.

Table 4.7. *Direct investment by U.S. companies in individual countries, 1973–85: mineral-processing industries*

	1973	1974	1975	1976	1977	1978	1979	1980	1981	1982	1983	1984	1985
Canada	779	916	1,010	1,052	1,114	—	1,516	1,645	1,641	1,375	1,491	1,589	1,856
United Kingdom	343	394	396	404	433	—	692	902	888	730	595	517	565
Germany	291	319	350	355	357	—	550	600	612	574	543	574	649
Mexico	162	194	224	213	216	—	393	511	584	322	301	333	348
Brazil	84	109	130	153	176	—	410	441	466	676	697	762	756
Australia	102	103	123	140	153	—	245	299	343	117	102	94	68
Netherlands	148	170	187	172	191	—	255	283	307	201	216	217	225
France	119	137	129	122	126	—	226	248	261	205	183	175	193
Italy	73	90	59	—	—	—	142	173	149	108	89	82	76
Belgium	72	76	76	74	87	—	132	149	127	99	98	83	85
Norway	—	142	146	—	180	—	6	6	7	2	<0.5	<0.5	<0.5
Spain	—	63	80	—	—	—	—	—	−3	100	70	48	—
Japan	11	18	19	13	10	—	67	82	80	67	79	42	50
Argentina	—	63	68	72	—	—	64	72	66	91	99	110	99
Sweden	30	38	42	37	37	—	55	56	52	6	−2	—	−20
South Africa	35	39	42	37	37	—	55	91	94	159	154	148	176
Ireland	17	19	19	18	21	—	43	51	61	50	66	65	81
Venezuela	32	42	43	48	55	—	55	54	67	64	45	78	46
Switzerland	53	53	53	—	—	—	—	7	6	21	19	75	—

Note: Dash means figures not available.

Source: "U.S. Direct Investment Abroad," *Survey of Current Business* 54–66, no. 8 (August 1974–August 1986). Mineral processing includes both primary and fabricated metals.

Table 4.8. *Direct investments by U.S. chemical and mineral-processing industries in key rapidly industrializing countries, 1980 and 1984 (in millions of dollars)*

	Chemicals		Mineral processing	
	1980	1984	1980	1984
Total direct investment by U.S. companies outside of Canada, Japan, and industrialized Europe[a]	6,633	6,533	2,160	1,757
Total in underindustrialized Europe[b]	1,362	651	115	118
Total in Ireland and Spain	1,250	621	98	113
% of total underindustrialized Europe in Ireland and Spain	91.8	95.4	85.2	95.8
Total in less-developed countries	4,462	4,275	1,652	1,390
Total in Brazil, Mexico	2,094	2,021	952	1,095
% of total less-developed countries in Brazil and Mexico	46.9	47.3	57.6	78.8

[a]Excludes Ireland, Spain, Portugal, Greece, and Turkey.
[b]Includes Ireland, Spain, Portugal, Greece, and Turkey.
Source: Compiled from figures in "U.S. Direct Investment Position in 1980," *Survey of Current Business* 61, no. 8 (August 1981), table 12; and "U.S. Direct Investment Position in 1984," *Survey of Current Business* 66, no. 8 (August 1986), table 14.

Western Europe (Ireland, Spain, Greece, Portugal, and Turkey). Mexico and Brazil alone account for 49 percent of all U.S. chemicals and almost 58 percent of all U.S. mineral-processing investments in the Third World (see Table 4.8). Between them, as Tables 4.6, 4.7, and 4.8 emphasize, these rapidly industrializing countries account for much of the major chemical and mineral-processing investments that U.S. companies have made outside the highly advanced industrial nations. If U.S. firms have fled the United States in search of pollution havens outside the advanced industrial countries, these few rapidly industrializing countries are the prime suspects.

One interesting inquiry is whether within this small subset of countries, the chemicals industries are dominant as a portion of total U.S. investment in manufacturing industries and whether the portion expanded during the 1970s. Table 4.9 shows that chemicals and metals now account for a little more than 28 percent of all U.S. manufacturing investments abroad, up nearly 3 percentage points from 1970. While the portion of chemicals and metals investments increased commensurately in the developed countries,

Table 4.9. *Percentage chemical and mineral-processing industries of total U.S. direct investment in manufacturing for selected rapidly industrializing countries, 1973–85*

	1973	1975	1977	1979	1981	1983	1985
All countries	25.7	26.4	26.5	28.5	28.9	28.7	26.5
Developed countries	24.0	24.8	24.7	27.0	27.7	28.3	26.0
Developing countries	33.3	33.8	34.2	34.7	33.5	30.1	28.3
Rapidly industrializing countries							
Ireland	61.5	62.3	59.2	49.4	54.3	19.5	21.1
Spain[a]	21.7	19.3	20.0	22.8	23.7	20.5	21.3
South Africa	24.0	23.4	21.8	32.9	29.2	35.3	44.0
Argentina	—	32.7	—	30.6	26.6	22.6	24.0
Brazil	21.0	21.5	25.5	28.6	28.0	30.6	28.7
Colombia	36.3	38.7	34.6	38.8	35.6	34.1	26.9
Mexico	37.0	38.9	38.7	36.6	33.4	27.8	27.5
Venezuela	31.0	31.0	31.6	38.7	40.3	27.9	28.0
India	46.8	45.3	—	63.3	60.8	56.2	56.5
Philippines	28.5	30.7	31.5	28.9	31.6	42.9	47.6

Note: Dash means figures not available.
[a]Chemicals only.
Source: Calculated from figures in "U.S. Direct Investment Abroad," *Survey of Current Business* 54–66, no. 8 (August 1974–August 1986). Mineral processing includes both primary and fabricated metals.

it remained relatively stable for developing countries, at just over one-third of all U.S. manufacturing investments. When the rapidly industrializing countries with the most U.S. direct investment are isolated, an extremely wide range is apparent. Five were just below the average for all developing countries in 1980, two were just above, and two were significantly above average. In Ireland the mineral-processing and chemicals industries clearly are dominant among U.S. manufacturing investments, but this predominance declined over the decade. In India the trend was almost exactly opposite: chemicals and mineral processing significantly increased their combined share of total U.S. manufacturing investments.

Overall, however, the rough percentage share for the metals and chemicals industries was relatively stable. The large percentage fluctuation upward in India is not very large in terms of total investment, because India still does not host a high absolute portion of U.S. chemical and mineral-processing investments, as Tables 4.6 and 4.7 show. Thus the sharp percentage increase of chemicals and metals in the share of total U.S. investment in India seems more attributable to a slowdown in growth in other manufacturing sectors than a sudden change in its attractiveness to high-pollution industries. Indeed, confrontations with U.S. companies in the computers and electronics industry led to major disinvestments in the 1970s that probably boosted the percentage shares of other sectors.

In most other countries, other U.S. manufacturing industries expanded their investments at rates approximately equal to or higher than chemicals and mineral processing. This indicates that, at the least, the comparative advantage for these rapidly industrializing countries is more broadly based than the differential in environmental regulations between them and the United States.

Annual overseas capital expenditures

The aggregate values of foreign investments can be influenced by deviations in currency values that may not reflect comparative capital expenditures on a year-to-year basis. Consequently, annual capital expenditures abroad by U.S. affiliates are also examined for certain trends: faster growth for key polluting industries than for overall manufacturing; a marked shift upward in the percentage of expenditures in developing countries; and unexplained jumps in expenditures made in particular countries.

Table 4.10 shows annual overseas expenditures by firms in the two high-pollution industries and compares them to those of all manufacturing industries. As can be seen, the share of total expenditures for the three industries fluctuated between about 19 and 31 percent. Although somewhat erratic on a year-by-year basis, the years after 1976 show a definite dropoff in percentage terms for the chemicals and mineral-processing industries. Thus, contrary to what would be expected if pollution-control costs and other environmental factors were pushing U.S. industries abroad, expenditures of lower-pollution manufacturing industries took larger shares of total annual manufacturing expenditures abroad in the second half of the decade than in the first.

However, when one looks at the breakdown of these expenditures between advanced developed and less-developed countries (Table 4.11) one can observe a marked increase in the share of expenditures in both the chemical and the mineral-processing industries going to LDCs. Of course, this shift was evident in all manufacturing industries, but it was more pronounced for chemicals and mineral processing.

There are no clear explanations for these changes in expenditure patterns, although for chemicals the shift to a larger portion of capital expenditures in developing countries was relatively gradual. In the mineral-processing industries, successive large annual jumps abruptly increased the portion of annual capital expenditures going to developing countries dur-

Table 4.10. *Annual capital expenditures by majority-owned foreign affiliates of U.S. corporations, 1973–86 (in millions of dollars)*

	1973	1974	1975	1976	1977	1978	1979	1980	1981	1982	1983	1984	1985	1986
Chemicals	1,355	2,126	2,712	2,745	2,435	2,484	4,351	3,623	2,968	2,776	2,319	2,620	2,632	3,218
Mineral processing	779	783	777	658	695	705	772	836	804	868	895	1,003	915	725
Total of chemicals and mineral processing	2,134	2,909	3,489	3,403	3,130	3,189	5,123	4,459	3,772	3,644	3,214	3,623	3,547	3,943
Total of all manufacturing	9,247	11,730	11,384	10,930	12,730	15,164	18,830	23,353	19,164	16,755	13,724	14,048	15,251	17,347
Chemicals and mineral processing as % of total manufacturing	23.1	24.8	30.6	31.1	24.6	21.0	27.2	19.1	19.7	21.7	23.4	25.8	23.3	22.7

Source: "Capital Expenditures by Majority Owned Foreign Affiliates of U.S. Companies," *Survey of Current Business* 54–62, no. 10 (October 1974–October 1982); 63–66, no. 3 (March 1983–March 1986).

Table 4.11. Percentage of annual capital expenditures by majority-owned affiliates of U.S. corporations made in less-developed countries, 1971–86

	1971	1972	1973	1974	1975	1976	1977	1978	1979	1980	1981	1982	1983	1984	1985	1986
All manufacturing	11.8	14.3	14.0	13.6	16.1	16.8	14.3	15.0	14.8	14.1	19.5	19.8	17.0	18.9	18.5	17.8
Chemicals	11.8	14.9	17.1	16.1	17.0	16.7	15.6	20.1	16.7	18.2	22.4	19.3	18.0	18.1	18.3	18.0
Metals	13.1	10.2	8.3	10.5	19.4	30.7	27.1	23.8	18.5	20.5	26.9	42.2	42.3	27.8	24.2	18.9

Source: "Capital Expenditures by Majority Owned Foreign Affiliates of U.S. Companies," Survey of Current Business 52–62, no. 10 (October 1972–October 1982); 63–66, no. 3 (March 1983–March 1986).

ing the second half of the 1970s. This trend, in particular, may bear further investigation for possible correlation with environmental regulations being instituted at the time in the United States, especially because it reinforces the trends already observed in total foreign direct investments by the mineral-processing industries.

The figures for annual capital expenditures in individual countries (Tables 4.12 and 4.13) emphasize that there is still a preference in most cases for other advanced industrial nations. For both chemicals and mineral processing, however, it is clear that a small number of rapidly industrializing countries – led by Brazil, Mexico, Spain, and Venezuela – have consistently registered high levels of new capital expenditures in recent years.

U.S. imports of manufactured goods

If U.S. companies were shifting more production facilities abroad as a result of increased environmental regulation, imports into the United States should be rising, particularly in those industries bearing the highest pollution-control costs and making the highest demands on a country's environmental factor endowment. In fact, Table 4.14 shows that although U.S. imports did rise significantly for all manufacturing industries between 1971 and 1981, they did not expand as rapidly in the two manufacturing industries with the greatest environmental problems. The percentage share of total manufactured imports for these two industries actually declined during the decade. However, once again, the separate figures for the mineral-processing industries indicate that imports for them did rise faster (in percentage terms) than the average for all manufactured imports.

A better set of figures than overall U.S. manufactured imports is the subset of these imports sent from abroad by U.S. affiliates. Unfortunately, since 1977 the Department of Commerce has not collected annually the data on exports to the U.S. by overseas U.S. affiliates. In order to delineate a reasonable trend line, then, the figures in Table 4.15 show the years 1966–1977 for the chemicals and mineral-processing industries. As with overall imports, these figures show a slight decline for the pollution-troubled industries in the aggregate but a more rapid rate of growth for exports to the United States by affiliates from the mineral-processing industries. The growth in exports to the United States by U.S. industry affiliates abroad is particularly pronounced between 1971 and 1976, a period that overlaps with the period during which U.S.-based mineral processors were expending considerable sums of money to comply with new

Table 4.12. *Annual capital expenditures by majority-owned foreign affiliates of U.S. companies, 1976–86: chemical industry (in millions of dollars)*

	1976	1977	1978	1979	1980	1981	1982	1983	1984	1985	1986
Canada	798	1,036	894	921	795	655	575	425	507	471	625
United Kingdom	591	675	673	514	317	419	420	460	410	—	420
Brazil	402	222	182	186	170	247	165	128	170	171	221
Netherlands	349	249	142	106	149	215	205	181	280	247	222
Germany	264	264	349	254	138	243	196	188	220	305	359
Spain	237	51	82	49	52	105	223	52	50	52	71
France	218	140	107	84	81	165	131	122	152	168	195
Belgium	192	300	289	261	179	110	111	114	110	130	190
Argentina	134	—	30	23	16	80	42	34	43	51	51
Australia	133	74	55	47	39	77	72	79	72	75	88
Mexico	129	132	100	90	64	100	78	45	99	89	91
Italy	107	87	68	65	61	105	86	79	91	120	127
Venezuela	75	122	134	75	109	58	66	55	20	25	14

Japan	71	79	124	163	66	70	90	78	100	99	129
Ireland	38	31	71	87	32	49	38	40	76	27	28
Greece	25	—	—	—	—	14	6	—	7	14	—
Colombia	25	52	43	33	18	32	28	25	31	16	23
Sweden	21	41	31	24	29	25	25	5	11	14	12
South Africa	30	39	22	17	18	23	24	31	21	19	17
Philippines	18	19	16	15	10	21	17	15	22	29	36
Taiwan	17	—	—	—	—	13	8	12	6	9	8
Switzerland	16	5	3	5	5	8	10	7	4	11	10
Korea	—	21	20	—	2	2	3	2	8	3	1
Jamaica	—	9	11	11	—	—	—	—	—	—	—
India	7	7	14	11	6	5	4	8	7	10	18
Hong Kong	9	—	—	—	—	8	3	5	2	2	5
Peru	10	—	4	2	8	2	2	1	1	1	1
Chile	11	—	2	2	2	5	2	2	1	2	3

Note: Dash means figures not available.

Source: "Capital Expenditures by Majority Owned Foreign Affiliates of U.S. Companies," *Survey of Current Business* 57–62, no. 10 (October 1977–October 1982); 63–66, no. 3 (March 1983–March 1986).

Table 4.13. *Annual capital expenditures by majority-owned foreign affiliates of U.S. companies, 1976–86: mineral-processing industries (in millions of dollars)*

	1976	1977	1978	1979	1980	1981	1982	1983	1984	1985	1986
Canada	58	82	83	100	106	201	170	230	450	373	245
Brazil	13	22	25	38	28	88	273	—	234	174	101
Germany	58	72	96	79	77	122	123	111	90	102	99
United Kingdom	203	221	207	267	279	132	70	69	70	100	99
Mexico	25	14	21	37	57	50	34	12	13	17	13
Netherlands	26	35	46	61	61	27	23	16	24	32	40
Australia	2	5	9	13	8	—	11	10	6	8	11
France	38	43	32	48	59	27	14	14	16	23	25
Italy	26	6	11	18	24	19	24	26	16	11	13
Belgium/Luxembourg	3	3	8	8	5	7	10	9	11	11	19
Norway	25	17	10	17	28	<0.5	0	0	0	0	0
Spain	3	6	8	12	—	6	6	4	4	5	8
Japan	2	3	6	4	4	—	4	3	6	4	8
South Africa	2	3	3	7	2	12	33	10	6	5	3
Argentina	3	12	—	5	6	—	7	7	5	5	3
Sweden	4	7	4	3	2	2	3	1	2	1	1
Ireland	1	1	1	1	1	2	2	2	3	4	5
Venezuela	68	88	65	30	21	7	2	1	1	1	1
Switzerland	2	2	5	2	2	1	1	2	2	4	7
Austria	1	1	1	1	—	3	3	4	5	6	5
Greece	1	2	1	1	1	<0.5	<0.5	<0.5	<0.5	<0.5	<0.5
Chile	2	2	3	2	1	2	3	1	3	3	3
Colombia	3	3	—	4	7	3	—	3	4	1	2
India	1	1	1	1	2	0	0	0	0	0	0
Philippines	21	13	18	8	10	<0.5	<0.5	<0.5	<0.5	<0.5	<0.5
Singapore	1	1	1	1	—	5	2	1	1	3	2
Peru	1	1	1	1	2	3	2	<0.5	<0.5	<0.5	<0.5

Note: Dash means figures not available.

Source: "Capital Expenditures by Majority Owned Foreign Affiliates of U.S. Companies," *Survey of Current Business* 57–62 no. 10 (October 1977–October 1982), 62–66 no. 3 (March 1982–March 1986).

Table 4.14. U.S. imports, 1970–84: all imports, chemicals, and processed minerals (in millions of dollars)

	1970	1971	1972	1973	1974	1975	1976	1977	1978	1979	1980	1981	1982	1983	1984
Chemicals	1,251	1,406	1,842	2,331	4,126	3,550	4,495	5,353	6,437	7,495	8,131	8,948	9,005	10,735	12,847
Processed minerals	3,814	4,283	4,904	5,451	9,433	6,597	7,777	9,499	11,954	13,472	13,821	17,643	12,998	14,830	18,366
Total of imports of chemicals and processed minerals	5,065	5,689	6,746	7,782	13,559	10,147	12,272	14,852	18,391	20,967	21,952	26,591	22,003	25,565	31,213
All imports	39,024	45,096	54,684	69,202	99,339	93,471	117,108	144,096	168,297	205,378	242,045	250,826	228,751	254,618	312,566
% of chemicals and processed minerals in total imports	13.0	12.6	12.3	11.2	13.6	10.9	10.5	10.3	10.9	10.2	9.1	10.6	9.6	10.0	10.0

Note: Iron and steel and non-ferrous metals are included as processed minerals.
Source: "World Trade by Commodity Class and Region, Developing Market Economies and Centrally Planned Economies," in United Nations Department of Economic and Social Affairs, Monthly Bulletin of Statistics, May 1977, 1979, 1983–86.

109

Table 4.15. Exports by majority-owned U.S. affiliates to the United States, 1966–77: all manufactured goods, chemicals, and processed minerals (in millions of dollars)

	1966	1967	1968	1969	1970	1971	1972	1973	1974	1975	1976
Chemicals	171	132	149	158	198	191	202	298	451	445	562
Processed minerals	47	69	102	128	100	182	208	226	394	383	555
Total of all manufactured exports sent by U.S. companies to U.S.	2,679	3,172	4,064	5,040	5,352	6,539	7,752	9,457	11,228	11,371	11,114
% of chemicals and processed minerals in total manufactured exports to U.S.	8.1	6.3	6.2	5.7	5.6	5.7	5.3	5.5	7.5	7.5	7.9

Source: "Sales by Majority-Owned Foreign Affiliates of U.S. Companies," Survey of Current Business 47–57, no. 8 (August 1967–August 1977) (discontinued).

110

pollution regulations. This again points to the need for further investigation.

Breaking the figures for U.S. imports down further, as in Table 4.16, points up several other considerations. First, although Table 4.14 shows that imports for chemical and allied industries did increase rapidly during the past decade, the percentages coming from LDCs remained relatively stable. Thus it appears that rapid expansion of U.S. chemical imports resulted more from a boom in OECD countries' trade in chemicals than from a shift in trade and investment patterns. One anomaly can be pointed out in the figures presented in Table 4.16. Although not large in aggregate terms, the percentage of U.S. chemical imports from European countries with centrally planned economies did rise substantially in the 1970s and into the 1980s. An interesting question is whether these chemicals have a higher "pollution content" than overall U.S. chemical imports. As would be expected on the basis of previous tables, Table 4.15 shows U.S. imports of processed minerals from LDCs rising in percentage terms.

Specific industries affected

Despite the predictions of industrial flight, the evidence in the mid-1980s reveals that there are only a relatively small number of American industries whose international location patterns have been significantly affected by environmental regulations in the United States. A recent in-depth study of the particular industries most susceptible to industrial flight, conducted by the author, concludes that they tend to fall into three categories.

First, manufacturers of some highly toxic, dangerous, or carcinogenic products have not yet developed safer substitutes or adapted their technologies to meet environmental, workplace, health, and consumer standards in the United States. For these few industries, pollution and workplace-health standards have led to declining production in the United States and increasing production overseas. Strict regulation and growing public awareness of the dangers of hazardous and toxic substances has disrupted or halted production in the United States of asbestos, arsenic trioxide, benzidine-based dyes, certain pesticides, and a few other known carcinogenic chemicals.

Second, stricter American environmental regulations have contributed to the international dispersion of some basic mineral-processing industries, such as copper, zinc, and lead processing. This trend is enhanced by other factors, such as the changing availability of raw materials, other nations' requirements that minerals be processed in the country where they are mined, and various economic factors including low prices, high interest rates, and recessions.

Table 4.16. *Percentage of U.S. imports from less-developed countries and centrally planned economies, 1970–84: chemicals and metals*

	1970	1971	1972	1973	1974	1975	1976	1977	1978	1979	1980	1981	1982	1983	1984
Chemical imports															
% from LDCs	11.8	12.1	15.0	12.3	13.2	13.1	12.9	14.1	12.0	11.0	12.6	14.1	14.8	14.5	14.2
% from centrally planned European economies[a]	0.6	0.7	0.9	1.3	2.1	2.3	1.5	1.2	1.8	2.2	3.2	1.4	1.6	1.8	2.4
Processed minerals[b]															
% from LDCs	15.9	11.5	13.7	16.1	16.2	12.1	17.4	16.3	18.2	17.6	18.1	16.2	17.7	25.7	21.8

[a]Includes USSR and Eastern European nations. Imports of processed minerals from these countries are negligible.

[b]Iron and steel and non-ferrous metals are included as processed minerals.

Source: "World Trade by Commodity Class and Region, Developing Market Economies and Centrally Planned Economies," in United Nations Department of Economic and Social Affairs, *Monthly Bulletin of Statistics*, May 1977, 1979, 1983–86.

Finally, environmental regulations may have increased, at least slightly, the trend toward worldwide purchasing of "intermediate" organic chemicals – that is, organic chemicals needed for the manufacture of other chemical products. This shift is partly attributable to stricter pollution-control laws, but more significantly to workplace health regulations. Although whole industries have not fled the United States, some large American chemical companies have increasingly gone abroad to produce or purchase intermediates needed for chemical production in the United States.

But this study, entitled *Are Environmental Regulations Driving U.S. Industry Overseas?*, emphasizes that these are exceptions to the norm. Most individual industries have responded to environmental regulations with technological innovations, changes in production processes or raw materials, more efficient process controls, and other adaptations that in the United States have proved more economical and less drastic than flight abroad. Even when these adaptations have not reduced regulatory burdens, the environmental problems have generally not been substantial enough to offset more traditional factors – market considerations, transportation, availability of raw materials, labor costs, political stability – that determine how most firms select overseas locations for branch-plant construction.

Importance of domestic demand and the product cycle

A most important point emphasized by the study is noted above: there are no instances of industrial flight from the United States in industries where domestic demand is expanding and U.S. producers enjoy technological superiority. Polyvinyl chloride and acrylonitrile are two notable examples of industries in which intense environmental regulatory pressures and adverse publicity in the 1970s did not prompt significant movements by U.S. producers to other countries. This is true even though both are produced by major chemical firms with worldwide operations and even though other locational factors such as availability of raw materials and transportation costs have not severely hampered industry mobility. Ultimately, rapid expansion of domestic demand for these two chemicals and the concomitant incentives to invest in new technological developments have given these industries large cushions to help weather the onslaught of new regulations and public concern.

Thus, the study concludes that long-term domestic demand and technological outlook are significant variables affecting the way an industry responds to intense regulatory pressures and public concern. If demand is forecast to remain strong in spite of environmental problems and if technological gains appear possible through the application of research-and-development resources, flight is unlikely to occur. On the other hand, if demand is static or declining and no significant technological breakthroughs can be envisioned to reduce workplace-health, pollution, and other environment-related hazards, chances are greater that in its waning stages the industry will produce and source more and more abroad.

In short, many of the industries that appear particularly susceptible to industrial flight have experienced slow growth or no growth in domestic demand in recent years. They have tended also to share several other related characteristics that have made it more likely that individual firms will respond to strict environmental standards by relocating productive facilities abroad. In these industries:

1. the actual costs of complying with the environmental regulations are not the only barrier to production in the United States; the logistics of complying tend to be complicated because many pollution or hazard problems are so acute that it is difficult to ensure safety even with large infusions of capital;
2. the regulations inhibit production of the product (workplace health and pollution control) more than final consumption, meaning that the hazards or pollution associated with the product can be "left behind" in a new producing country;
3. the regulations and procedures, as well as local opposition and lengthy public participation, have had the effect of severely limiting the number of sites where new facilities in the industry may be located;
4. demand for the product, although not expanding, is relatively inelastic; that is, substitute raw materials, intermediates, and final products are unavailable or uneconomical and the product is essential to some consumer sector or industry;
5. production tends to be more labor intensive rather than capital intensive, decreasing the likelihood that all environmental and safety difficulties can be solved with technological innovation or closed productive process systems; and
6. shipping costs are low relative to production costs and the weight and volume of the product.

Taken together, the characteristics indicate that the industries most likely to move abroad to avoid environmental regulations are either (a) dying industries that manufacture products for which consumption is declining, or (b) industries at an advanced stage of the international product cycle where competitiveness is determined more by direct production and shipping costs than by possession of technological advantage.

These trends, over the long term, may have appreciable implications for the U.S. economy and the overall industrial outlook. Nevertheless, as already noted, in most instances environmental regulations and public concern are only partly responsible for these movements. These trends are in accord with those predicted by theories of the product cycle, foreign direct investment, and the stages approach to comparative advantage by underindustrialized countries.

In most cases where environmental regulations and public concern appear to be directly responsible for an industry's flight from the United States, the industry is no longer a dynamic force within the U.S. economy. Although localized economic and employment disruptions are likely as these industries continue to decline, none of the clear-cut examples of industrial flight noted here are likely to have major deleterious effects on the U.S. economy or overall industrial base. Most of these industries will gradually be replaced by cleaner, safer products utilizing more technologically advanced manufacturing processes. More and more substitutes for harmful dyes, arsenic, highly toxic pesticides, and even asbestos are being introduced. Gradually these new products (or, alternatively, more advanced technologies for production and use) will absorb most of the intermediate and end-product uses for these hazardous chemicals and products. Relief from the workplace-health, pollution, and consumer-safety standards that are speeding the obsolescence of such hazardous industrial materials would be tantamount to holding back technological progress, as well as to increasing health hazards for workers and the public.

Conclusions

Taken in the aggregate, the investment and trade figures presented in this section indicate that the years immediately following emergence of stringent environmental regulations in the United States did not witness widespread relocation of pollution-intensive industries to countries with drastically lower regulatory requirements. Overall investments in developing countries by American firms have not expanded significantly faster for the two highly polluting industries examined than for all manufacturing industries. In the mid 1980s, environmental endowment has not become an overwhelming consideration for "footloose" U.S. industries seeking to minimize production costs and maximize their access to key world markets.

However, the investment and trade figures do point out some nascent trends among pollution-intensive industries, trends that could be correlated with increased environmental regulations in the United States. Of greatest potential significance are the large increases evident in recent years in overseas investment and refined imports by U.S. mineral processors. In addition, some of the incremental changes noted in the aggregate figures for the chemical sector as a whole could represent rather large increases of foreign investment and imports in a few particular chemical-producing industries.

Indeed, it does seem that, in response to stricter environmental regulations, a few industries are fleeing the United States rather than modernizing technology, finding substitute products, or installing expensive pollution controls. These industries have few incentives to improve production facilities and the quality of their products because demand for their products is static or reduced as a result of product obsolescence or hazards. By contrast, there are no documented examples of healthy, growing American industries that have been forced to move abroad because of environmental regulations or public concern in the United States. An important point, though, is that the flight of a few ailing industries from the United States is not likely to contribute in any significant way to the development of countries trying to build their industrial base.

Still, the data presented in this chapter also indicate that two small groups of countries should be examined in more detail in order to assess whether the lack of environmental regulations has played an integral part in their rapid buildup of chemical manufacturing and mineral processing and their increased ability to sell such goods in world markets. The first group is composed of the few rapidly industrializing, more or less capitalistic countries identified in the tables; these countries have been highly successful in attracting U.S. corporate affiliates in recent years. The second group is made up of the few centrally planned economies which, during the 1970s, began to figure more importantly as producers of chemicals destined for use in the United States. In particular, although the figures in Table 4.16 are not broken down, this means the rapidly industrializing economies of Eastern Europe: Poland (until recently), Hungary, Czechoslovakia, Romania, Yugoslavia, East Germany, and Bulgaria. While the trend toward increased East-West trade has suffered with the decline of detente, it may be that these countries did try to increase exports to the West by taking advantage of their environmental endowments.

5

Pollution and industrial strategy in four rapidly industrializing countries

The examination of international industrial-location trends presented in the last chapter leads to the conclusion that the environment probably has not been and will not become an important factor in determining the distribution of overall international comparative advantage in industrial production, even in the industrial sectors most profoundly affected by stringent environmental controls. There is no evidence that the industrial-flight hypothesis is valid in any but a very narrow range of industries, nor does it appear that the world is being divided into core countries that export industrial polluters and peripheral countries that accept these rejected industries.

Still, the general lack of evidence to support the industrial-flight hypothesis does not necessarily mean that its twin, the pollution-haven hypothesis, is also invalid. The fact that environmental regulations have not driven industries from the United States does not mean that U.S. firms locating abroad have not sought to take advantage of lower environmental standards in some countries and have not contributed to pollution problems arising in countries where they do locate. Nor does it mean that industrializing countries have not operated on the assumption that their overall industrial development will be enhanced by maintenance of lax environmental standards for incoming industries.

This chapter, therefore, evaluates the pollution-haven hypothesis by looking at the extent to which environment has become an important factor in the industrial development of countries outside the United States, Japan, and the most advanced industrial nations of Europe. To do so, it draws primarily on case-study research in four countries that fit the three categories identified in Chapter 4 as potentially having an increased comparative advantage in production of high-pollution products. That is, the less-industrialized, capitalistic countries on the periphery of Europe that have been notably successful in attracting U.S. direct investors (represented by Ireland and Spain); the dynamic group of newly industrializing countries (represented by Mexico); and the rapidly industrializing socialist countries of Eastern Europe (represented by Romania).

These brief case studies attempt to provide a broad overview of how environmental factors have been perceived to have affected the industrial-development strategies pursued by each of these four countries, particularly in the 1970s and early 1980s. The primary questions are whether these countries have sought to use their environmental factor endowments to lure multinational firms and build domestic industrial capacity in certain industries and, if so, whether such efforts have proven to be successful and enduring. Ensuing chapters describe in more detail how the broad approaches adopted by each country toward pollution and international trade and investment have affected the relationship between these countries and multinational corporations in specific instances.

Pollution and rapid industrial development

Despite the persistence of depressed world economic conditions, a number of countries outside the most advanced industrial nations achieved dramatic industrial progress during the time of greatest concern to this study – roughly, the period between the Arab oil embargo of 1973 and the onset of the debt crisis in about 1982. As noted in Chapter 2, rapid industrial development in many of these countries is correlated with the buildup of export-oriented industries to generate economic growth, provide large numbers of jobs, and improve the balance-of-payments outlook. The embracing of the export-promotion approach has prompted governments of underindustrialized nations to attempt to redefine comparative advantage in international trade by replacing their traditional role as suppliers of raw materials or sellers of simple, labor-intensive manufactures. Underindustrialized nations, in other words, have sought to quicken the pace of industrialization by stimulating what the United Nations calls the "redeployment" of industries away from the already heavily industrialized nations.

Transfers of technology and capital from the heavily industrialized countries have figured strategically in the industrial development of most of these countries, even the socialist countries of Eastern Europe. Some countries have been oriented toward attracting multinational corporations who would locate production facilities within their borders or establish joint ventures with domestic firms. Other countries have preferred not to depend on foreign ownership of industrial enterprises; they have sought instead to purchase licenses, technology, or even whole plants from abroad.

The spread of a wide variety of industrial technologies around the globe, as well as the speed with which industrial development is taking place in some countries, has tended to alter classical patterns of industrial development. In a world in which technology flows with considerable freedom and in which affluent consumers from developed countries demand esoteric items, underindustrialized, less affluent countries increasingly specialize in highly sophisticated and consumption-oriented industries before building up domestic technological capabilities or product markets. Many countries, in effect, create "last industries first," as the economist Albert Hirschman puts it.[1]

These strategies provide great economic opportunities for countries that do not have the technological sophistication, capital resources, and consumer demand necessary to sustain rapid increases in industrial output. At the same time, the internationalization of industry – which speeds up development and disperses industrial processes – has greatly increased the range and severity of pollution problems in many rapidly industrializing countries. The concentration of pollution problems resulting from the telescoping of the time sequence for industrial development is significantly complicated by several other trends in industrial development. For example, large, heavy industries of the sort that may generate problematical air emissions or water effluent tend overwhelmingly to be located in a very small number of heavily industrialized, urbanized enclaves in most underindustrialized countries. Although total industrial pollution for a country as a whole may still appear quite low, the level of pollution in these areas of concentrated industry is often far higher than the worst levels recorded in the most industrialized areas of the advanced countries.

In addition, as many observers of international industrial-location patterns have pointed out, firms in particular industries – especially those producing for world markets – have a remarkable propensity to locate close to each other. They tend to cluster not only in the same countries but often at factory sites near one another. There are many reasons for this "piggyback" effect: availability of raw materials, marketing opportunities, oligopolistic behavior, enticements from governments, labor force specifications, and so forth. The result is that in a particular area total industrial pollution may again be relatively low, but it may consist primarily of a few high-volume pollutants.

Because they often import technology and intermediate materials from abroad and perform the final touches for reexport, newly industrializing nations may soon confront the more subtle and pervasive forms of industrial pollution from certain highly sophisticated industries that have burgeoned in the advanced developed countries since World War II.[2] Thus,

1. Albert O. Hirschman, *The Strategy of Economic Development* (New York: Norton, 1958), p. 111.
2. For an analysis of the categorical differences in pollution generated by major smokestack industries and by postwar leading sectors such as petrochemicals, see Barry Commoner, *The Closing Circle* (New York: Bantam, 1972).

along with the more obvious forms of pollution from so-called smoke-stack industries – forms like thick black smoke, noxious water effluent, and hazardous industrial work conditions – many industrializing countries today must cope with "invisible" pollution problems such as industrial carcinogens and toxic substances. This is particularly true for countries that are building industries relying on organic chemistry: petrochemicals, plastics, pesticides, dyes, fuels, solvents, pharmaceuticals, man-made fibers, paints, and the like.

All these factors help make industrial pollution in developing countries highly concentrated in location and type but widely diversified in scope and complexity. At an early stage in their industrial development, many rapidly industrializing countries are being confronted with a range of environmental-pollution and industrial-health problems equally as broad and severe as those that have provoked intense concern in the advanced industrial countries in the past two decades. These problems are further exacerbated in very poor countries by the fact that the sheer numbers of people and the volumes of pollutants associated with the urban environment – sewage, solid waste, air pollutants – are exponentially greater in many Third World cities today than they were in the cities of Europe and America during their periods of helter-skelter development.[3]

The ability of governments in most rapidly industrializing countries to cope with these problems is severely limited. Prevailing levels of affluence, technical capability, scientific know-how, and institutional specialization in most Third World countries are obviously far below those in the advanced countries. Moreover, development planners, economists, industrialists, and even some environmentalists often contend that countries still in need of rapid economic development cannot and should not imitate the United States and other industrial nations by passing extensive regulations to control pollution. It is argued that industrializing countries can no more afford to pay pollution-control costs than they can afford to pay high labor costs, that poor people are not concerned about pollution when they do not have enough to eat, and that underindustrialized countries generally have large, unused "assimilative capacities" for "natural" disposal of wastes on land and in the air and water.[4] Indeed, as Chapter 3 noted, many observers seeking to assist developing countries to increase their industrial development, particularly those associated with the UN Industrial Development Organization, explicitly urged LDCs to take

3. H. Jeffrey Leonard, "Politics and Pollution from Urban and Industrial Development," in H. Jeffrey Leonard, ed., *Divesting Nature's Capital: The Political Economy of Environmental Abuse in the Third World* (New York: Holmes and Meier, 1985), 263–291.
4. Ibid.

advantage of their high social and natural assimilative capacities to attract industry.

On the other hand, pollution problems in some rapidly industrializing nations have become too severe to be ignored or put on the shelf until greater affluence is attained. Specific instances of human suffering and economic disruption caused by industry-related pollution in many developing countries have stirred public concern and prompted governments to formulate new policy responses.[5] Industrial-development planners in most rapidly industrializing countries have thus been forced to respond in one way or another to the growing importance of pollution factors. In many instances the responses have been conflicting, reflecting both a desire to take advantage of any possible means of attracting industry and a nascent understanding that courting some high-pollution industries may prove to be a Faustian bargain.

In short, the increasing number of countries competing to move up the industrial ladder by redefining their international comparative advantage and importing Western technologies has heightened the possibility that environmental factors will affect a country's overall industrial-development strategy. The choice of which industries to build up and what products to sell on the international market, for example, may be influenced by a country's willingness or unwillingness to accept technologies and productive processes that cause high levels of pollution or are associated with other environmental hazards. Some countries may choose to compete for Western industries on this basis; others may refuse to accept industries that appear to be searching for a convenient haven from stringent environmental regulations in their home countries.

That rapidly industrializing countries often adopt nervous and contradictory approaches to pollution is evidenced clearly in the cases of Ireland, Spain, Mexico and Romania presented in the rest of this chapter. In the 1970s and early 1980s, each of these countries sought to integrate pollution factors into their industrial-development planning under very different economic and political circumstances. Of particular interest are the questions of whether these countries embraced the pollution-haven hypothesis and whether industrial-development planners have understood the significance of pollution factors in their countries' industrial-development strategy. These are particularly interesting questions in the case of these specific countries because several unique political and economic factors coincided during the period of greatest interest to this study, and

5. See H. Jeffrey Leonard and David Morell, "The Emergence of Environmental Concern in Developing Countries: A Political Perspective," *Stanford Journal of International Law* 17, no. 2 (Summer 1981):281–313.

these factors encouraged considerable new industrial expansion and favored (particularly in the mid 1970s) increased relations between these countries and U.S. companies. These included the flowering of East-West detente in the case of Romania, the entrance of Ireland and the impending entrance of Spain into the European Common Market, and the huge windfall that accrued to Mexico during the 1970s as a result of increased petroleum revenues.

Ireland

Although traditionally underindustrialized, Ireland is an interesting case to study because it is a small country with a highly educated population and in recent decades it has become an important producer of certain chemical products for European and U.S. markets. As the figures in Chapter 4 showed, U.S. chemical firms have made substantial investments in Ireland in recent years, especially since Ireland became a member of the European Economic Community in 1972.

The Republic of Ireland is an independent nation occupying about 80 percent of the island known as Ireland. Until 1922 the whole island was part of the United Kingdom, when it was divided into the Republic of Ireland and Northern Ireland (which remains part of the United Kingdom). Although only the Irish Channel separates Ireland from the first major centers of the industrial revolution (Birmingham, Liverpool, and Manchester) relatively little industrial development took place in Ireland until after 1922. Except for the machinery and textile industries, which grew up in the northeastern part of the island (in what is now Northern Ireland), Ireland remained predominantly an agrarian colony whose role was to supply food, timber, and other raw materials to Great Britain's industrial centers.

With this colonial legacy, it is no wonder that soon after independence the Irish government instituted a policy of import substitution in the hope of industrializing the Irish economy to provide jobs, halt emigration, improve the country's balance of payments, make it less vulnerable to the cyclical fluctuations of commodity trade, and reduce the country's dependence on Great Britain for manufactured goods.[6] The first three decades of independence were dominated by extraordinary circumstances that

6. See Garrett Fitzgerald, "Economic Evolution Up to 1958," in J. W. O'Hagan, ed., *The Economy of Ireland: Policy and Performance* (Dublin: Irish Management Institute, 1978), pp. 4–17; Frank Long, "Foreign Direct Investment in an Under-developed European Economy: The Republic of Ireland," *World Development* 4, no. 1 (1976):59–84; and T. R. A. Magee, W. R. Murphy, and P. O'Flynn, "The Development of the Process Industries in Ireland," *The Chemical Engineer* (August–September 1978):648–650.

made broad industrial development difficult – civil war, the depression, "economic warfare" with Great Britain, and the Second World War. Nevertheless, industrial output expanded and the nation achieved population stability in the years up to 1950. In fact, in the years 1944–1950, after industrial protection was reintroduced at the end of World War II, industrial output actually doubled.[7]

However, by 1950 Ireland had reached the limits of its import-substitution strategy for industrial development. Because the Irish market is small, further increases in industrial output and industrial employment sufficient to compensate for declining agricultural employment depended upon increasing exports from Irish industries. At the same time, traditional manufacturing industries, set up behind the cushion of protective barriers, lagged technologically, often produced at a low level of efficiency, and were unable to take advantage of economies of large-scale production. These circumstances made it very difficult for Irish manufactured goods to compete openly on the international market. In addition, the economic expansion that followed the war had driven Irish imports up rapidly as consumers demanded a greater variety of nonagricultural goods, and Irish industries depended increasingly on imported technology and parts. This trend was creating a serious balance-of-payments problem.[8]

As a result, the 1950s were marked in Ireland by economic stagnation. While economic growth was rapid in nearly every nation in Europe during this time, Ireland's growth in national output was less than 2 percent per annum between 1950 and 1955 and virtually zero between 1955 and 1958. Employment declined, inflation increased, and emigration once again climbed, reaching forty thousand a year by the middle of the decade.[9]

By the late 1950s many Irish policymakers were convinced that new economic-development strategies were necessary. Early in 1958 a comprehensive study of the economy noted the factors inhibiting economic growth and suggested radical new policies to overcome the obstacles.[10] These policy measures became the basis for the First Programme for Economic Expansion, adopted by the Irish government in late 1958.[11] Although the program covered all the major sectors of the economy, it centered on spurring industrial output by attracting foreign capital and

7. Fitzgerald, "Economic Evolution Up to 1958," pp. 11–14.
8. P. N. O'Farrell, "An Analysis of New Industry Location: "The Irish Case," *Progress in Planning* 9, pt. 3 (1978):136; and Fitzgerald, "Economic Evolution Up to 1958," pp. 14–15.
9. Fitzgerald, "Economic Evolution Up to 1958," p. 13.
10. T. K. Whitaker, *Economic Development* (Dublin: Stationery Office, 1958).
11. W. J. L. Ryan and M. O'Donoghue, "The Republic of Ireland," *Journal of Industrial Economics,* supplement no. 2, ed. Thomas Wilson (1965):90.

encouraging investment in export-oriented industries. To accomplish these goals, the government outlined new policies that offered large capital grants toward the costs of new industrial investments, extended facilities for industrial credit, and provided tax relief on exports.[12]

To promote the expansion of foreign industry and implement the new package of industrial incentives, several new institutions were set up by the Irish government. The Industrial Development Authority (IDA) was reorganized to attract foreign investors to Ireland through promotional work in major Western nations and to provide assistance to would-be investors in Ireland. The government also formed the Export Board to assist in marketing exports; the Industrial Training Centre to train Irish workers for a variety of manufacturing jobs; and the Industrial Credit Company to offer credit and underwrite facilities for manufacturers. Finally, a series of industrial estates was set up around the country to facilitate the provision of infrastructure and the establishment of industrial complexes for certain types of manufacturing industry.[13]

Since the 1960s the IDA, which has been responsible for administering the system of financial incentives to attract foreign industries, has gained a reputation as one of the best industrial-promotion agencies in the world. It has offered complete services to foreign investors interested in setting up a new enterprise, including the selection of sites, providing for services and infrastructure for sites, banking land for future industrial sites, building advance factories for future occupancy, organizing the construction of industrial estates and nearby housing for new employees, helping with worker training, and troubleshooting for industries having difficulties after locating in Ireland.[14]

But in addition to providing these services, IDA has been responsible for formulating the overall industrial strategy that will best serve the four major goals of Irish economic policy: rapid economic growth, high generation of new jobs, increased exports to improve the balance of payments, and the reduction of economic inequalities among the different regions of the country. In the process IDA has had to make certain choices about what types of industry to attract to Ireland. Should industries be labor intensive or capital intensive? Foreign-owned, joint ventures, or wholly Irish? Large or small? Based on indigenous raw materials or part of international supply and assembly lines?

12. *First Programme for Economic Expansion* (Dublin: Government of Ireland, 1958), pt. 5.
13. Ibid. These are summarized in Long, "Foreign Direct Investment," p. 61; and Ryan and O'Donoghue, "The Republic of Ireland."
14. Industrial Development Authority (IDA), "Industrial Development in Ireland" (Dublin: IDA, August 1978).

Actually, because its choices have not necessarily been mutually exclusive options, IDA has had to define the particular mixture that best meets the needs of the Irish economy. During the past two decades, IDA has gone through three relatively distinct phases in seeking this balance, concentrating first on labor-intensive industries, looking then to heavy basic industries, and finally stressing high-technology, light manufacturing industries. Environmental factors played an important role in influencing IDA's evolving choices. Ireland's high environmental factor endowment was offered as one reason for the belief that the country's comparative advantage was evolving into heavy industries, and, conversely, rising concern about pollution helped to push IDA in the direction of lighter manufacturing industries.

A *dustbin strategy of development*

The magnitude of Ireland's unemployment problem prompted the IDA to concentrate on trying to attract labor-intensive industries into the country during the early 1960s. Thus IDA usually marked for increased foreign investments those industrial sectors that already accounted for about 70 percent of Irish manufacturing industry in 1960: textiles, clothing, footwear, paper and printing, food, drink, and tobacco.[15]

By the late 1960s the shortcomings of an industrial strategy based on labor-intensive industry – whether foreign or Irish – were also apparent. Labor-intensive manufacturers were increasingly vulnerable to stiff competition from cheaper-labor countries in the Third World and were highly sensitive to rapid obsolescence in a changing world market. This prompted IDA, which was reorganized again in 1969, to look for another means of comparative advantage for Ireland. One IDA report noted:

> An industrial strategy must recognise the profound changes taking place in industry. Traditional industries in Europe face intense competition from the newly industrialised countries using up-to-date equipment, which combined with low labour costs can undercut European producers. By comparison, Ireland is not a low labour cost producer. Ireland's strength lies in our comparatively well developed business and institutional infrastructure and our generally high level of education and skills which provides a workforce capable of employment in more technologically advanced industry.[16]

15. J. W. O'Hagan, "Industrial Policy," in J. W. O'Hagan, ed., *The Economy of Ireland: Policy and Performance,* 2d ed. (Dublin: Irish Management Institute, 1978), pp. 255, 256.
16. Industrial Development Authority, *IDA Industrial Plan 1978–82* (Dublin: IDA, 1979), p. 17.

Thus IDA began to emphasize new criteria for determining which types of manufacturing industries should be attracted to Ireland. These included high value-added content; high value per unit volume, to permit Ireland to supply world and European markets competitively in spite of sea-transport costs; high content of skilled labor and trained technicians; strong future growth potential; and commitment within the industry for continuous advancement through research and development.[17]

One of the industries that appeared to meet these criteria best was, of course, the international chemical industry. IDA formulated ambitious plans to integrate into the world chemical-production network, particularly in two areas: chemicals and chemical products manufactured from raw materials in Ireland, and downstream development in the petrochemical sector. Included in these plans were zinc and lead smelters to process Irish ores; petroleum refineries to complement the Whitegate Refinery, built by a consortium of multinationals in Cork Harbor in 1958; and the secondary development of large-scale organic-chemicals projects, especially to take advantage of Cork's deep-water port and available petrochemical feedstocks.[18] Expansion of Ireland's one steel plant, as well as production of sulfuric acid, ammonia, urea, and other fertilizer-related chemicals, were also included in IDA's plans. However, these sectors were primarily targeted as the domain of already-established Irish companies.

From an environmental point of view, the professed intention to emphasize the attraction of foreign companies to engage in large-scale processing and petrochemical production was not particularly controversial at the time, even though these were among the industries most under pressure from antipollution groups and new government regulations in both Europe and the United States. Because unemployment was such a severe problem nationwide, few people were willing to criticize the Irish government's plans to bring in industries with significant job-creation potential. One local official says the Irish government and much of the population were at the time willing to become a "dustbin" for industries from Europe and the United States if it meant more jobs. This local official quotes an old Irish politician who supposedly said: "All my life I've seen the lads leaving Ireland for the big smoke in London, Pittsburgh, Birmingham, and Chicago. It'd be better for Ireland if they stayed here and we imported the smoke."[19]

Some argued that Ireland's physical characteristics – an island nation in the Atlantic Ocean, it has frequent rainfall and high wind velocity – would

17. O'Hagan, "Industrial Policy," p. 256.
18. T. M. Whelan, "County Cork: Growth Centre of the Irish Chemical Industry," *Chemical Engineer* 29 (August–September 1978):658–659.
19. Interview with David Byrne, environmental officer, Dublin Corporation, Dublin, March 23, 1980.

help the country avoid severe pollution problems without the necessity of imposing stringent environmental standards on industries attracted to Ireland. Austin Burke, an Irish meteorologist, contended in a 1972 lecture that the Irish climate was a valuable national resource because it ensured a high assimilative capacity for pollutants released into the country's air and water. The fact that pollution of air and inland waters was a less acute problem in Ireland than elsewhere, he said, "is due not at all to our foresight but almost entirely to our climate." Burke argued that Ireland "should not accept as automatically valid for Ireland the order of priority in attacking environmental problems which may well be the right one for the U.S.A. or for Sweden or wherever the current agitation is most active. . . . Instead," he concluded, "we must make for ourselves a cold and balanced assessment, free of emotional overtones, of Ireland's pollution problems against the background of the *Irish* economy and the *Irish* climate."[20]

At this time, IDA officials were not much concerned with assessing the environmental implications of most industrial projects for which overseas firms were seeking grant assistance. Although IDA made no explicit effort to attract industries that were causing severe environmental problems in other countries, the agency generally assumed that some of the industries migrating to Ireland would be ones that faced an inhospitable climate at home owing to concern about pollution. To ensure the cooperation of the local governments actually responsible for approving specific industrial proposals, IDA officials held a series of closed-door meetings to advise local officials that, for the sake of the economy and jobs, some of the dirtier industrial facilities from the advanced industrial nations might have to be sited on terms that offered less stringent pollution controls than in Europe or the United States.[21]

One American company, though perhaps not actually lured to Ireland by the promise of lax environmental regulations, at least benefited from the sentiment in IDA and among local officials that a tradeoff was inevitable between jobs and the environment. Twice during the late 1960s Pfizer made plans to locate a large chemical facility in Ireland and in both cases was granted pollution restrictions that were significantly lighter than those it would have faced either in the United States or in most other countries in Europe. Pfizer's organic-chemicals and organic-synthesis complex, located on IDA-owned land at Ringaskiddy, near Cork, was originally granted permission in 1970 to dump large amounts of untreated

20. Austin Burke, "The Climate of Ireland as a Natural Resource," text of the fourth Kane Lecture, sponsored by the (Irish) Institute of Public Administration and delivered in the Royal Dublin Society on November 16, 1972, pp. 4–5.
21. Interview with James Shine, chief planning officer, Waterford County, Dungarvan, Ireland, April 1, 1980.

organic waste directly into Cork Harbor.[22] When the Waterford County Council approved Pfizer's proposal for a joint-venture magnesite facility in Dungarvan in the late 1960s, it outlined what turned out to be grossly inadequate provisions to prevent water and air pollution. Both of these cases will be discussed in Chapter 6 in more detail.

As a result of such developments, critics of IDA's industrial-development strategy began to allege that Ireland was deliberately being turned into a pollution haven in order to accomplish its industrial-development goals. The Socialist party in Ireland, Sinn Fein, charged in 1973 that the industrial-development strategy of IDA was geared to attract the "dirty outcasts" from other European countries and to permit them to pollute at will in Ireland. Sinn Fein's policy statement on environment and technology pointed out "the threat from the international capitalists" to the Irish environment:

> The fact is that several countries in Europe have learned the hard way about the environmental effects of certain types of heavy industry smelters, oil refineries, and chemical plants, have either banned extra plants from being built or introduced regulations and controls which, even where they may be inadequate, still eat into the profit margin of the big multinational corporations which operate these industries. Several concerns which now find it difficult to operate with maximum profit in Holland or Sweden now see Ireland as an ideal EEC base. . . . Not only do we try to get the dirty outcasts of European industry to come to Ireland. We pay them large grants to come. We have totally inadequate pollution control standards and we are prepared to allow the construction of such technological time-bombs in the most beautiful and scenic parts of our country. Sinn Fein says that the prostitution of the environment and the amenities of Ireland in this manner must be resisted. . . . We can not allow the capitalists of Europe and North America to unload the filth, which is no longer tolerated in their own countries in many instances, on our door-step in return for jobs which it would be the duty of any proper Irish government to provide in the first place.[23]

In 1977 the chairman of An Taisce, the National Trust for Ireland, wrote in a widely quoted article that "it is worth noting that permission to pollute may well be more valuable in economic terms than any I.D.A. grants."[24] Taking their cues from these and other allegations, U.S. publi-

---

22. Industrial Development Authority, *A Survey of Pollution in Ireland* (Dublin: Institute of Public Administration, 1976), p. 2.
23. "The Quality of Life in the New Ireland," Sinn Fein Policy Document, May 1973, pp. 9–10.
24. Phillip Mullaly, "Viewpoint," *An Taisce: Ireland's Conservation Journal* 1, no. 4 (August–September 1977):12.

cations also began to raise the question of whether IDA was dangling permission to pollute as one of the primary incentives for U.S. corporations to relocate in Ireland.[25]

Forsaking the big smoke

Between 1970 and 1978, however, rapid changes were taking place in IDA's overall industrial strategy, in the attention it was paying to the potential environmental impacts of industries considering location in Ireland, and in concern for carefully selecting sites that would minimize adverse environmental impacts of industries actually locating in Ireland. Although these changes did not alleviate all environmental problems relating to foreign industry in Ireland, they clearly moved IDA to reject the "dustbin" theory of industrial development that it had, at least tacitly, previously embraced. There were a number of reasons for the evolution in IDA's industrial-development strategy and its heightened concern for the environment.

In the first place, the boom that IDA expected in heavy industrial development relating to mineral processing and petroleum-based industries never did occur during the early 1970s. With the 1973 Arab oil embargo and the subsequent downturn in the worldwide economy, many large industrial proposals that IDA had been attempting to negotiate were canceled. In particular, the changed economic situation significantly slowed IDA's grand scheme to build up industry around Cork Harbor, already Ireland's largest concentration of heavy industry.[26] At Ringaskiddy, for example, where IDA purchased over a thousand acres for heavy industrial development, only the Pfizer complex and a much smaller light chemical plant owned by Penn Chemicals were built during the 1970s. Several proposals for petroleum refineries, along with IDA's long-planned zinc and lead smelter, were all put on the back burner by the economic situation of the mid-1970s.[27]

These developments were probably not enough by themselves to alter IDA's strategy, but during the interim period several other trends tended to make IDA more wary of resuming an intensive heavy-industrial strategy when the international economic situation improved. Even though many heavy industrial projects were shelved between 1973 and 1978, IDA

25. For example, Mary Holland, "The Pollution of Killarney," *Washington Post,* August 6, 1978, p. A5; Colman McCarthy, "Foggy Mists for Ireland, Inc.?" *Washington Post,* September 15, 1978, p. A10; and Con Power, "Progress and/or Beauty: Ireland's Environmental Crossroads," *Cry California* 10, no. 3 (September 1975):3–12.
26. O'Sullivan interview; Whelan, "County Cork"; Cork Harbour Plan.
27. Ronan Foster and Dick Ahlstrom, "Cork: Special Report," *Irish Times,* March 26, 1980, pp. 11–14.

continued to have striking success in luring foreign companies to Ireland during this period. Most importantly, the health-care industries generally, and specifically the pharmaceutical and fine-chemicals industry, proved to be even better suited for the Irish industrial-development strategy than the heavy industrial chemicals industry.[28] IDA's grant and tax-relief package turned out to be extremely attractive to firms in this industry, because their products tend to be highly research intensive and sell at a high price per unit. The entrance of Ireland into the European Economic Community proved to be an additional attraction for U.S. pharmaceutical companies, as they were searching during the 1970s to gain a foothold in European drug markets that were expanding even faster than the more mature markets in the United States.[29]

Pharmaceutical and fine chemical manufacturers also were better situated than large-volume chemical producers to take advantage of IDA's gradual shift to stressing more regional development by spreading middle-sized plants around the country. The purpose of the shift was to bring jobs to people living outside of Ireland's larger cities and to reduce migration to already heavily congested areas such as Cork and Dublin.[30] In addition, while these industries generally require large amounts of fresh water and are not free of pollution problems, they do not produce the volumes of solid waste, effluent, and air emissions that larger, heavier industrial chemical plants produce.[31] From a public-relations point of view, light chemical and pharmaceutical plants generally do not have the billowing smoke-stacks and extensive exterior pipe networks that often make heavy chemical plants seem ominous. Although this was probably only a secondary consideration for IDA, it was an opportune one, because public concern about the contributions of industrial development to worsening pollution problems in Ireland rose very quickly during the mid-1970s.

Even if the Irish government had persisted in its plan to become a "dust-bin" for Europe and the United States, it is likely that growing popular awareness would have prevented it. In fact, survey research conducted by An Foras Forbartha (the National Institute for Physical Planning and Con-struction Research) advised the IDA that public concern was very high even about the pharmaceutical plants and light chemical industries that were located in the country.[32] By the early 1980s, then, IDA officials were citing environmental concern as a primary reason for discouraging a num-

28. Desmond J. Green, "The Pharmaceutical/Fine Chemical Industry in Ireland: A Decade of Phenomenal Growth," *Chemical Engineer* 56 (August/September 1978):651.
29. Ibid.
30. Ireland, Industrial Development Authority, *IDA Industrial Plan, 1978–1982.*
31. Green, "Pharmaceutical/Fine Chemical Industry," p. 652.
32. "Proposed Industrial Development at Keenaghan, Carrick on Shannon, County Lei-tram" (Dublin, Ireland: An Foras Forbartha, January 1979).

ber of different types of industries that had inquired about locating new plants in Ireland.[33]

Thus, as the decade progressed, the IDA became much more discriminating about the types of industry it would consider for Ireland and much more active in assisting local governments to evaluate what types of pollution controls were necessary for incoming industries. Rising public concern about pollution and awareness inside IDA that the failure to consider pollution issues in the Pfizer and a few other siting decisions had created long-term problems were influential in this shift. Equally important was IDA's growing confidence that Ireland did not have to become a dustbin but instead could compete in attracting lighter, cleaner, more dynamic industries.

One local official describes the evolution that took place both within IDA and among county officials throughout the country between about 1972 and 1982:

> Seven to ten years ago, we did not have much industry in this county. The county was poor and unemployment was the major problem. The first thing we cared about was to get some industry – any industry – to come here. We would have done just about anything for them and would have let them do just about anything in exchange for a few jobs. Before, we would have mortgaged ourselves to the hilt, for instance, to get a big industry enough water to operate the plant; and we probably wouldn't have worried too much about what pollutants they were sending back out of the plant with the waste water. Now we're much more choosy.[34]

A former head of the IDA says that when the new IDA came into being in 1969 after reorganization, "there wasn't much planning, we just assumed we would have to take what industry we could get and that dear Ireland would have to make some tradeoffs." And, he adds in retrospect, Ireland is "fortunate that none of the really bad industries came to us then; had they, there is a good chance they would have been welcomed in."[35]

This analysis is echoed by Kenneth McGuire, former economic attaché in the U.S. embassy in Dublin. IDA, McGuire says, has been so successful in attracting high-technology industries that it has not had to worry about bringing in "the big smoke." Now, McGuire says, "much more than 10 years ago, Ireland can afford to be choosy."[36]

33. Interviews with Matthew Lynch, manager, Environmental Department, Institute for Industrial Research and Standards, Dublin, March 1980; and Ken Gunn, manager, Heavy Industry Division, Industrial Development Authority, Dublin, March 26, 1980.
34. Interview with Sean Lucy, Westmeath County Council, Mullingar, Ireland, April 9, 1980.
35. Interview with John Gannon, An Bord Planeola, Dublin, April 8, 1980.
36. Interview with Kenneth McGuire, U.S. Embassy, Dublin, March 25, 1980.

Of course, several circumstances have enabled Ireland to reject the dustbin approach and become more discriminating. These may not exist in other rapidly industrializing countries intent on attracting foreign manufacturing companies. Ireland is a small country with a small population and a small economy. Thus it cannot and need not aspire to build a full industrial base or a complete chemical industry from basic bulk chemicals to finished chemical products. Since it will always be highly dependent upon imports to feed its manufacturing and consumer sectors, it can pick and choose which industries to develop and which not to develop. It can import many dangerous chemicals rather than produce them if such chemicals are needed for industrial use. For example, while the Asahi plant in county Mayo uses acrylonitrile and the GAF plant in county Westmeath uses polyvinyl chloride, neither chemical is manufactured in Ireland; both are imported in the necessary quantities.

In addition, the fact that Ireland is an English-speaking country, with a highly educated and skilled workforce has given it an enormous advantage over many other countries that would also like to be able to specialize in high-technology industries. Finally, Ireland has been able to augment these advantages with a package of incentives that is perfectly suited for pharmaceutical, fine chemical, and other high-tech firms. Not every industrializing nation can benefit from such advantages; obviously, the industries Ireland has been steering away from in recent years have been locating somewhere.

Spain

In most industrializing countries pollution has probably not played as important a role in the debate about industrial strategy as it has in Ireland. Few countries began the 1970s by outlining an explicit "dustbin" strategy, and even fewer ended the decade by actively screening out industries on the basis of potential pollution problems. At the same time, environmental concerns have played an increasing secondary role in the industrial-development planning process in most industrializing countries.

The example of another rapid industrializer on the periphery of Europe, Spain, is probaby more representative than Ireland in terms of the relationship between pollution and industrial strategy. There do not appear to have been any significant instances when Spanish industrial-development planners have sought to use pollution as a negative incentive for attracting foreign industry in the same manner as they offer tax relief and direct grants. Nor has the government refused to bring in firms in particular industries solely on grounds that the environmental disruption associated with the industry would be too severe. And Spanish industrial planners have not become nearly as attuned as Irish planners to identifying and mitigating in advance the future economic and social consequences associated with certain industries. Still, pollution problems and antipollution sentiment have combined with many other factors in recent years to influence the shaping of industrial-development strategy in Spain.

Spain's economy, like Ireland's, grew rapidly in the 1960s and 1970s, averaging 4.7 percent growth per annum between 1960 and 1979. Thus, Spain's gross national product jumped from the equivalent of $8 billion in 1960 to more than $160 billion in 1979. And, also as in Ireland, much of this growth has been accounted for by a rapid increase in the share of industry in GNP – especially by substantial growth in nontraditional sectors of industry such as transport, machinery and metal products, and chemical manufacturing.[37]

But the evolution of Spain's industrial development strategy, as well as the role of foreign investment and environmental factors in it, differs from Ireland's in several crucial ways. First, although poor and underindustrialized in the early postwar years, Spain was heavily industrialized in several areas – particularly along the northern Atlantic coast and in the Barcelona area on the northern Mediterranean coast – and possessed well-developed, largely state-controlled productive facilities in iron and steel, petroleum refining, and several other heavy industries.

Demographics and politics have pushed Spain's industrial policies in different directions, as well. As the second largest country in Europe (slightly smaller than France) and with a population of about 40 million, the real or potential market in Spain itself has often been reason enough for foreign investors to want to locate production facilities in Spain. In fact, into the 1970s the economic policies of General Francisco Franco made it difficult for foreign firms to use Spain as an export platform or to integrate Spanish subsidiaries into inter-European or international production networks. Because of the size of its economy and its national economic aspirations, Spain's industrial-development strategy concentrated much more than Ireland's on building productive capacity across the whole range of the chemical and related industries, rather than foregoing production in certain industries and relying on imports to supply domestic markets. Specialization primarily in clean, export-oriented high-technology industries, while a possibility for a small nation like Ireland, has been viewed as an unrealistic strategy for a would-be industrial giant like Spain.

37. U.S. Department of State, "Background Notes: Spain" (Washington, D.C.: Government Printing Office, December 1979).

Foreign investment first became an important element of Spain's indus-trial-development strategy in 1959, when new laws were issued encour-aging the inflow of capital from other countries.[38] Despite Franco's pre-vious antipathy to foreign investment, the new laws seemed necessary because of three problems in the Spanish economy: Spanish imports con-sistently ran much higher than exports, creating serious balance-of-pay-ment problems; domestic investment continued to lag, making new indus-trial growth difficult because of the lack of available capital; and technological innovation and overall research and development in Spanish industries remained low.[39]

Although Spain encouraged foreign investment in the industrial sector after 1959, it was strictly controlled. Foreign companies desiring to set up production facilities in Spain were generally required to establish joint ventures with majority-controlling Spanish firms and to adhere to strin-gent regulations concerning imports and the degree of local content. In addition, foreign investment was relegated to specified sectors in which there was insufficient domestic activity, in order to prevent foreign firms from directly competing with state-owned or private Spanish firms.[40]

Franco's economic policies and foreign-investment rules had several significant implications for foreign firms. His protectionist policies made it difficult for foreign firms to sell in the Spanish market without produc-ing in Spain as well. The local-participation and local-content rules made it difficult for firms to export from Spain to worldwide markets. However, in many instances the quid pro quo offered foreign firms was that they would be the sole producer (or one of very few) in the Spanish market. As a result, although Spanish subsidiaries of foreign companies tended before the 1970s to be small (by the parent companies' standards) and not partic-ularly efficient (because they enjoyed protection from external competi-tion), they generally prospered and contributed to the Spanish economy. Foreign direct investment, with American firms accounting for about 40 percent of the total, increased steadily to a value of $5 billion at the time of Franco's death in 1975.[41]

38. Overseas Business Reports, "Investing in Spain," *OBR 76-49* (Washington, D.C.: U.S. Department of Commerce, December 1976), p. 3.
39. Ministry of Commerce and Tourism, *Foreign Investments: A Guide to Business in Spain*, 2d ed. (Madrid: Ministry of Commerce and Tourism, October 1978), p. 5. For a broad discussion on Francoist and post-Francoist economic policies, see Ray Alan, "All the Spains: A Survey," *Economist* 273 (November 3, 1979):29–34. For an early critique of Francoist policies, see International Bank for Reconstruction and Development, *The Economic Development of Spain* (Washington, D.C.: World Bank, 1963).
40. These and other conditions are described in Ministry of Commerce and Tourism, *Development Incentives and Export Promotion: A Guide to Business in Spain*, 2d edi-tion (Madrid: Ministry of Commerce and Tourism, April 1979), p. 5.
41. Overseas Business Reports, "Investing in Spain," p. 3.

Pollution and post-Franco investment policies

In the years just before and after Franco's death, the rules governing foreign investment in Spain were reformulated to encourage more foreign investment, particularly for export-oriented industries. The "Reformulated Code on Foreign Investment," issued by the Council of Ministers in 1974, consolidated many previous policies governing the foreign-investment process and eased some of the complex administrative procedures that had been necessary to obtain government approval of proposed foreign investments. The new code also permitted majority participation by foreign firms in some industries without prior approval of the Council of Ministers, simplified the process for obtaining council approval for greater than 50 percent ownership in other industries, and granted foreign companies almost complete freedom to subscribe up to 50 percent of a Spanish company's capital in all but a few strategic industries.[42]

In the years following Franco's death, the incentives offered for new investments in a wide range of industries were upgraded. The government also greatly expanded its system of extra incentives for industries locating in preferential zones for industrial development. These special zones were of two types: individual industrial poles, called *poligonos,* were located in secondary cities throughout the country, where industrial agglomerations were encouraged; and entire regions were deemed priority regions by the government because of their lack of industrial activity.[43]

The liberalization of foreign-investment laws was necessary in the eyes of industrial and economic planners because of several factors. They thought that rigid limitations on foreign investment hindered progress in developing important advanced-technology industries. As well, the continued persistence of balance-of-trade problems increased the pressure for stimulating exports, which the government thought foreign firms would do. Moreover, Spain's petition to become a member of the European Common Market raised the possibility that soon the Spanish economy would be forced to open up considerably and its industries would be forced increasingly to compete in European and world markets. Indeed, although Spain's membership was delayed for quite a while, until 1985, it had maintained preferential trade agreements with the EEC since 1970.[44]

Increased foreign participation was seen as an important means of meeting long-term objectives for key-growth industrial sectors, particu-

42. The post-Franco foreign-investment rules are described in Overseas Business Reports, "Investing in Spain"; and Ministry of Commerce and Tourism, *Foreign Investments.*
43. Overseas Business Reports, "Investing in Spain," p. 3.
44. Spain, Ministry of Commerce and Tourism, *Economic Outlook: A Guide to Business in Spain* (Madrid: Ministry of Commerce and Tourism, 1977), pp. 12–14.

larly chemical and automobile manufacturing. Spectacular growth had been achieved in the production of basic organic and inorganic chemicals during the 1960s, as is shown in the following tabulation:[45]

Tons produced	1962	1971
Sulphuric acid (monohydrate)	1,319,999	2,470,000
Chlorine	44,500	180,000
Ammonia (tons of N)	166,000	666,000
Sodium carbonate	161,000	345,000
Caustic soda	154,000	290,000
Calcium carbide	87,300	184,000
Ethylene	–	249,000
Propylene	–	83,000
Benzene	5,400	145,000

However, several structural defects were seen as major obstacles in the quest to increase exports and open the Spanish industrial economy to international competition. Chief among them was the proliferation of small, nonspecialized, and increasingly obsolete production facilities, a problem that industrial technocrats hoped would gradually be reduced if increased foreign-capital participation in existing Spanish companies stimulated industry consolidation.

Similarly, in order to shift the Spanish affiliates of major international companies from the role of small domestic producers to that of large-scale exporters, the government realized that large new foreign investments would be necessary on entirely new terms.[46]

As a result of these changes, foreign companies, particularly those from the United States, came increasingly in the 1970s to view Spain as a potentially important outlet to Common Market and other European countries. Many multinational firms bought shares in existing Spanish firms or initiated efforts to secure permission to open a new subsidiary in Spain. At the same time, already-established foreign companies faced increasingly clearer prospects of future difficulties because they operated plants geared primarily for small-scale markets. Some multinational firms, therefore, were actually in the position of closing and consolidating production facilities during the same time they were initiating negotiations with the Spanish government about new investments in the country.[47]

During the mid-1970s, Spanish officials were concerned about maintain-

---

45. Organization for Economic Co-operation and Development, *The Industrial Policies of Fourteen Member Countries* (Paris: OECD, 1971), p. 166.
46. Ibid., pp. 157–158, 166–167.
47. U.S. Foreign Service, "Foreign Economic Trends and Their Implications for the United States: Spain," (Washington, D.C.: Government Printing Office, April 1980), pp. 4–8.

ing the country's position as a low-cost producer of industrial goods in the eyes of foreign investors. The cost advantage – owing to lower expenses for labor, employee benefits, and the overall cost of living – coupled with Spain's proximity to vast European markets were the most important elements stressed by Spanish officials to foreign investors.[48]

Maintaining this advantage had to be balanced against the perceived political need to permit substantial real wage increases and pursue expansionist monetary policies in the years before 1977, when the first general elections in forty-one years took place. Thus, inflation, propelled by the spectacular rise in world energy prices as well as by the government's easy-money policies, spiraled to nearly 30 percent in 1977. In October 1977 all major political parties initialed the Moncloa Pact on economic policy. In so doing they promised to support austerity measures and economic reforms in 1978 to help reduce inflation, hold down wage and price increases, and slow the growth of the money supply. But this pact was not renewed, and, with large wage hikes going to industrial workers, some of Spain's comparative cost advantages vis-à-vis other European countries were reduced in the years 1977–1980.[49] Presumably, if the government had perceived that giving industry permission to pollute would have helped offset other increases in industrial production costs or helped preserve Spain's low-cost advantage, it would have felt intense pressure to use this advantage during this period in the mid- and late 1970s.

Even though Spain's efforts to attract foreign investors focused heavily on the chemical and metallurgical industries, industrial planners seem to have had no particular inclination to offer the right to pollute as an incentive to potential investors from the U.S. and advanced European countries. Even though government industrial planners emphasized Spain's relative cost advantage over other European locations more than any other factor, the relative cost saving due to lax environmental laws apparently was not among their selling points. Several domestic political, economic, social, and geographical circumstances help explain why Spanish authorities did not consider the pollution-haven approach expedient.

First, in contrast to Ireland, Spain had already suffered serious industrial pollution before it began its efforts to stimulate exports, integrate more thoroughly into world industrial-production networks, and increase foreign investments. Historically, Spanish industrial development took place in concentrations, with the iron, steel, and metal-processing industries

---

48. See Banco de Santander, "Business Opportunities in Spain for the 1980s" (Madrid: SOFEMASA, 1980), p. 1.
49. U.S. Department of State, "Background Notes," pp. 4–5; U.S. Foreign Service, "Foreign Economic Trends," pp. 1–7; and "Spain," in *The Europa Yearbook 1981: A World Survey*, vol. 1 (London: Europa, 1981), pp. 1089–1090.

bunched in three centers (Bilbao, Asturias, and Valencia) and the chemical industries heavily concentrated in Barcelona, Madrid, Huelva, and Tarragona. In all of these areas, water and air pollution have long posed serious problems. As a result, in the 1960s the national government passed legislation to control air and water pollution, as well as to discourage new industry from locating in areas that were already polluted and congested.[50]

The problems of heavy industrial pollution in Spain were compounded by two other factors that have long made the pollution of inland rivers a matter of greater concern than might be expected. Spain is an arid country, and the capacity of most major rivers to receive and flush pollutants varies greatly with season and rainfall. Furthermore, Spain's agricultural processing industries – especially paper and pulp manufacturing in the north; olives, sunflowers, and similar products in the south; and leather-tanning operations throughout the country – have long contributed vast amounts of waste materials to rivers, even in rural areas where heavy industrial pollution has been low. For these two reasons, some of Spain's inland waterways were among the most polluted in Europe even before the country embarked on a large drive to stimulate export-oriented industrial development by attracting foreign investors in advanced manufacturing industries.[51]

On top of the physical problems arising from pollution, the government also was sensitive to possible political problems. The period of intense efforts to attract more foreign participation in Spanish industries coincided with the period of renewed political activity on the part of the Spanish population in the wake of Franco's death. The sentiment for regional autonomy was strong, not only in the Basque region but in others as well; and popular resentment of external influence in regional economics and politics grew. National industrial planners, assuming that anything that focused public attention on foreign investments could become highly politicized, sought to keep a low profile in relationships with foreign companies. In addition, contemporary international political concerns, such as pollution and nuclear power, often were among the most important to newly politicized factions in Spain.[52] Thus, as will be discussed further in Chapters 6 and 7, regional politics had significant effects on the ways in which the Spanish government dealt with the issues of foreign capital and industrial pollution.

The fact that pollution was a matter of concern to government officials trying to devise policies to attract foreign investors does not necessarily

---

50. Organization for Economic Development and Cooperation, *Economic Surveys: Spain* (Paris: OECD Publications, 1977), pp. 175–176.
51. Ibid.
52. Alan, "All the Spains," p. 7; and "Spain," *Europa Yearbook 1981*, pp. 1088–1089.

mean that they sought actively to impose stringent antipollution requirements or screen out heavy polluters. As in many underindustrialized countries, the overwhelming preoccupation was with creating jobs and increasing exports. Little effort was made to measure the potential pollution problems to be expected from certain types of industrial pursuits or to assess the actual role that foreign capital might play in increasing pollution.

Government officials apparently considered it most important that they and the Spanish public not feel that foreign investors were taking advantage of them. Such an ambiguous attitude was summarized in 1980 by the government official in the Ministry of Industry and Energy who was responsible for evaluating all new investment proposals and assigning antipollution requirements. Alfonso Ensenat, subdirector general for industrial environment, pointed out why Spain would never allow itself to be perceived as a pollution haven for foreign companies, even though the government was unwilling to crack down on existing polluters:

> There are two types of technology: pre-ecological ones and ecological ones. We have to be very careful to make sure that a foreign company will use the second type here, because if not, the public opinion will sooner or later turn against the company. Spaniards are very proud people. If we permit our industries to pollute our rivers, that is our business. But if a foreign company comes here and makes contamination, it is an insult to Spain.[53]

Mexico

As with Spain, the role of environmental factors in Mexico's industrial-development strategy has not been as clear-cut as in Ireland. Hundreds of U.S.-based companies now operate plants south of the border, including most of the largest U.S. chemical producers and many mineral processors discussed in previous chapters as having been among the industries hardest hit by U.S. pollution-control regulations. For a variety of reasons, many of these facilities have proven in recent years to be lagging behind their counterpart manufacturing plants in the United States when it comes to pollution control. At the same time, Mexico's proximity to the United States, its emphasis on petroleum-based industries to utilize domestic feedstocks, and the concentration of industrial development in three major urban areas have combined to elevate the level of concern about industrial pollution in recent years.

53. Interview with Alfonso Ensenat, subdirector general for industrial development, Madrid, June 18, 1980.

The economy of Mexico was dramatically transformed between 1940 and 1970, a period during which it expanded at an annual rate of more than 6 percent. The first major stimulus for this period of sustained economic expansion was the outbreak of World War II, which opened markets for Mexican manufactured goods in Latin America and thereby stimulated production and enabled Mexico to increase its imports of capital goods.[54] Although many of the wartime markets for Mexican goods dried up when prewar suppliers from the United States and Europe resumed shipments, the pump had been primed for rapid postwar industrial development.

In the early postwar years, the Mexican government sought to intensify the pace of industrialization through capital investments in industry and infrastructure and more direct coordination of public-sector investments with the needs of the private sector. Public-sector investment, which totaled more than 50 percent of all gross fixed capital formation in the late 1940s, concentrated on the provision of infrastructure (transportation, electricity, and communications) and the expansion of strategic industries that could supply basic materials to the rest of the economy (petroleum, steel, fertilizers, and heavy capital goods).[55] This public investment, combined with a political and economic stability that increased confidence among Mexican entrepreneurs and foreign investors, stimulated a large outpouring of private-sector investment in a wide variety of consumer-goods industries. The production of automobiles and accessories, electrical equipment, machinery, televisions, processed foods, and numerous household items increased rapidly in the 1950s and 1960s.[56]

Much of the expanded output by consumer and capital goods industries replaced manufactured products that had previously been imported. These import-replacement activities were assisted by a broad range of government policies and subsidies, including tariff protection, licensing arrangements to further restrict competing imports, tax incentives, preferential treatment with national banking and capital-lending institutions, and subsidized prices on fuel, electricity, and other public services.[57]

By 1970 Mexico had reached a high level of industrial production in

54. See Robert E. Looney, *Mexico's Economy; A Policy Analysis with Forecasts to 1990* (Boulder, Colo.: Westview Press, 1978), pp. 12–13.
55. Roger D. Hansen, *Mexican Economic Development: The Roots of Rapid Growth* (Washington, D. C.: National Planning Association, 1971), pp. 43–44.
56. Ibid., p. 42.
57. See Leopoldo Solis, *Economic Policy Reform in Mexico: A Case Study for Developing Countries* (Elmsford, N.Y.: Pergamon Press, 1981), pp. 4–9; Bernard S. Katz, "Mexican Fiscal and Subsidy Incentives for Industrial Development," *American Journal of Economics and Sociology* 31 (1972):353–358; and L. Antonio Aspra, "Import Substitution in Mexico: Past and Present," *World Development* 5 (January–February 1977):118–120.

major public industries such as petroleum and steel and was approaching self-sufficiency in many consumer industries. Industrial production as a share of the national product had risen from 21 percent in 1955 to 27 percent in 1970.[58]

Moreover, the manufacturing activities undertaken in Mexico had also become much more diverse. Import substitution expanded continuously to cover more capital goods, intermediate inputs, and sophisticated consumer products. This growth is reflected in the fact that nearly thirteen thousand new import categories were created between 1964 and 1970, primarily as a result of entrepreneurial requests for protection of products being manufactured in Mexico for the first time.[59]

Mexico's postwar import-substitution industrial-development policies were highly successful in inducing foreign manufacturers and Mexican firms to produce in Mexico not only more finished goods, but also more of the inputs, parts, and intermediate goods needed in manufacturing operations. But this rapid progress in stimulating inward-oriented industrialization exposed, exacerbated, or created a number of economic problems for which the Mexican government has been forced to seek a remedy in the last two decades.[60]

Three difficulties have particular relevance to this study and to the shape of the Mexican government's evolving industrial-development strategy.[61] First, the protectionist policies necessary to stimulate domestic production in many industries created a strong bias against exports. Few of the expanding Mexican industries were producing efficiently enough or at a high enough level of quality to be competitive in international markets.

Second, despite huge successes in import substitution for key basic industries and for many industries manufacturing finished products for consumption, Mexico's dependence on imports in the manufacturing industries was not substantially reduced. Little effort was made to control imports of the capital goods required by the industries themselves. The

58. Looney, *Mexico's Economy*, p. 16.
59. Solis, *Economic Policy Reform in Mexico*, p. 5.
60. Sober evaluations of Mexico's future growth potential if it continued its import-substitution policies were offered in the 1960s by Raymond Vernon. See Raymond Vernon, ed., *The Dilemma of Mexico's Development* (Cambridge, Mass.: Harvard University Press, 1963); and Raymond Vernon, *The Dilemma of Mexico's Development: The Roles of the Private and Public Sectors* (Cambridge, Mass.: Harvard University Press, 1965).
61. Many of these problems relate to balance of payments, public-sector debt, currency valuation, and government fiscal and economic policy – considerations that are not elaborated here. See Solis, *Economic Policy Reform in Mexico,* and Looney, *Mexico's Economy,* for detailed accounts. See also Gustavo Garza and Martha Schteingart, "Mexico City: The Emerging Megalopolis," in *Latin American Urban Research*, vol. 5 (Beverly Hills, Calif., Sage, 1977); and Robert E. Looney, *Income Distribution Policies and Economic Growth in Semi-Industrialized Countries: A Comparative Study of Iran, Mexico, Brazil and South Korea* (New York: Praeger, 1975), pp. 115–116.

very success of the import-substitution strategy in finished-consumer-goods sectors bred a continually growing need for new imports of capital goods to maintain and expand production equipment and to provide needed materials. The producer-goods sectors remained weak in Mexico, and little success was achieved in stimulating domestic industrial research, product innovation, or technological development. Thus, while dependence on foreign-produced consumer goods dropped sharply in the postwar years, Mexico remained heavily dependent upon imports of machinery and other capital goods to generate its industrial expansion.

Third, governmental policies greatly intensified preexisting tendencies toward the centralization of industrial and commercial activities in Mexico. Because industrial development was geared to supply final domestic demand, new industries clustered close to traditional markets and population centers, especially Mexico City. This propensity was merely reinforced by patterns of public investment in infrastructure – skewed toward Mexico City, Monterrey, and Guadalajara – and by subsidized transportation and public services that reduced the importance of spatial cost factors in industrial-location considerations in Mexico. Thus, by 1970 almost three-fourths of Mexico's GDP was generated in the nation's three largest urban areas, with nearly half accounted for by the Federal District (Mexico City) alone.

Starting from a very low base, Mexico's manufactured exports have expanded very rapidly since 1970. In fact, excluding petroleum and primary metal products, the value of manufactured exports grew by almost 30 percent per annum between 1970 and 1975, going from $600 million to almost $2.1 billion in this period.[62] Despite this rapid and continuing increase in manufactured exports, Mexico remains a relatively small generator of exports when compared either with European countries of similar populations or with the most successful of the export-oriented industrializing nations.[63] Yet its export growth in particular industrial sectors of relevance to this report has been substantial.

About half of Mexico's manufactured exports come from plants in the border region that assemble products for the U.S. market from components or raw materials imported in bond from the United States. By special U.S. tariff provisions, import duties for these finished goods when they enter the United States are limited to the value added in Mexico. The other half of Mexico's manufactured exports are diversified but have been especially strong in several areas. Exports of parts and components (espe-

---

62. The World Bank estimates that over half of this growth represents real growth, while the rest is accounted for by price increases. See World Bank, *Mexico: Manufacturing Sector* (Washington, D.C.: World Bank, 1979), pp. 10–11.
63. Ibid., p. 11.

cially automobile engines and other parts, non-electrical machinery, electrical machinery, and transport equipment) to the United States have expanded rapidly. Large expansions of exports have also been achieved in recent years for textiles, chemicals, and processed minerals.[64]

During the 1970s industrial-development planners in Mexico also took increasing note of the structural imbalances that had resulted from previous industrialization efforts. In March 1979 the Mexican government, under President José López Portillo, released a new National Industrial Development Plan (NIDP) in order to speed industrialization and to correct or compensate for the structural imbalances created by previous government-influenced industrial development.[65]

In an effort to reduce urban and industrial concentration, the government developed fiscal incentives to encourage Mexican industry to locate away from the most congested urban areas. A major goal of NIDP was to channel 70 percent of new industrial development away from Mexico City. In 1981 special fiscal incentives ranging from 5 to 20 percent of the investment costs, plus employment incentives, were announced for enterprises relocating to other parts of the country. The incentives were designed to encourage regional decentralization, the development of priority industries, and the creation of employment opportunities, and they include tax credits on investments, depending on the priority of the product category and geographic zone. Top priority was given to the development of four "industrial ports" (Lazaro Cardenas, Salinas Cruz, Coatzacoalcos, and Tampico).[66]

To slow its industrial growth, the Federal District was designated as the "zone of controlled growth" and the nearby regions as a "zone of consolidation." Investments in these areas are excluded from receiving many incentives. The Committee to Control Industrial Growth in Zone IIIA was also created to consider and implement specific actions to reduce Mexico City's industrial growth. Any new plant or expansion of existing plants now needs the specific authorization of this committee.[67]

Obviously, concern about pollution and congestion in Mexico City has been one major factor in the government's efforts to steer industry into other areas. Moreover, the incentive system has been extended to the purchase of pollution-control equipment. Special tax-payment certificates can be issued to companies for the installation of pollution-control equipment

64. See Bernhard Fischer, Habil Egbert Gerken, and Ulrich Hiemenz, *Growth, Employment and Trade in an Industrializing Economy* (Tubingen: Mohr, 1982).
65. Secretaria de Patrimonio y Fomento Industrial, *Plan Nacional de Desarrollo Industrial, 1979–82* (Mexico City: SEPAFIN, March 1979).
66. Ibid., p. 26.
67. Ibid.

on existing plants. This is one of the few fiscal benefits available to plants remaining in Mexico City. On the other hand, new plants are eligible for pollution-control tax benefits only if they are located outside the Mexico City area.[68]

A haven across the border?

Probably more than any other country, Mexico has witnessed dynamic growth within virtually all of the potential problem industries identified in Chapter 4: those in which U.S. firms have adopted a direct strategy of industrial flight or in which environmental factors have been a significant contributing factor in the increase of production abroad by U.S. firms. Mexico's capacity for smelting copper, lead, and zinc has continued to increase rapidly in recent years, as has its production of hydrofluoric acid. Though not increasing substantially, production of arsenic trioxide has remained high enough to fulfill demand for exports to the United States. Production of some hazardous chemical products that are banned or regulated strictly in the United States, particularly pesticides, has also expanded. And, among the low-technology, labor-intensive industries attracted by Mexico's Border Industrialization Program are a number of plants that utilize asbestos fibers or produce other asbestos products.

The Border Industrialization Program, which permits so-called *maquiladora* industries to operate in special export-processing zones, was instituted in 1965 to reduce illegal immigration into the United States and to stimulate industrial development on the Mexican side of the border. U.S. investors can take advantage of large pools of inexpensive labor without paying import duties on raw materials and equipment shipped into Mexico, and the production takes place near their principal suppliers, markets, and administrative headquarters. In effect, many U.S. companies have divided up their production process, constructing *maquiladora* operations in Mexico for labor-intensive portions and maintaining the more capital-intensive portions at existing plants on the U.S. side of the border.[69]

Particularly well-suited for the *maquiladora* program are industries that combine three features: high labor intensity within an easily separable portion of the productive process, moderate transportation costs and easily transportable goods, and a need for fast turnover and rapid delivery to U.S. markets. Thus textiles and fashion-sensitive clothing, perishable food

68. These pollution-control benefits are most clearly described in World Bank, "Staff Appraisal Report: Mexico, Pollution Control Project," April 28, 1982, pp. 21–22.
69. See Donald W. Baerreson, *The Border Industrialization Program of Mexico* (Lexington, Mass.: Lexington, 1971).

products, building materials, household items, furniture, glass and pottery products, and a wide range of simple metal products have proven to be the leading industries participating in the *maquiladora* program.[70]

For many of these industries, pollution control is not a major factor. On the other hand, since these are all labor-intensive industries, concern has focused more and more in recent years on the workplace-health dangers associated with some of the *maquiladora* industries. Most significant for this study have been the numerous reports that industries using asbestos for textiles, building supplies, and other consumer goods have relocated across the border and that workers in these plants are subjected to almost uncontrollable exposure to asbestos fibers in the working environment.[71]

The Mexican government seems not to have explicitly encouraged this migration of hazardous industries under the Border Industrialization Program. Nor has the crucial reason for the relocation in Mexico been the absence of workplace-health controls in Mexico. The labor intensity of the products has been the decisive element on both accounts. Nevertheless, the Mexican government has not yet taken concerted action to require substantial improvements in the occupational health field in such industries, and thus it continues to offer U.S. companies added subsidies above their labor-cost savings.

Pesticide production is another instance in which Mexico's proximity to the United States and its relatively lax or ineffective system of pollution controls apparently have affected what is manufactured. Although FERTIMEX, the state-owned fertilizer monopoly, produces many of Mexico's most widely used pesticides, many foreign companies also produce pesticides in Mexico.[72]

FERTIMEX produces most of the organochlorines and organophosphates used in Mexico, while foreign firms tend to produce the more sophisticated pesticide products such as all the carbonates and synthetic pyrethroids used in Mexican agriculture. The most problematical pesticides manufactured in Mexico, especially the older and more dangerous pesticides discussed in Chapter 4, are produced by FERTIMEX or wholly Mexican-owned companies. Mexican exports of some of these products have filled the void between the cessation of production in the United States and the final prohibition of all use (DBCP and lindane are two key examples). In addition, a great deal of concern has arisen in recent years about illegal exports by Mexican-based companies of pesticide products

70. Ibid. Also, World Bank, *Mexico: Manufacturing Sector*, pp. 11–15.
71. See especially the sources listed in nn. 27, 28, and 29 of Chap. 3.
72. See Louis Goodman and Belfor Portilla, "Foreign Toxins: Multinational Corporations and Pesticides in Mexican Agriculture" (Draft paper, Spring 1984).

manufactured and used in Mexico but banned in the United States, such as DDT, BHC, and Toxafene.[73] Some of these products are manufactured by U.S. affiliates in Mexico, although no evidence exists to indicate that these affiliates are responsible for suspected illegal border traffic.

Mexico thus appears to have been used as a pollution (or workplace-hazard) haven by a few of the industries participating in the *maquiladora* program and by some companies engaged in the production of hazardous chemical substances. It is impossible to obtain export figures that break down how much this has increased the totals of manufactured exports achieved under the border industrialization program or by the chemical industry. Although the significance in terms of total Mexican exports of manufactured goods to the United States is small, there is little doubt that the impact for worker and public health in local areas that have "benefited" from these developments may be substantial in the future.

In the mineral-processing industry, too, Mexico's increased comparative advantage vis-à-vis the United States may be at least partly attributable to environmental factors. Recent U.S. government reports have confirmed that Mexican mineral processors, especially in the copper industry, operate smelters with much higher levels of sulfur dioxide emissions than those permitted in the United States.[74] State-owned companies, as well as private Mexican firms separately and in conjunction with foreign partners, have increasingly built smelting and refining capacity in Mexico to process domestic ores rather than exporting them.[75]

Many observers in the United States have contended that the difference in Mexican and U.S. environmental controls has encouraged this backward integration process. It is also clear, however, that new Mexican government policies restricting the export of unprocessed minerals, coupled with increased incentives to industries for the export of processed minerals, and (most significantly) Mexico's position as one of the world's leading mining countries for fourteen minerals and ores have been the dominant factors encouraging the growth of Mexico's mineral-processing industries.[76] Lack of stringent environmental controls has been, at best, a secondary factor in establishing Mexico's comparative advantage as a producer and exporter of processed minerals.

73. Ibid., p. 44.
74. Comptroller General, "The U.S. Mining and Mineral-Processing Industry: An Analysis of Trends and Implications" (Report to the Congress of the United States, October 31, 1979).
75. Camara Americande Comericio de Mexico, *Localizacion Industrial en Mexico* (Mexico City: Amcham, 1983).
76. The array of incentives set out by the government and the strength of Mexico's mining industry are described in U.S. Embassy, Mexico City, "Industrial Outlook Report: Minerals CERP" (Unclassified report prepared by the Department of State, August 6, 1981).

Romania

As a socialist country, Romania has built up its chemical industry and its relations with multinational corporations by following a very different path from that of Mexico, Spain, or Ireland. Nevertheless, Romania's interactions with Western corporations, in the form of technology transfers, technology licenses, and joint ventures, increased rapidly; and the volume of trade between the United States and Romania grew fivefold between 1970 and 1980. There is some evidence to suggest that environmental issues have played a role in the Romanian industrialization strategy and have influenced the choice of goods produced for export to the U.S. and other Western markets.

Before World War II, Romania was one of the least developed countries in Europe. The economy was predominantly agrarian, with three-fourths of the work force living in rural areas and working in agriculture. In 1938, for example, only 8 percent of the work force was employed in industrial production, and the only large-scale, quasi-modern industry was oil, of which Romania had large domestic reserves.[77] After the war, when a Communist government gained power under the umbrella of the Soviet Union, rapid industrialization became an overwhelming priority for Romania. The basic industrial-development strategy pursued in the early years after the war followed closely the Soviet model: centralized direction of publicly owned enterprises; concentration on the heavy capital-goods sector of production; forced savings for capital-goods investment through collectivization and government-controlled terms of trade in the agricultural sector and through drastic limitations in the consumer-goods sectors; and integration into a system of cooperative and specialized production with the Soviet and other Eastern European economies.[78]

Today, Romania is still a member of the Soviet-dominated Council for Mutual Economic Assistance (CMEA) and still trades heavily with the Soviet Union and other Eastern bloc countries. But, especially during the flowering of detente in the mid-1970s, it steered a more independent industrial-development course than most of the other Eastern European countries. Beginning in about 1961, the Romanian government asserted increasingly nationalistic policies aimed at achieving a "de-Russification"

77. Andreas C. Tsantis and Roy Pepper, *Romania: The Industrialization of an Agrarian Economy under Socialist Planning* (Washington, D.C.: World Bank, 1979), p. 24.
78. See Trond Gilberg, *Modernization in Romania since World War II* (New York: Praeger, 1975); American University, *Area Handbook for Romania* (Washington, D. C.: U.S. Government Printing Office, 1972); U.S. Department of State, *Romania: Background Notes* (Washington, D.C.: U.S. Government Printing Office, 1978); and Tsantis and Pepper, *Romania*, for more details on early postwar industrial-development strategy under Soviet direction.

of the country. In addition to refusing to take part in Warsaw Pact military maneuvers, in 1962 Romania's Communist leadership rejected Soviet proposals to subordinate economic-development planning to CMEA's supranational authority, insisting on the prerogative of each Communist party to work out its own economic policies on the basis of national self-interest.[79]

Since that time, Romania has constantly been increasing the number of its non-Communist trading partners and the percentage of its overall trade with these nations. From 1947 to 1959, more than 85 percent of all Romania's foreign trade was with the Communist world. Between 1959 and 1969, however, trade with non-Communist countries grew three times faster than trade with other Communist countries. In 1973 Romania became the first Warsaw Pact country to conduct less than one-half of its foreign trade with other Communist nations. By 1980, over 55 percent of Romanian trade was with the industrialized free-enterprise countries or with developing countries.[80] Important in stimulating these developments have been Romania's membership in the General Agreement on Tariffs and Trade, its entrance into the International Bank for Reconstruction and Development (World Bank) in December 1972, the extension of U.S. Overseas Private Investment Corporation facilities and U.S. Export-Import Bank credits in 1972; the 1975 U.S.-Romania trade agreement that accorded Romania Most Favored Nation (MFN) status; and a number of other bilateral trade agreements between Romania and countries in Europe and the developing world.

With over 50 percent of all investment devoted to industry, Romanian industrial output grew rapidly between 1951 and 1975, averaging 13 percent per annum.[81] A key to achieving such high overall growth rates in industrial output during this period was the channeling of the bulk of investment, technology, and skilled labor into important production sectors: metallurgy, machine building, energy production, engineering, and chemicals. The share of these goods in total industrial output rose from less than 25 percent in 1950 to more than 50 percent by 1975.[82] During this time, the share of total output from chemicals and engineering goods alone climbed from about 16 percent to almost 45 percent.[83]

Output in the chemical industry by itself grew even faster than overall industrial output from 1950 to 1975, with an average annual growth rate

79. U.S. Department of State, *Romania: Background Notes,* pp. 4–6.
80. Documentation supplied by U.S. Department of State, U.S. Embassy in Bucharest, Romania, "Romania: Key Economic Indicators" (undated).
81. Ibid.
82. *Romania Yearbook: 1977* (Bucharest: Scientific and Encyclopaedic, 1977), p. 71.
83. Tsantis and Pepper, *Romania,* p. 6.

of nearly 21 percent. Total chemical production in Romania expanded more than five times in the ten-year period from 1966 to 1976.[84] Growth in the chemical industry has been tailored to take advantage of opportunities for processing and refining Romanian raw materials that before industrialization were exported or underutilized: hydrocarbons, salt, coal, timber, and various mineral resources. In particular, the chemification of methane gas and other oil products has been a high priority. The petrochemical sector accounted for about 49 percent of Romanian chemical production in 1975 and long-range planners have targeted this figure to increase to 75 percent by 1990.[85]

Industrial progress in the chemical sector, as well as other priority sectors, has depended on the application of new technologies and emerging scientific knowledge. Although the Romanian engineering sector has grown rapidly and technological research and development have made significant advances, the Romanians have still relied heavily on the import and licensing of foreign technology in the continuing development of their chemical industry. This, plus a growing demand by Romanian industry for raw materials unavailable in the country, has led to dramatic increases in imports in the last two decades.

The necessity of importing advanced technology has probably been a major factor in Romanian efforts to steer an independent economic and political course and to cultivate amicable relations with a broad spectrum of nations. In the 1970s President Nicolae Ceausescu's rhetoric certainly stressed the importance of Romanian integration into the world economy and the international division of labor more than did that of most other leaders of socialist countries. According to Ceausescu, "Romania could not 'ensure the building of an advanced society such as should be the socialist and the communist society, unless we actively take part in the world division of labour, unless we promote a broad exchange of material, technico-scientific and cultural values with other people.' "[86]

Paying for increased imports, which has not been an easy task for Romania, has necessitated a growing emphasis on stimulating exports during the last two decades. Through the 1950s and 1960s export promotions centered primarily on commodities in which Romania had traditionally maintained a comparative advantage, especially raw materials such as coal, wood, oil, and agricultural products. Beginning in the early

84. *Romania Yearbook, 1977,* pp. 73–74.
85. Ibid.
86. Nicolae Ceausescu, Opening Speech Delivered at the Colloquium on the Science of the Management of Society, March 6, 1972, reprinted in Nicolae Ceausescu, *The Development and Modernization of the Techno-Material Basis of Socialism in Romania* (Bucharest: Meridiane, 1979), p. 169.

1970s, Romanian export strategy placed a much greater emphasis on industrial goods. Ceausescu, speaking in 1971, described the changing relationship between Romanian exports and imports:

> The impetuous development of our national economy, the growth of industry at a sustained rate posed new problems to our foreign trade, and led to important changes in the structure of export and import. . . . At the same time, essential changes took place and will be further accentuated in the structure of Romania's exports; the share of raw materials and auxiliary materials in the country's exports is decreasing and the proportion of products of the machine-building industry, chemicals, and products of the light and food industries is increasing. These changes also pose to the producers and foreign trade workers new and highly responsible tasks.[87]

In essence, in order to increase its revenue from export trades and enhance its position in world markets, Romania made in the early 1970s a concerted effort to redefine its comparative advantage in international trade. The first priority was to upgrade the value added to Romanian raw materials before exportation: for example, instead of exporting crude oil, emphasis was put on exporting more refined petroleum products or downstream petrochemicals. In addition, Romanian officials sought to take advantage of new elements of comparative advantage: textile and footwear exports have increased because Romania could sell cheaply in the West on account of its low labor costs; and Romanian engineers found increasing demand for their services and technological know-how among Third World countries that wished to import technologies appropriate to their stage of development. But it also appears that during the 1970s environmental factors became an important consideration for Romanian industrial-development planners who believed they could help bestow a comparative advantage upon Romanian producers of heavy industrial chemicals.

Targeting the West's untouchables

Officially, Romanian spokesmen contend that environmental protection has become a high priority and that they consider it important to reduce the adverse consequences of the country's rapid industrial development. In addition to maximizing economic growth, they claim, careful selection of industries and applications of the most advanced technologies have enabled Romania to adhere to an ecologically sound industrial-develop-

---

87. Nicolae Ceausescu, Speech Delivered at the Conference on Foreign Trade Activity (February 5, 1971), reprinted in Ceausescu, *Development and Modernization*, p. 172.

ment strategy. An article by the deputy scientific director of the Romanian Institute of Industrial Economics noted that although Romania has a large-scale program of industrialization in order to overcome its status of a developing country, it "is one of the countries which pay particular attention to environmental protection ... and which promptly and efficiently prevent and detect any phenomena of environmental degradation which might be the result of the high economic growth rates in the conditions of the techno-scientific revolution."[88]

To ensure that industrial development is in accord with the environmental as well as economic goals of the Romanian government, all industrial projects are subject to the approval of the National Council for Environmental Protection. According to *Lunea,* the Romanian foreign-policy weekly, because no industrial activity is initiated or developed outside the state plan and no investment is financed without approval by the National Council for Environmental Protection, "it follows that new polluting projects are killed before they are really born."[89]

Despite this official view, when the list of key Romanian exports to Europe and the United States is examined, it is difficult to avoid the conclusion that in the late 1970s Romanian officials did not see environmental factors as influencing Romanian comparative advantage in a different manner. Along with several other Eastern European countries, Romania became an exporter of a variety of chemicals and chemical products whose production is banned or facing significant regulatory restraints in Europe and the United States.[90]

A number of the major chemical companies from the United States, Japan, and Europe maintain offices for buying and selling chemicals with state-owned firms in Eastern Europe. Spokesmen for several of these corporations in Bucharest, the capital of Romania, note candidly that the production of many of the basic chemicals that they purchase there for use in Europe and the United States causes severe pollution or industrial

88. Aurel Iancu, "Economic Growth and the Environment," in Ceausescu, *Development and Modernization.*

89. Teodor Brates, "Reason and Ecology: The Place of Romanian Progress," *Lunea: Romanian Foreign Policy Weekly,* no. 15 (April 11–17, 1980), p. 3.

90. The exports from Chimimport-export's affiliated factories are soda ash, caustic soda, various chlorosodium and petrochemical products, methanol, butanol, octanol, phenolacetone, sodium bichromate, acetic acid, carbide, fatty acids, cellophane, ammonia, azotic, sulphuric, polyethylene, acrylonitril, vinyl polyacetate, polystyrene, bakelite, plastic carpets, slabs, tubes, hoses and gaskets, other plastic products, insecticides, aklylamines, medical drugs for human use and pharmaceuticals, cosmetics and raw materials thereof, dyestuffs and intermediates, lacquers and paints, detergents, soap and other similar products, plasticisers and other chemicals. This list is taken from Foreign Trade Publicity Agency (Publicom), *Your Commercial Partners in Romania* (Bucharest: Publicom, 1979), p. 23.

workplace hazards.[91] Even though this phenomenon is not a simple matter of capital flight on the part of multinational corporations hoping to avoid environmental regulations, it does raise a host of questions of relevance to this study, particularly since Western corporations contracted with Eastern European governments to build or sell technology for some of the new industrial plants that came onstream in Romania in the late 1970s and early 1980s.[92]

It appears that Romanian choices of which chemical products to sell in the West have, in some instances, been affected by an analysis of changing environmental constraints on industry in Europe and the United States. In fact, an official with one of Romania's state trading companies said in an interview that Romania's decisions about what types of chemical products to produce for sale on the world market have been influenced in part by the tightening of environmental and workplace health standards in the West. He said:

> We have representatives in many countries; we send people all over the world for negotiations and to get data about the market and exchange information with clients about tendencies of the market.... On the basis of all this input we try to adjust our strategy to penetrate Western markets as much as we can.... We see products where we have a competitive advantage. Regulations that restrict production of certain commodities in other countries affect our comparative advantage. Your regulations help us make our decisions about what to produce for export.[93]

The spokesman added, however, that although restrictions in the West may have influenced Romanian marketing decisions, it is not the lack of regulations and pollution technology but other price factors that give Romania its competitive production advantage in benzidine dyes, polyvinyl chloride, and other pollution-intensive chemicals being sold in the West.[94]

---

91. American companies that buy and sell chemicals in Romania include Dow Chemical; DuPont; Monsanto; Diamond-Shamrock; Stauffer; Merck, Sharpe, and Dohme; Phillip Brothers; Atlanta. Representatives of all major U.S. companies with offices in Romania were interviewed by the author in July 1980. All requested anonymity.
92. "U.K. Raps MNCs for Exporting Jobs to Eastern Europe," *Business International,* March 9, 1979, pp. 73–74; "Chemicals in the East Explode West," *Economist,* February 10, 1979, pp. 84–85; "Chemicals Threaten West," *Financial Times World Business Weekly,* November 13, 1978, p. 61; "Western Know-How Comes Home to Roost," *Chemical Week,* July 28, 1976, pp. 39–40.
93. Interview with Sorim Niculescu, assistant to the president of Chimimport-export, Bucharest, Romania, July 7, 1980.
94. Ibid.

In the case of products where the primary danger is that workers may be exposed to hazardous substances at certain stages of the productive process, Romanian officials say technological innovations have enabled them to reduce industrial hazards dramatically. For example, they contend that the production of benzidine dye is totally automated, so that no workers are exposed to health hazards. Recent investments, the officials contend, have also reduced the level of vinyl chloride monomer in polyvinyl chloride from five to one parts per million, bringing Romanian PVC within U.S. standards.[95]

The representative of one American chemical company with an office in Bucharest, however, notes that low environmental expenditures may be a significant aspect of Romania's price advantages: "We don't really ask how the Romanians can afford to sell us some products as cheaply as they do, but, having seen some of their chemical plants, I can tell you that they spend a heck of a lot less than we do in Europe or the United States on pollution control or workplace health."[96]

Whether or not the lack of environmental controls on industrial chemical plants has enhanced Romania's comparative advantage, several factors have reduced the degree to which Romanian chemicals have penetrated U.S. markets during the 1980s. First, trade with Romania has leveled off as a result of increased East-West tension in recent years. But of more relevance to this study, spokesmen for the Romanian chemical industry say that in the cases of benzidine dyes, polyvinyl chloride, B-naphthylamine, and certain pharmaceuticals, U.S. purity standards have also hindered Romanian exports to the U.S. But the spokesmen add that overall production of most of these commodities has not been reduced by restrictions in the U.S. market, because new markets have been opened in countries (developing countries in particular) with regulations that are not so strict.[97]

95. These assertions were made in a group interview with the following representatives of the Ministry of the Chemical Industry: Paul G. Mgravescu, general inspector; Joan Tiberiu Hudea, chief of Fertiliser Department; John Mandravel, engineer in the Petrochemical Department; Corneliu Craiu, technical director of the Research and Design Institute for Wastewater Treatment; and Pavel Mariana, engineer. The interview was conducted at the ministry on July 9, 1980. It should be noted that the author was not permitted to verify any of these assertions and that Western diplomats and spokesmen for several American companies expressed considerable doubt that benzidine-dye production has been automated to this extent.
96. See n. 93.
97. Interviews with Sorim Niculescu, the representatives listed in n. 97, and Matei Nicolau, secretary of the National Council for Environmental Protection, Bucharest, July 9, 1980.

Conclusions

Pollution and explicit consideration or passive acceptance of the pollution-haven hypothesis have played a role in the evolving industrial strategies of all four countries briefly examined in this chapter. But this fact does not in itself validate the hypothesis or recommend a pollution-haven strategy as a means of stimulating industrial development. Indeed, the experiences of the four countries suggest the opposite. Officials in Ireland, the country that most clearly considered styling itself as a pollution haven when the potential implications of U.S. environmental controls first became apparent, today consider themselves fortunate that intervening circumstances kept them from successfully attracting a large number of heavy polluters. Spain has not been particularly adept at dealing with its industrial-pollution problems, but Spanish resentment of foreign polluters is strong in the bureaucracy, among ambitious politicians, and in the public at large. This sentiment has reduced the degree to which Spain has been willing to use the assimilative capacity of its environment as an element of comparative advantage.

The example of Mexico shows how industrial pollution can have conflicting impacts in terms of the country's industrial-development strategy. Although not fundamentally responsible for Mexico's rising position as an exporter of manufactured goods, the relative dearth of effective environmental and health controls has enhanced Mexico's attractiveness to some U.S. firms participating in the *maquiladora* program, in the mineral-processing sector, and in certain types of chemical manufacturing. On the other hand, stifling pollution and congestion problems in Mexico City, and increasingly in Monterrey and Guadalajara, have been integral in the government's growing perception that future industrial growth must be decentralized into new port cities and other priority zones around the country.

Romania's mixed record of success in exporting hazardous chemical products to the United States suggests that comparative advantage in international markets secured by the absence of pollution controls may be overridden by international political factors (the decline of detente), and more significantly by import standards and product-use standards designed to protect consumers in the industrialized nations. This is likely to be a growing problem for some of the *maquiladora* industries and pesticide producers in Mexico that are currently exporting hazardous products to the United States. This is especially true for the asbestos-related industries, since both the use and the production of asbestos products are more and more heavily restricted in the United States.

In the countries studied, in fact, industries in which increased comparative advantage in production appears to be related to environmental factors are those that fit the problem categories identified in Chapter 4: hazardous substances; low value-added, low-technology, labor-intensive goods; and goods for which locally abundant minerals make in-country processing a logical pursuit anyway.

Two critical questions are raised by the general experiences of the four rapidly industrializing nations described in this chapter. First, since some multinational companies have obviously sought to find convenient havens for certain highly polluting industries, and since some industrializing nations appear to have become more aware of the potential pitfalls, how have these developments affected the bargaining process over time between multinational corporations and industrializing countries? Second, in light of the fact that some developing countries have changed the standards for the level of pollution they are willing to accept and are also discovering the existence of pollution problems that they had not anticipated when they solicited particular industries, have pollution concerns further politicized the relationship between multinational corporations and host countries?

To examine these questions, the next two chapters draw on a number of individual case studies of the relationship between multinational corporations, host-country governments, and the public in these countries.

6

Bargaining for the right to pollute

Political scientists and economists have focused a great deal of attention in recent years on the nature of the bargaining relationship between multinational corporations in search of a hospitable country for a new production facility and nation-states depending on foreign businesses for the economic benefits they generate. Often, companies play different countries off against each other to extract maximum concessions, offering their technological, capital, and managerial resources and their job-creating potential in return. Countries more and more often attempt to conduct negotiations with a number of companies from a variety of countries to increase their bargaining strength.

Still, as noted in Chapter 2, most studies of the bargaining relationship between countries and companies conclude that in the initial phase, before a company actually builds a plant in one or another country, the upper hand generally belongs to the corporation. Indeed, there has been sharp criticism of the process wherein many large multinational corporations make little secret of jurisdiction shopping, eliciting large monetary concessions from governments desperate for jobs and foreign-exchange revenues. The process is hardly confined to poor countries in need of rapid industrial development; it has reached its apogee in Europe, where large companies now tender proposals to several countries and wait to see which government bids the most. In 1979, for example, Ford finally agreed to build a new European car plant in Austria, after soliciting simultaneous offers from Spain, Belgium, Britain, France, and West Germany. The *Economist* criticized this and similar deals, noting that the calculated and careful gamesmanship practiced by many big companies "shows up the structure of grants, loans, tax holidays, interest subsidies, and other promises and caresses that underlie so much of western Europe's big investment schemes these days." The *Economist* concluded that "governments which offer ever-higher bribes to get firms to bring them jobs have no grounds for complaint when the companies play one country off against another." However, it went on to note the short-term exigencies and political pressures that operate on most governments and give big corporations the upper hand in "the international jobs auction."[1]

An obvious question of relevance to this study is how environmental issues enter into this bargaining relationship. Do companies and countries negotiate over pollution control as part of their attempts to strike the initial bargain that will bring a company to locate in a particular country? Do companies hold an edge in such negotiations as well, and can they therefore extract larger pollution concessions from governments by dealing with several at once?

Negotiations with national governments

It is clear that multinational corporations involved in industries where treatment of wastes and other environmental precautions may impose substantial expenses do seek to negotiate agreements that will hold down such expenditures. J. B. O'Sullivan, the deputy general manager and harbor engineer for Ireland's Cork Harbor, for example, says that virtually every large company that has made contact with the board about locating in Cork has sought to negotiate over the amount of effluent it will be permitted to discharge into Cork Harbor.[2] However, as O'Sullivan points out, companies invariably initiate the bargaining process over pollution-control standards only after making the commitment to locate in Cork.

This seems generally to be the case in rapidly industrializing countries: negotiations over specific pollution controls do not occur at the same time as negotiations over tax holidays, grants, and other forms of assistance offered by national governments. In part, this is because pollution-control regulations, especially outside of the United States, Japan, and Europe, tend to be site specific and variable according to the wishes of local governments. Few countries have national pollution standards for more than a few general categories of pollutants. As a result, several complicating factors make it difficult for a national government to negotiate with a foreign corporation over specific effluent and emissions standards as part of the initial bargaining to determine whether the company decides to locate in that country.

In both Ireland and Spain, for example, local and regional governments devise most environmental restrictions as part of the overall land-use-planning process that determines where and on what terms all new development takes place. Since this process is initiated only after a company

1. "The International Jobs Auction," *Economist*, February 25, 1980, p. 74.
2. Interview with J. B. O'Sullivan, deputy general manager and harbor engineer, Cork Harbour Board, Cork, Ireland, April 3, 1980.

decides to locate in Spain or Ireland, the bargaining parameters on pollution control may not even be clear when a company weighs the incentives offered by a national government. Moreover, at least in Ireland and Spain, national government authorities have no means of assuring that the pollution concessions they do offer will in fact be endorsed in the local planning-and-permit procedures which lie ahead.

Screening of industries

Nevertheless, a bargaining process over environmental issues, albeit an informal one, frequently does take place between officials of the national government and company officials before the company offers a site-specific proposal and seeks planning permission at the local level. At this stage bargaining is not necessarily over specific effluent or emission standards, nor are national governments usually in a position to promise what these standards will be. Instead, the early give-and-take on environmental issues tends to center on broad questions of process and technology. Generally, the purpose of such negotiations is to set a basic accord on the productive processes, raw materials, and types of technology that will be used by the proposed industrial plant.

Government officials often use this process to set out the minimum conditions that they will accept in return for the fiscal concessions they are offering a company. For example, in keeping with its evolving industrial-development strategy, the Irish IDA has bargained actively with companies about the environmental impacts of overall process and technology choices. Because of its success in attracting high-technology industries, and because it has offered such attractive packages of fiscal incentives, IDA has frequently had the upper hand in these dealings, effectively screening out a number of industrial proposals by striking an intransigent bargaining position.

In 1975 IDA claimed negotiations had been called off on six major industrial proposals in the chemical, agricultural, food-processing, and smelting sectors on the basis of concern about the pollution they concluded would result even if local governments imposed stringent regulations.[3] Since then, negotiations with several other foreign companies have broken off after IDA concluded that the proposed industrial facility would entail too much risk of pollution. One American company, a well-known producer of fragrances and flavors, was prohibited from manufacturing in Ireland after officials discovered that the effluent expected from its plant

---

3. Interview with Ken Gunn, manager, Heavy Industry, Industrial Development Authority, Dublin, March 26, 1980.

affected the homing system of salmon, which run in most of Ireland's rivers and streams, and the company decided against altering its process or treatment technology.[4] The Imperial Chemical Industries, a British-owned company that is one of the largest chemical producers in the world, proposed to build a chlorine plant several years ago, something IDA had long considered since there were no domestic facilities for chlorine production. However, Imperial Chemical claimed that the plant would be economical only if it used the mercury-cell process. IDA rejected the proposal, deciding that any chlorine plant built in Ireland would have to use the diaphragm process in order to avoid mercury contamination of Ireland's waters.[5] Matthew Lynch, who is in charge of evaluating industry for the Institute for Industrial Research and Standards, says that IDA also refused to offer financial assistance to a large U.S. chemical company to construct an organochlorine herbicide plant in Ireland unless the company agreed to utilize an activated-carbon treatment system to remove potentially harmful chemical substances from the effluent. The company reportedly argued strenuously with IDA officials that it was not using activated carbon even in similar plants operating in the United States. When IDA refused to negotiate further on the matter, the company withdrew its proposal and began searching for other European locations, eventually siting its plant in Scotland.[6]

Although Mexican officials had previously appeared unconcerned about the potential long-term implications of some firms' relocating across the border, they too began in the early 1980s to screen out certain industrial proposals on environmental grounds at a preliminary stage. For example, there are indications that the Mexican government no longer views the transfer of labor-intensive, low-technology asbestos industries from the United States to Mexico as a desirable trend. Thus, Manuel Medellin Milan, then the director general for the chemical industry in the Secretariat of National Patrimony and Industrial Promotion (SEPAFIN), said in 1982 that SEPAFIN had rejected a proposal from a U.S. company to build a new plant to produce asbestos products in Mexico because "we did not accept the company's motives for wanting to come to Mexico." Although Medellin said that Mexican officials thought that the problems of asbestos have been exaggerated in the United States, they decided they did not want to get involved with a company if it was running away from those problems. He added: "We are prepared to live with the risks asso-

---

4. Interview with Liam Kearney, industrial promotion analyst, Industrial Development Authority, Dublin, March 24, 1980.
5. Interview with Ken Gunn.
6. Interview with Matthew Lynch, manager, Environmental Department, Institute for Industrial Research and Standards, Dublin, March 27, 1980.

ciated with asbestos if it is for our own domestic needs, but we will not accept asbestos companies anymore if they want solely to produce for export."[7]

So although negotiations over environmental issues at the national-government level take place within the overall context of bargaining between the host country and the multinational corporation, they do not generally determine the particular pollution standards that will eventually be assigned. Instead, this process tends to determine the broad environmental parameters of industrial production (processes, technology, raw materials used) and the financial assistance to be made available to companies to help overcome potential environmental problems and meet whatever pollution standards are imposed.

The primary purpose of these negotiations, then, is to set broad minimum requirements about technologies, production processes, and raw materials to be used, as well as types even if not precise quantities of waste products to be permitted. The government of the host country may therefore have the upper hand in such negotiations if it is willing to forgo industry that cannot meet these minimums. Obviously, the strength of a country's bargaining position is heavily influenced by its ability to find alternatives: other companies in the industry that will accede to the government's parameters or other industries that do not pose potential environmental hazards and health risks.

But a country's bargaining position in talks about processes, technologies, and raw materials may also be strengthened by its other bargaining chips. Governments have often sweetened the overall array of financial incentives for incoming industry by offering to subsidize a portion of pollution-control expenses, giving tax breaks on imported pollution technology, or assisting in waste disposal. For example, IDA offers to pay up to 30 percent of capital expenditures on pollution-control equipment, and the Spanish government offers up to 20 percent. Both governments often make promises about assisting companies with water treatment and solid-waste disposal.[8]

To some extent, then, it is true that host countries often end up inducing companies to accept whatever minimum pollution constraints they establish by subsidizing pollution-control costs. If the country wants a particular project badly, a multinational firm may find itself in a good position to extract substantial financial concessions to prevent pollution.

7. Interview with Manuel Medellin Milan, director for the chemical industry, Secretariat of National Patrimony and Industrial Development, Mexico City, July 16, 1982.
8. Industrial Development Authority, *IDA Industrial Plan 1978–82,* p. 22; and interview with Jeronimo Angulo Arambura, director general of chemical and textile industries, Ministry of Industry and Energy, Madrid, June 17, 1980.

But this is true only if the firm is willing to meet the minimum technology and process constraints set down by the host country.

The dilemma for technology importers

Sometimes, however, technology transfer and import restrictions set by host countries prohibit foreign companies from utilizing the most advanced pollution-control equipment or the cleanest available production processes. For example, Celanese Mexicana inaugurated a new industrial complex during the early 1980s at La Cangrejera, near the port city of Coatzacoalcos, with eight different chemical plants drawing petrochemical feedstocks from a nearby PEMEX facility. At the complex Mexican officials required an elaborate system for activated-carbon treatment and oxidation lagoons for water effluent, and installation of equipment to reduce air pollution from the plants. Yet engineers from the parent company in the United States say that, as a result of Mexican restrictions on technology imports, Celanese is using a production process for vinyl acetate that is less efficient and causes more pollution than the process used in the United States.[9]

Mexico's concern to limit the importation of capital goods to essential goods not available in Mexico forced Celanese to rely on less efficient production technology for its new plant. Mexican officials accepted a sacrifice in terms of efficiency and added pollution burdens instead of granting Celanese's request for a license to import technology from the United States. If the sacrifice had been thought to be too substantial, the Mexican government could have permitted the technology transfer as part of the package deal for assistance and concessions to Celanese, which has operated chemical plants in Mexico since 1942.

The dilemma posed when pollution-control technology or the most efficient production technology available must be imported is even more pointed in the case of countries that import technology and whole production plants without permitting foreign ownership. Ireland, Spain, Mexico, and other countries relying on multinational corporations to build and operate production facilities may set out technology and process constraints that the companies must adhere to if they wish to locate in the country. Part of the cost of complying with these constraints, as well as with specific pollution-control guidelines, is subsidized in part by various government grants and tax breaks, but the rest is subsumed into the com-

---

9. Interivew with Doug Staley, production superintendent, Celanese Chemical Co. (USA), Coatzacoalcos, Mexico, July 29, 1982.

pany's overall capital-expenditure horizon for the project. If the country seems hospitable and the long-range profit potential appears bright, a multinational firm may be quite willing to absorb extra capital costs related to pollution control as the price for getting into the country.

For technology importers, however, negotiations on every item center around price. Romanian officials do not bargain with companies building a turnkey plant about whether regulations require pollution-control technology to be installed. They decide what pollution-control technology they desire and whether to pay the added costs of this technology, and then bargain about the price. Thus one representative of an engineering firm that has built a factory for Romania said in an interview:

> The Romanian government hires us to design and build a plant. We tell them what is best from a technical viewpoint, but they make the choice. Since they are the ones paying the bill, they may have us build a different – perhaps less sophisticated – plant than we'd build for ourselves. If they want a plant with no atmospheric emissions we could build it for them, but they'd have to pay the bill.[10]

Because of the substantial added costs, Romanian officials say they have frequently not purchased pollution-control technology for new plants. Foreign currency is scarce, and they do not wish to spend it unless the investment will lead directly to increases in productivity. But the Romanian officials say that Romanian engineers have developed highly sophisticated pollution-control technologies and adapted them to imported production facilities in almost all instances. The officials contend that Romanian pollution-control technology is as advanced as that of any country in the world. An official of the National Council for Environmental Protection boasted: "We import very little environmental technology. Over 90% is made here. This percentage will be even higher in the next five years because of intense technological research here."[11]

Such contentions are difficult to corroborate, since access to industrial complexes in Romania is heavily restricted. Nevertheless, interviews with spokesmen for several firms that have constructed plants in Romania and for an international organization that has helped finance Romanian industrial-development projects indicate that cost-cutting considerations have often led the Chemical Ministry to cancel the installation of pollution-control technology even on some new plants.[12]

10. Interview, Paris, July 14, 1980 (anonymity requested).
11. Interview with Matei Nicolau, secretary, National Council for Environmental Protection, Bucharest, July 9, 1980.
12. This point was made in an interview with Jean Tixhon, industry analyst, Office of Environmental Affairs, Washingtion, D.C., June 25, 1982. The other interviews were conducted in Bucharest, Paris, New York, and Washington. These respondents requested anonymity.

The point to emphasize is that if Ireland, Spain, and Mexico often end up paying part of the bill (in the form of investment subsidies) when they require a company to install pollution-control equipment, Romania must pay the whole price, in hard currency, if it desires to include pollution control in its technology import deals. Thus the bargaining position of technology importers such as Romania is actually weaker when it comes to negotiations regarding the transfer of added technology for pollution abatement.

Channeling industry

Another important pollution-related aspect of the negotiation process between national governments and foreign companies is the selection of general location within the country. As pointed out in Chapter 2, spatial planning for the location of industry has become increasingly integral in the overall development plans of many countries. Governments in most rapidly industrializing countries are struggling to reverse strong centralizing tendencies for industrial location by seeking to encourage or force new industries to be built in less heavily developed areas. Indeed, the industrial-development strategies of Ireland, Spain, and Mexico described in the last chapter all stress the dispersion of industry to underindustrialized zones or growth-pole regions as major goals.

In all three cases, foreign investors have been among the first to feel the subtle "channeling" pressures of national government officials in addition to the explicit rewards and incentives offered to invest in outlying areas. In part, this is because incoming foreign companies tend to have fewer business ties and less "social" need to locate in one area or another. In addition, since many foreign companies are export oriented, it may not be as important for them to be strategically located near existing domestic population and industrial centers as it is for industries dependent on domestic demand. But many foreign companies do have other needs that often can be filled only in the most developed areas in underindustrialized countries: modern communications and transportation, suppliers of peripheral industrial goods and economic services, skilled-labor pools, and managerial expertise are a few. Without some basic guarantees that these amenities will be available in outlying areas, even substantial incentives and location restrictions may not encourage foreign investors to locate away from traditional industrialized areas.

Ireland has followed a strategy of spreading industrial plants built by foreign companies around the countryside, and the combination of fiscal inducements and active salesmanship by the IDA has been strikingly successful. The main reason for this strategy has been the Irish government's desire to halt migration from small villages to Cork and Dublin for employment. But in the course of steering different industries to particular areas around the country, pollution issues have also been important to IDA officials.

In the chemical industry, for example, pharmaceutical companies, with medium-sized plants and relatively small amounts of water effluent, have been guided by IDA to seek sites near villages located on inland streams. Conversely, industries that need larger plants and have greater amounts of effluent have been guided into two areas: Cork Harbor, in particular the Ringaskiddy area; and along the Shannon estuary in the western part of the country. Thus, when DuPont was negotiating with IDA about construction of a titanium dioxide plant in Ireland, IDA indicated that a six-hundred-acre site at Ringaskiddy was the only one suitable. And Alcan was instructed by IDA to find a site for its alumina plant within the tidal area of the Shannon.[13] Although no IDA policy makes the distinction mandatory, this channeling of industries has resulted in the creation of what one Irish lawyer describes as "mental pollution parks,"[14] areas in which the most heavily polluting industries can be cordoned off.

Industrial and automobile pollution, coupled with heavy traffic congestion, have forced Spanish officials to place major restrictions on the types of new industries that can be built in the Madrid and Barcelona areas. Particularly when a proposed plant will be owned by a foreign company, the government has been actively involved in steering industry to other regions. In 1979, Smith, Kline and French initiated planning-permission procedures to build a new plant to produce semitidyne in Alcala, a heavily industrialized area near Madrid. However, national officials intervened, forcing the company to move its new plant to Zaragoza, because they felt the industrial estate outside of town was a better location to absorb the air pollution the plant might generate.[15]

But, while Zaragoza was deemed a suitable location for Smith, Kline and French, Spanish officials have not been willing to allow new industries that may contribute significant amounts of water pollution there. Foret, the Spanish subsidiary for FMC Corporation, proposed in the late 1970s to build a new chlorine dry bleach plant in La Zida, near its existing peroxide plant in the Zaragoza area. Spanish government officials asked FMC not to file for planning permission because the Ebro River, which runs

13. Interviews with J. B. O'Sullivan, Ken Gunn, and Matthew Lynch.
14. Interview with Yvonne Scannell, professor of law, Trinity College, Dublin, March 25, 1980.
15. Interviews with Alfonso Ensenat, subdirector general for the industrial environment, Ministry of Industry and Energy, Madrid, Spain, June 18, 1980; and John Keeler, managing director, Smith, Kline and French (España), in Madrid, June 19, 1980.

through Zaragoza, is already heavily polluted and officials are trying to reduce the pollution. Eventually, Foret constructed the plant in Huelva, at the mouth of the Rio Tinto in southern Spain.[16]

Despite such actions, and the insistence by Spanish officials that multinational companies with the potential to generate pollution will hereafter have to build any facilities outside of already polluted areas, some observers express skepticism that the government would actually carry this to the point of turning away potential foreign investors. Foret executive Daniel O'Brien says:

> If we were to go to [the government regulators] and say that we were thinking about putting a silicates plant in near Madrid, they would at first say to move it somewhere else. But, if we insisted, I think they'd finally come back to talking about Madrid. It wouldn't be easy to accomplish, and the pollution restrictions would be tight, but right now they are absolutely desperate for new projects and I just don't see them turning one away in the end.[17]

As discussed in the last chapter, Mexico's problem with overconcentration of industry is probably as intense as in any country in the world. This situation has forced the government to try to channel new polluting industries to other areas. Deane Woods, regional director for Cyanamid, says Mexican government officials have radically changed their attitude toward what industries they want where in recent years. If Cyanamid proposed to build a phenolic resin plant in the Mexico City area, for example, Woods ways that government officials "would blow us away; there's no way they'd let us now, even though a few years ago they would not have batted an eye."[18]

The government has also introduced substantial incentives for new industries to locate in industrial port cities and other preferential industrial areas. And government officials have begun seriously to contemplate carrot-and-stick policies to encourage certain existing industries in the Mexico Valley to close up and move elsewhere. Already several domestic cement plants that were engulfed by rapid urban expansion and were causing serious health problems in Mexico City have been forced to close down.[19]

Of more concern for multinational corporations is the fact that the metropolitan Mexico City area now surrounds the entire industrialized strip in Naucalpan and Tlalnepantla, an area in the state of Mexico where

16. Interview with Daniel O'Brien, executive director, Foret, Barcelona, June 25, 1980.
17. Ibid.
18. Interview with Deane Woods, regional director, Cyanamid, Mexico City, July 27, 1982.
19. Interview with Guillermo Diaz Meja, director general for investigation of the effects of environment on health, Secretariat of Health and Welfare, Mexico City, July 15, 1982.

many foreign investors in the chemical industries operate plants. When this industrial area was set aside several decades ago, it was sufficiently removed from the urban area so as not to pose serious health and environmental hazards. But the explosive growth of Mexico City in the 1960s and 1970s pushed the contiguous metropolitan area well beyond Naucalpan. Today thousands of poor urban residents now live so close to industrial facilities that many yards or temporary dwellings share their back walls with heavy chemical plants. In 1981, an official with the Lopez Portillo administration announced that PEMEX's Azcapdtzalco refinery adjacent to Naucalpan would be required to close because of the serious health problems and dangers it posed for urban residents in the area. Although no date has been set for the closing, officials reiterated this claim in interviews in 1982 and 1983, and again in 1986.[20]

Industrial-location experts in Mexico doubt whether the government's incentives package is substantial enough to induce big companies to close still-profitable plants in the Mexico City area and move them to outlying priority zones, and Mexican officials have thus far been reluctant to decree a forced exodus. But Edward Wyegard, director of the Arthur D. Little office in Mexico, says that many foreign companies now considering future expansions or new investments are asking Arthur D. Little to study the economics of locating in areas outside the Mexico Valley. Wyegard contends that a prolonged economic recovery in Mexico is likely to be accompanied by the first serious wave of moves by major companies away from Mexico City.[21]

In fact, one problem is that Mexican officials are so concerned with stimulating growth away from Mexico City that they may be overly lax about environmental restrictions in areas of industrial growth. Wyegard says, for example, that his recent experience has been that when it comes to negotiating about pollution, government officials "don't care so long as a plant is going to built away from Mexico City and will create a lot of jobs."[22]

The obsolescing bargain

Most bargaining over precise pollution standards and discharge levels does not take place until after a general agreement has been reached

20. Manuel Lopez Portillo, subsecretary for environmental improvement, Secretariat for Health and Welfare, as quoted in "Pollution in Mexico City," unclassified cable from the U.S. Embassy in Mexico City to the State Department, June 18, 1982.
21. Interview with Edward Wyegard, director, Arthur D. Little (Mexico), Mexico City, July 28, 1982.
22. Ibid.

between a corporation and a national government about the financial terms for the project. Then the company submits a proposal for a specific site to the proper regional and local authorities and begins obtaining the necessary building and operating permits. Of course, discussion about possible pollution regulations is often initiated on an informal basis, with representatives of the national government acting as go-betweens, before a company officially finds a site and submits a proposal. In addition to steering industry toward or away from different regions, national industrial-development officials are often instrumental in helping foreign companies find the best potential sites in a region and in advising the companies on the political mood toward pollution and foreign companies at the local level.

Still, in spite of all the efforts to establish coordinated and uniform procedures, inherent flaws remain when countries rely primarily on bargaining about pollution guidelines on a plant-by-plant basis, either at the national level or within the structure of the local land-development process. Quite often, the problems that arise make it more difficult for the host country to extract concessions from foreign companies.

One problem is that companies, whether deliberately or not, sometimes make falsely optimistic promises about the environmental-quality standards they can meet, only to renegotiate when the plant is operating and they can hold jobs and government revenues as ransom. In Ireland, for example, local governments have driven very tough bargains with many pharmaceutical companies in recent years about the level of biochemical oxygen demand (BOD) that effluents may create in receiving waters. Some of the companies, in part because of the lack of municipal wastewater-treatment facilities, actually agreed to BOD levels below those attained in similar plants in the United States. Yet, in a number of cases, these companies subsequently encountered problems in meeting their agreed-upon levels. Once operational, at least four major pharmaceutical plants – Wellman International; Merck, Sharpe, and Dohme; Syntex; and Penn Chemicals – sought to renegotiate the BOD standards that had been agreed upon in negotiations with local officials before the plant began operation.[23]

A major difficulty often is that national and local governments do not have adequate information to determine the potential pollution problems from a proposed industrial plant or to evaluate the information provided by and promises made by company officials. Thus, even when they gather the conviction to strike a tough bargain on pollution control, government officials may be at a significant disadvantage. The outcome is often that

---

23. Based on interviews with IDA and local government officials and each of the companies named.

by the time a new plant is completed, either the government or the company feels the bargain is obsolete and seeks renegotiation.

Trial and error

Before about 1974 the tendency of local governments in Ireland was to bargain without much conviction on pollution control, for fear of losing the potential jobs and because of a general lack of knowledge about industrial process and wastes. Officials usually accepted company claims about the air and water discharges and often even imposed standards recommended by company officials. Invariably, local officials had neither the expertise nor the political will to bargain hard once a company indicated an unwillingness to go beyond a minimum level of treatment or meet stricter waste standards.

In 1968 the Quigley Company (a subsidiary of Pfizer) and an Irish company entered into a joint venture to construct a magnesite plant at Dungarvan, county Waterford, along Ireland's east coast. Local officials, while excited about the prospects of bringing several hundred jobs into Dungarvan, were apprehensive enough about the Pfizer proposal to request assistance from the Institute for Industrial Research and Standards (IIRS) in assigning pollution-control requirements. The letter from the county engineer to the IIRS said of the proposed plant:

> The points which give us concern are atmospheric pollution from the two chimneys each of which will be about eighty feet high, and forming part of the kiln installation, nuisance from noise which may be important as this is close to a tourist area and the golf course, and the deposit of silt in the harbour through the waste effluent from the factory. The applicants have informed us that these will be down to negligible levels but in such an important application the County Council feels that they could not rely on such vague terms and would wish that these items be quantified and standards fixed so that checks can be carried out periodically throughout the working life of the plant to ensure that nuisances do not develop.[24]

With the help of IIRS, local officials pushed the company to modify the design to prevent air pollution along the coast and in town, and to ensure that silt did not build up in the Dungarvan Harbor. However, county officials say today that they were forced at the time to rely heavily on information provided by and promises made by Pfizer. Local officials say that, on the basis of information from the company, they assumed that the main

24. Letter dated March 6, 1968, obtained from the Waterford County planning file on record in Dungarvan, Ireland.

effluent would be twenty tons per day of calcium sulfite $(CaSO_3)$ which they thought would be soluble in large quantities of water. Their main concern was to require Pfizer to run the discharge pipe out of Dungarvan Harbor into the open sea. They also sought to get Pfizer to adjust the height of the plant's chimneys and to install scrubbers to reduce air pollution.[25]

Pfizer agreed to run its discharge pipe to a point offshore where the currents would disperse the effluent and to raise the height of its smokestacks. Pfizer's consulting engineer had promised in a 1967 letter to the Waterford County Council that these methods were more than adequate to prevent any pollution problems: "The amount of silt would be negligible. The waste water would be discharged into the outer Harbour and will not have any polluting effect. . . . there would not be any atmospheric pollution due to the height of the chimney stack and the standard of the fuel oil which it is proposed to use, and . . . the noise would not cause any unpleasantness."[26]

Waterford County officials accepted Pfizer's claims and authorized construction of the plant subject to the agreed-upon modifications in the effluent pipe and the height of the stacks. It did not take long for Waterford officials, and people in and around Dungarvan, to realize they had made several mistakes. Several years after the plant began operations, a large area of the seabed adjacent to the plant's outfall, including a once-renowned fish-breeding area, was coated with a thick crust of calcium sulfate $(CaSO_4)$, commonly known as gypsum, a substance that is not very water soluble. Local officials even today insist that Pfizer originally said they would not have gypsum in the effluent. The entire area adjacent to the Pfizer plant is frequently covered with fine gray dust from Pfizer's stacks. Farmers more than five miles from the plant have complained about the effects of the dust on their crops. Several recreational beaches up the coast from Pfizer have sometimes been shrouded in thick haze even on sunny days. And golfers at the country club next to Pfizer complain that their shoes and clothing are sometimes coated with dust before they finish eighteen holes.[27]

25. Interview with James Shine, chief planning officer of Waterford County, Dungarvan, Ireland, April 1, 1980.
26. Letter dated December 18, 1967, obtained from the Waterford County planning file, on record in Dungarvan, Ireland.
27. The water pollution caused in Dungarvan Bay is noted in W. K. Downey and G. Ni Uid, *Coastal Pollution Assessment* (Dublin: National Board for Science and Technology, 1978). The complaints about Pfizer were echoed by several Waterford and Dungarvan officials in a public meeting attended by the author on April 1, 1980. Some of these problems are further detailed in a confidential report prepared for the Waterford County Council by the Planning Division of the National Institute for Physical Planning and Construction Research, October 1976.

James Shine, the chief planning officer of county Waterford, says of the Pfizer case:

> The county was just as concerned in 1968 about the possibility of adverse environmental impacts as we would be now. We were a lot less sophisticated then, though. Our main problem turned out to be that we had to rely quite a bit on the company's estimates about what pollution they would generate, how to reduce it, and how much that would cost. A number of the specifications outlined by the company later turned out to have been somewhat less than accurate.[28]

Concerned about both the environmental problems that could arise if local governments were not alert and the potential economic consequences if industrial-development proposals were long delayed by local haggling over pollution controls, the Irish Industrial Development Authority took steps in the 1970s to remove some of the uncertainties from the local pollution-control bargaining process. In 1970, after local authorities and various public groups complained that little information was available for evaluating the potential environmental impacts of incoming industries, the IDA had already begun to contract on an ad-hoc basis with the IIRS, a quasi-governmental research agency, to assess the environmental impact of all industrial projects requesting grant assistance from IDA. This practice became a formal procedure in 1972. IIRS gathers information from all incoming companies about proposed industrial processes, raw materials, wastes, and final products, in addition to information about the proposed site of the industrial facility. IIRS and An Foras Forbartha, the National Institute for Physical Planning and Construction Research, issue recommendations about the standards that should be met if the facility is approved by local governments and assisted by IDA.[29]

Although these recommendations are not mandatory for local governments, they have provided a useful benchmark. In addition, since the standards are frequently accepted at the local level, this procedure has added a measure of predictability to the process of allocating pollution-control standards, so that incoming companies can gain some idea about the eventual standards in advance. In recent years IDA has made it a condition of any grants to industry that the terms set by local authorities be fully met. For example, IDA on several occasions threatened to hold up disbursing final grant installments for the Pfizer-Dungarvan facility until the company made promised improvements to reduce pollution.

Similarly, the Spanish government made efforts in the late 1970s to improve the institutional processes for bargaining over pollution-control

28. Interview with James Shine.
29. Industrial Development Authority, *A Survey of Pollution in Ireland*, pp. 1–2.

standards. It established standardized procedures whereby national officials would recommend certain pollution standards to local governments.[30] In both Ireland and Spain, such steps were intended to ensure that industries would receive relatively similar pollution restrictions, to reduce the uncertainties created by the need for incoming companies to negotiate with local officials, and to provide local governments with badly needed technical assistance in evaluating industrial proposals. In Mexico, where the national government has been largely responsible for assigning basic pollution restrictions for new industries, the procedures also were standardized in the late 1970s. All foreign investors proposing industrial facilities must submit detailed information concerning wastes to be generated and waste-disposal facilities needed to the Secretariat of National Patrimony and Industrial Promotion and the Secretariat of Urban Development and Ecology.[31]

In all three countries, the efforts to develop better procedures for deciding on pollution controls apply to all industrial proposals, whether foreign or domestic. However, pollution-control standards for industrial plants are still allocated on a case-by-case basis, according to the whim of local or national officials, the amount of public pressure, and some rough calculation of local "assimilative" capacity. One result of the continuing ad-hoc nature of these processes is that an unspoken distinction is drawn between domestic and foreign companies. It appears that multinational corporations are often being asked to abide by stricter standards in these countries than they would have to meet if they were locally owned or if the same regulations applied to all industry. International investment codes and multilateral treaties would make this disparity impossible if national pollution standards for all new industrial plants were established.

Russian roulette with invisible pollutants

But there are also serious long-term risks that can result from the lack of uniform criteria for protecting workers and the public from industrial hazards. Not only are industrializing countries plagued by problems resulting from a lack of general environmental knowledge in the past, those seeking to attract international capital find continuing difficulty in generating adequate information to project the long-term environmental

30. Interviews with Alfonso Ensenat and Jeronimo Angulo Arambura.
31. Interviews with SEPAFIN officials: Amado Vega, subsecretary for the automotive and transport industries, July 16, 1982; and Rafael Martinez Conteras, chief of analysis and technical control, in the Subsecretariat for Automotive and Transport Industries, July 19, 1982. The procedures have been updated since 1982, when the Secretariat of Urban Development and Ecology took over responsibilities formerly held by the Secretariat of Health and Welfare.

impacts of proposed new industrial facilities. Some industries at first appear more benign by traditional measures of pollution than they eventually prove to be.

Authorities in most successful industrializing countries are much more adept (both at the national and the local level) than they were a decade ago at driving a hard bargain when a productive facility might pose obvious, significant, and unacceptable dangers to water and air quality, the general public, or workers in the plant. If a proposed factory has the potential to create black smoke, make loud noise, smell excessively, explode, or discharge chemicals that could kill fish or threaten public health, there is not much likelihood that the foreign company that plans to build it will be permitted significantly more leeway in Ireland or (to a somewhat lesser extent) Spain than in the home country. In both countries officials, as well as growing numbers of the general public, have access to information and technical data to enable them to assess the obviously detrimental environmental impacts and to prescribe the technologies and treatments they desire. Even in Mexico the most visible and dangerous types of pollution are no longer permitted when foreign investors open new production facilities.

But when it comes to more subtle forms of environmental hazards posed by certain types of industrial facilities, none of these countries is adequately equipped to evaluate proposals or to make reasonable assessments about the long-term implications of accepting the industry. For example, host countries are still not generally well informed about the problems that may develop when small amounts of chemicals build up in receiving waters or human bodies over the long term or when workers and the public are exposed to hazardous substances that do not smell or burn.

Many countries are now discovering that some industries that appeared to have no significant pollution problems are being linked to major public-health or pollution problems after they have been in operation for a long period. It is very difficult for industrial-development authorities in rapidly industrializing countries to conduct enough research on their own or be aware of all the latest research in the United States, and thus they find it difficult to anticipate such problems when they sit down to bargain with a foreign company over a particular industrial proposal. People who live and work around industries where later evidence shows the potential for serious health problems often react angrily and cannot easily be reassured by new safety standards or procedures. Such real and public-relations problems are illustrated by the cases in Ireland involving the use of asbestos by Raybestos Manhattan and the use of acrylonitrile by a Japanese firm, Asahi, which operates a large facility on the west coast of Ireland in Killala, county Mayo.

Neither the Raybestos plant nor the Asahi plant seemed likely to pollute or to cause dangers to public health when they were built in the mid 1970s. Both brought a large number of jobs to depressed areas and appeared to fit well into the IDA's evolving industrial-development strategy. In the case of Asahi, which is one of Ireland's largest manufacturing plants and produces acrylic fiber from acrylonitrile, methyl acrylate, and nitric acid, the remoteness of the plant, an advanced water treatment unit, and the fact that none of these chemicals would actually be produced in Ireland muted most of the environmental objections to the plan. Irish officials envisioned the Asahi plant as a chemical-industry version of an off-shore electronics component-assembly plant that would import all the components in prefabricated form and simply put them together for reexport.[32]

It was only after the Raybestos and Asahi plants were operational that scientific evidence from the United States and Great Britain began to alarm local officials, workers, and the general public about the potential long-term hazards of exposure to acrylonitrile and asbestos. The resulting controversy at Raybestos is described in the next chapter. At Asahi the concern that has arisen since DuPont announced in the late 1970s that high-level exposure to acrylonitrile can cause cancer has been more sporadic and muted. County officials claim that Asahi is enforcing strict safety and exposure rules inside the factory.[33] But the workers, many of whom would be left unemployed in a remote and depressed region if Asahi were to close, remain apprehensive about the long-term health problems they may face. Moreover, they have frequently contended that the Asahi management is indifferent to their health and safety.[34]

Today, although many officials in Ireland continue to defend the safety records of both Raybestos and Asahi, it is difficult to find officials who do not say they would at least scrutinize the two plant proposals more closely now because of the new information. Matthew Lynch of the IIRS, which is charged with evaluating the environmental risks of industries for local governments and the IDA, says:

> It is safe to say that if we had had the information we have today about asbestos and acrylonitrile, neither Raybestos nor Asahi would

32. Interview with Matthew Lynch.
33. M. O'Malley, "The Asahi Experience" (Paper presented at the Annual Conference on "Planning for Industrial Development," Dublin, Ireland, November 17, 1978).
34. John Mulcahy, "What Worries the Asahi Workers," *Hibernia*, July 26, 1979; and John Mulcahy, "Asahi Booms despite Problems," *Hibernia*, September 20, 1979.

have been permitted to come to Ireland except under very restrictive circumstances. But we cannot generate the information on long-term health hazards here in Ireland. We are still dependent on the United States and Britain; sometimes it takes several years before new scientific information reaches us.[35]

The lack of advanced research capabilities, particularly in environmental carcinogens and the imperfections in information-transfer networks from the more advanced nations sometimes leave industrial-development officials and local governments in industrializing countries playing a sort of Russian roulette with the new industries they accept. Now, although officials in both Ireland and Spain do not speak about it very openly, there is a growing concern about the pharmaceutical industry, which has played such an important part in the industrial-development strategies of both countries in recent years.

The Spanish seem only vaguely concerned as yet. Alfonso Ensenat says that Spanish regulatory officials do receive information through the World Health Organization, and the U.S. Environmental Protection Agency, and the European Economic Community about the more subtle forms of environmental hazards that may arise in an industry like pharmaceuticals. But, he says, his department does not have the capability to stay abreast of all the latest developments. "Only a very underindustrialized country would purposely industrialize by risking the health of its population," Ensenat says. However, he acknowledges, "our problem is that we cannot always see into the future." A pharmaceutical plant may seem attractive now, he says, because it has only a trickle of effluent and a puff of white smoke as compared to a big chemical plant, "but let's hope that we do not have to pay the price later."[36] Despite Ensenat's interest, Evilio Quinones, general manager of Merck, Sharpe, and Dohme, España, noted in the early 1980s that there was not much outward concern in Spain about possible long-term problems from his industry. "Our industry is very concerned about the potential for discovering more links with cancer, but I don't see anyone within the Spanish government particularly aware," he says.[37]

In Ireland the concern about the pharmaceutical industry has been more widespread, not only among officials of the central government but also among local officials and the general public. This is partly because of the odor problems that have plagued several prominent U.S. firms, the concern about industrial plants being built in the rural countryside, and the

35. Interview with Matthew Lynch.
36. Interview with Alfonso Ensenat.
37. Interview with Evilio Quinones, general manager, Merck, Sharpe, and Dohme (España), in Madrid, June 17, 1980.

rise of "social blockage" in Ireland. Public fears of the unknown have been especially marked in the case of a plant operated by Syntex in county Clare. Most national and local officials are sympathetic with Syntex in its running battles with local citizens who have taken the company to court for creating a smelly nuisance. The odor itself is not objectionable; it is similar to a sweet perfume. However, local officials are not sure how far they should go in fighting for Syntex because they are uncertain whether nerolin – the by-product in Syntex's emissions that creates the sweet, acrid smell – may prove to cause adverse long-term health effects.[38] The company says categorically that there are no known health hazards from nerolin. But some Irish officials are alarmed by the conflicting evidence cited in the controversy between Syntex and the U.S. Food and Drug Administration in the late 1970s over premarket testing performed on the arthritis drug Neprosyn, which is what Syntex makes in its Irish plant.[39] Ultimately, Irish officials have no way of knowing whether in the long term the workers and local residents will pay for the employment generated by Syntex with their health. They must simply wait either for definitive research findings from the United States or for long-term data to provide a statistical picture of workers and local residents in comparison with national norms.

Obtaining information

A problem related to the inability to conduct adequate basic research is that multinational firms are frequently very guarded in the information they will provide to national and local officials. Sometimes, as Dungarvan officials claim was the case with Pfizer when it proposed to build the magnesite plant in 1968, corporate officials appear to have offered misleading or at least confusing information to local officials. But the problems arise more often from the omission of relevant information than from blatantly false statements. Corporate spokesmen, claiming the need to protect proprietary information, are reluctant to discuss certain aspects of their production processes with outside officials. Tom Kilgarrif, chief assistant

38. Les Crowley, "Syntex in Bad Odour in U.S. and Co. Clare," *Hibernia*, May 25, 1978; and "High Court Asked to Prevent Plant from Emitting Offensive Chemical Stench," *International Environment Reporter*, March 3, 1981.
39. See "Suit Is Filed against Syntex," *New York Times*, September 2, 1976, p. 49; "F.D.A. Acts to Remove Painkiller from Market," *New York Times*, October 15, 1976, p. I-12; "Syntex Assails F.D.A. over Report of Concern's Anti-Arthritis Drug," *New York Times*, October 20, 1976, p. 17; "Calandra Out as Bio-Test Head; Concern under Study by F.D.S.," *New York Times*, March 26, 1977, p. 29; "Syntex Unit Enters Accord with Philips," *New York Times*, June 15, 1977, p. IV-14; and "Syntex Reaches Settlement on Suits," *New York Times*, February 17, 1979, p. 28.

county engineer for sanitary services in county Westmeath, says that his office always has trouble getting adequate information from the foreign firms located in the county:

> We have a problem getting enough information to help us evaluate a proposal or identify the source of a problem that develops downstream [from Mullingar] because the companies claim thay cannot divulge trade secrets. Sometimes we have to assemble a whole team of experts and go through a number of tests just to find out basic things that the companies could tell us in a minute. We have to be trusted with some of this information if we are going to be able to make reasonable judgments and answer to our own public. Besides, I believe that in many cases if the companies were more forthcoming, a lot of rows that occur later on could be avoided. People get upset when they think a company is hiding some bit of information or leading them astray.[40]

This lament is reiterated by many local officials in Ireland who feel that multinational firms should make a greater effort to share technical and process-oriented data that would make it easier to evaluate the impact of the firms on the air and water around them. Up to a point, corporate officials tend to be very cooperative in providing information to local officials. Officials from local and national governments in Ireland and Spain, encouraged by company representatives, frequently travel to the United States to examine plants similar to the ones that a company proposes to build in their country. In the Syntex case, for example, local officials and representatives of IIRS visited the Boulder, Colorado, plant operated by a Syntex subsidiary, Arapahoe Chemicals, before granting approval for construction of a Syntex plant in Ireland. What companies are often slow to provide, however, is a detailed breakdown of all chemical inputs, intermediate and final products, and byproducts associated with the plant.

One problem is that dangerous intermediate chemicals are sometimes produced as a result of in-plant production processes and then are used or altered at a later stage of production. Since these chemical intermediates are neither transported into the factory nor expelled from it, officials charged with regulating the internal environment of the plant and the overall risks to the public may not even know of their existence. This could present serious problems, local officials contend, if, for instance, the local fire brigade were called in to help with a fire or explosion but had no idea what chemical substances to expect.

Another problem is that many multinational firms, particularly those in

40. Interview with Tom Kilgarrif, chief assistant county engineer for sanitary services for Westmeath County, Ireland, April 9, 1980.

the pharmaceutical and light chemical industries, frequently change processes, raw materials, and final products without informing local officials. From a company's standpoint, the ability to switch rapidly in response to changing market demands is essential. Corporate officials say it is impossible to predict at a particular time (especially during the initial planning process) all of the possible products and raw materials they will use in the future. Moreover, they contend that if they had to make a new application every time they changed some aspect of their production process, the burdens of delay and possible public controversy would be too great.

However, from the perspective of local officials, trouble often begins when a company makes process changes. For example, the odors at two pharmaceutical plants in Ireland – Merck, Sharpe, and Dohme in Carrick-on-Suir and Penn Chemicals in Ringaskiddy – did not begin until both plants had been in operation for some time. Although neither violated its planning permissions by later beginning to produce the products that resulted in the odors (in fact, both had listed the products that resulted in their original planning applications) the sudden appearance of the smells and the public outcries that arose caught local officials unprepared.

Public concern in Ireland has been particularly acute in county Cork (where a large number of foreign chemical and pharmaceutical companies are located), and it often centers on the companies' use of the blanket of proprietary information. Many contend that county officials have been manipulated into extending broad mandates to corporations to produce almost anything they want after receiving planning permission. Public concern peaked in 1978 when Eli Lilly's Irish subsidiary, Elanco, applied for planning permission to construct a $12 million pharmaceutical plant in Kinsale, county Cork. Lilly had discussed the construction of a facility to produce its leading herbicide, Treflan, but was discouraged by both local and IDA officials. When it did file its planning application, Elanco specified only that the plant would produce pharmaceuticals. When the county council requested more specific information, the company submitted a list of eleven broad categories, including semisynthetic antibiotics, antihistamines, analgesics, antibacterial agents, and antidepressants. Although the first condition of the subsequent planning permission restricted Elanco to the production of materials that fell into the eleven categories, critics charged that this in effect gave Elanco permission to produce virtually any one of thousands of chemical products at any time without notifying local authorities and the public.[41]

An Taisce, the National Trust of Ireland, objected to the county Cork

41. "The Harbour Board Commissioners Meeting with Elanco," *Kinsale and District News Pictorial,* August 1978, p. 15.

planning permission, arguing to both company and government officials that public confidence and the safety preparations of public agencies depended on knowing more specifically what the Elanco plant would produce. Subsequently, An Taisce convinced Elanco and the Cork County Council to sign a binding agreement amending the first condition and restricting the company to the production of a limited number of named chemicals unless it reapplies for a new planning permission from the county.[42] Since then, all planning permissions issued by county Cork have included a specific list of products and chemicals to be manufactured in the proposed plant.

The information gap between multinational companies and government officials generally works against the interests of the host country. The initial bargaining process often therefore culminates in an agreement with insufficient pollution-control measures. And, once a plant is operational, it may be difficult for a government to renegotiate the standards for a number of reasons: the need to maintain among international investors a reputation for keeping promises; the fear that the company will close the plant rather than amend its pollution-control procedures; the generally high costs of retrofitting industrial plants for pollution control.

But the uncertainty created by the lack of information available to government regulators in the bargaining over pollution control can also work against the interests of multinational investors in both the short and the long term. The short-term problems are illustrated by the difficulties encountered several years ago by Eli Lilly in Córdoba, Spain. Lilly had bought a large tract of land, completed discussions with national officials regarding fiscal assistance, and was preparing to begin construction on a new plant just outside Córdoba along the Guadalquivir River. In the process of obtaining final planning and zoning permits from municipal officials in Córdoba, the company began discussions with the local water authority about water-pollution controls.

Although unemployment was extremely high in Córdoba, local officials were also concerned that new industrial plants not contribute to further degradation of the Guadalquivir, which was already seriously polluted by agricultural wastes and municipal sewage. Since they did not have the scientific or technical ability to evaluate the Lilly proposal themselves, Córdoban officials relied on bits and pieces of information about pollution controls obtained from both the United States and Great Britain. As often happens in less-industrialized countries, officials sought to establish standards for Lilly's water effluent by borrowing from the documents of these

42. "An Taisce Signs Unique Agreement," *Taisce Journal* 3, nos. 2, 3, (May–October 1979):37.

advanced countries. However, they became confused about the distinction between discharge standards, which apply to the quality of the effluent, and ambient standards, which apply to the quality of the waters that receive the effluent. This confusion caused a series of arguments, first among the bureaucrats and later with elected officials, that delayed the issuance of Lilly's final construction permits.[43]

Eventually, Lilly canceled its plans for construction at the Córdoba site and bought an existing plant from a Spanish company north of Madrid. Lilly officials insist that the decision to renovate was prompted by changing economic factors and the availability of the already-built plant. They express confidence that they could have obtained the necessary permits to construct the Córdoba plant if they had persisted.[44] Nevertheless, the wrangling that resulted when local officials were poorly informed about pollution control and confused about the application of standards in the United States and Great Britain ended up working against Lilly's efforts to get its plant construction started expeditiously. The mayor of Córdoba, Julio Anguita, believes that the resulting delay was a major factor in Lilly's decision to cancel, as does the director of Procter and Gamble's Spanish operations, John Asher. In fact, Asher says that Procter benefited from Lilly's misfortune because the mayor's office stepped in to expedite the pollution-control bargaining process when Procter applied for permits for its new plant in Córdoba.[45]

Local politics and the bargaining process

As the last section emphasized, host-country officials at the local and national levels frequently must bargain about pollution control with less-than-perfect information about the immediate and potential long-term environmental problems associated with different industries. Sometimes this means that less-than-adequate environmental controls are assigned to a particular industrial plant, as appears to have happened in several instances in Ireland. However, as Eli Lilly found in Córdoba, the lack of knowledge available to government officials about pollution-control measures can also work against companies.

Poor information is not the only uncertainty that can destabilize the bargaining process. A problem with long-term repercussions for multi-

43. This account is based on interviews with Jesus Martin Filipe, general manager for Eli Lilly (España), Madrid, July 4, 1980; Julio Anguita, mayor of Córdoba, July 1, 1980; John Asher, director of Procter and Gamble (España), Madrid, June 19, 1980; and C. P. (Bert) Gorman, director of environmental affairs for Eli Lilly (USA), Washington, D.C., May 13, 1981.
44. Letter from C. P. (Bert) Gorman, dated May 22, 1981.
45. Interviews with Julio Anguita and John Asher.

nationals is that the multilevel, interdependent process by which pollution-control standards are ultimately assigned for individual industrial facilities is frequently more complicated and more politicized than the economic bargaining that primarily takes place between national governments and foreign corporations. The addition of another group of actors, regional and local governments, adds a great deal of uncertainty and potential for conflict to the bargaining process. Moreover, negotiations between local governments and companies over sites and industrial standards often are subject to much more public scrutiny than the initial negotiations at the national level.

The resulting negotiations at the local level can be complicated. Representatives of the national government, eager to bring in certain industries, may make informal promises or assessments about the eventual pollution standards to be applied by local governments. Agreements on grant money and infrastructure to be provided by the national government to assist in pollution control may be worked out on the basis of such assessments. Yet local governments, because they are under pressure from citizens or because they are controlled by a different political party from that of the central government, may confound or delay these agreements by striking a hard bargain on pollution controls. Sometimes, in fact, they go to extremes, ignoring economic and technical limitations. Alternatively, a local government under great pressure to create jobs and ease local unemployment and not having adequate scientific knowledge at hand may not make any effort at all to negotiate seriously with a company over effluent and emissions standards, even when national officials recommend certain standards.

Sometimes local politics prevents governments from upholding their end of the bargain to provide the services, infrastructure, or fiscal assistance that they have agreed to make available to help companies with waste disposal. Pfizer's experience at its other Irish industrial complex in Ringaskiddy, located in the outer part of Cork Harbor, illustrates how a local government may be forced by political pressures to renegotiate the deals it has struck with foreign investors. Pfizer received permission from the Cork County Council in 1970 to dump raw organic nutrients from its organic-chemicals and organic-synthesis complex directly into Cork Harbor. The permission was granted by Cork officials after analysis indicated that the assimilative capacity of Cork Harbor was very large and could without difficulty disperse and neutralize the Pfizer waste.

But county Cork officials came under pressure from local citizens, and An Taisce subsequently sought to revoke permission for Pfizer to dump its effluent in the harbor. At the time (in 1973) the argument used to renege on the original deal was not that the harbor was overly polluted, but that

Pfizer had been allocated more than 50 percent of the harbor's estimated assimilative capacity. Environmental and economic-development groups joined to argue that even though Pfizer was using only about one-third of its allowance, for one firm to tie up so much of the total capacity was unfair to other firms and might stifle future industrial-development plans.[46] Today, Pfizer no longer is permitted to discharge into Cork Harbor and instead barges its nutrient-rich wastes out to sea every day.[47]

The Pfizer-Ringaskiddy case demonstrates that changing local circumstances, political pressures, and public activism can bring about very different attitudes among local officials only a short time after negotiations on pollution control have been concluded. A classic illustration of how uncertain local circumstances can affect agreed-upon pollution-control plans of multinational companies occurred several years ago after the Ford Motor Company decided to build a major new automobile plant in Spain.

Renouncing the deal

Under the old Francoist autarchic international-investment policies, foreign automobile manufacturers were limited in the percentage of outstanding capital they could control, could produce only for the Spanish market, and could use only a small proportion of imports in their production process. Thus the major international automobile firms that owned a stake in production facilities in Spain – Chrysler, Fiat, Volkswagen, and British Leyland – not only operated relatively small plants but also had to produce nearly all their own accessories on all the models they sold in Spain. All of these restrictions made them relatively inefficient producers.

In the early 1970s, as Spain sought to reach trading agreements with the members of the EEC and to consider the possibility of eventual membership in the EEC, it became clear that when the high tariff barriers were reduced, the Spanish automobile industry would have a difficult time competing and could no longer attract international firms to produce solely for the Spanish market. Ford was one of the first major international firms, and the first automobile manufacturer, to make plans to build a new production facility in this changing environment. When negotiations began in 1972, the Spanish government was looking for three principal contributions from a Ford production plant: a very large foreign investment, at

46. Industrial Development Authority, *A Survey of Pollution in Ireland*, pp. 2–3.
47. Interviews with Phillip Mulally, chairman of An Taisce, Cork, Ireland, April 3, 1980; and Cashel Riorden, manager of pollution control for Pfizer, Ringaskiddy, Ireland, April 3, 1980.

least several thousand jobs for Spanish workers, and large amounts of foreign exchange generated through exports.[48] For its part, Ford bargained for three further changes in Spanish foreign investment rules: lower local-content requirements, since it wanted to integrate its proposed Spanish facility into its European production network; reduced or suspended duties on advanced technology imported for use in the Spanish plant; and the right to maintain 100 percent ownership by the parent company, Ford Motor Company USA.[49]

Ford proposed to build a $300 million automobile plant to employ over 7,500 workers and produce close to 250,000 cars annually, with at least two-thirds of these to be exported. This proposal met the government's three major needs. In return, a special decree promulgated on December 23, 1972, made the car industry an industry of preferential interest. It thus cleared the way for the exceptions to the foreign-investment rules that Ford desired. The decree also made Ford eligible under a 1963 law for substantial government tax breaks and subsidies in the building and operation of its plant.[50] These subsidies were important, because investment incentives have become major considerations in Ford's European location decisions in recent years. Carl Levy, director of Ford España, says of Ford's instigation of multicountry bidding wars: "It's simple. We go where the best incentives are because we need them. Maybe a richer company like General Motors needn't make this the top priority, but we cannot afford that luxury."[51]

Ford's formal proposal to build a Spanish plant was tendered on the same day that the special decree, which became known as the "Ford decree," was passed. The Spanish government announced its official acceptance of the proposal in April 1973.[52] During the time negotiations were going on with the national government, Ford was also narrowing down its choices for the actual site of the plant. Government officials put very few restrictions on the location of the plant. Levy says, for example, that the Ministry of Labor suggested only that Ford not locate in Madrid or Barcelona because these overcrowded areas were already the home of many foreign industries, and that the company stay away from the Basque

48. Interview with Angel Molina, subdirector general for transport, Ministry of Industry and Energy, Madrid, June 13, 1980.

49. Interview with Carl Levy, director of Ford (España), in Madrid, June 16, 1980.

50. The "Ford decree" as well as the 1963 law outlining the benefits offered to industries of preferential interest are described in *A Guide to Business in Spain (4): Development Incentives and Export Promotion,* 2d ed. (Madrid: Ministry of Commerce and Tourism, 1979), p. 6.

51. Interview with Carl Levy.

52. *Facts on File* 33, no. 1,682 (January 21–27, 1973):67, and no. 1,697 (May 6–12, 1973):387.

country in the north because of the political problems that were intensifying in that region.[53]

Ford did have certain criteria, though, that restricted the number of potential sites. It needed an area with good access to large port facilities for shipping its cars abroad, large amounts of land, a large surplus of skilled and unskilled labor, and provincial and local governments willing and able to install major new infrastructure for transportation, communication, power supply, water supply, and waste disposal. To Ford, the most attractive siting locations were in the province containing the country's third largest city and second largest port, Valencia, located midway down Spain's eastern Mediterranean coast.

Valencian authorities showed Ford three possible areas near the city and put Ford in contact with officials from local governments *(municipios)*. Ford, Valencian officials, and the local government of Almusafes finally agreed on a site located about fifteen kilometers south of Valencia in a hitherto predominantly agricultural area. Ford was left on its own to negotiate for the purchase of almost 650 small, privately owned farms that constituted the site. But the Valencian provincial government agreed to provide, with the assistance of central-government funds, the new infrastructure that would be needed to service the Almusafes plant.[54]

Pollution did not figure centrally in any of these negotiations with the regional and local governments, although one of Ford's selling points to the local population was that it was providing "commerce without chimneys."[55] No one expected any significant pollution problems, either real or from a public relations standpoint. Ford had plans to treat wastewater from its paint shop and other operations before discharging it, and the Valencian government promised to build a collector pipe to carry the treated water from the Ford site as part of its infrastructural plans.

Nevertheless, as the Ford plant neared completion in 1976, changing circumstances forced Ford to initiate hastily a new series of negotiations over plant discharges with Valencian and local officials. This bargaining process and its subsequent outcome illustrates clearly just how politicized such negotiations can become.

The Valencian provincial government's plan to provide an outlet pipe for Ford's treated wastewater was part of an ambitious scheme to alleviate water pollution around the city of Valencia and in the Albufera, a famous freshwater lake near the Ford factory. The original plan was for the Span-

53. Interview with Carl Levy.
54. As described by local and Ford officials and by "Ford Comes to Spain" (Barcelona: Ford, 1976).
55. Ibid., p. 23.

ish government, as part of the national antipollution program announced in 1971, to put up substantial appropriations for the construction of up to six waste-treatment facilities around the perimeter of the Albufera to treat agricultural, municipal, and industrial wastes before they went into the lake.[56]

In 1976 no construction had begun, and mounting costs had reduced the plan to the building of a canal that would channel water around the Albufera and directly out to sea. In addition, there were no indications that construction on the canal would begin soon, as the national and local governments were locked in a dispute over who would pay what share of the total costs. The central government balked at picking up the entire tab, wanting local governments to pay at least a small share. Although expressing great concern about pollution, Valencian officials and local socialist mayors were reluctant to spend money on any large programs that did not directly create significant numbers of permanent jobs.[57]

As it became clear that the collector pipe would not be ready when the factory opened, Ford began to make other plans for discharging its waste-water after it was treated. At first, the proposed alternative, letting the water run back into the drainage and irrigation ditches that flow through the marshy bottomland at the head of the Albufera, did not seem to pose problems, since the Valencian Rivers Board and the Spanish Ministry of Agriculture certified that wastewater samples from Ford's sister plant in West Germany were suitable for use in irrigation.[58] In any case, the entire area was already heavily polluted. Chemical wastes from many small chemical manufacturers located next to the Albufera, agricultural wastes and fertilizers from farmers in the area, and raw sewage from about eight different villages were all flowing through the drainage system or directly into the Albufera. But, at the same time that Ford was requesting permission from provincial and local government officials to discharge its waste-water into the Albufera network, local concern about pollution in the Albufera was growing rapidly.

The Lago Albufera, which is about twelve kilometers south of Valencia, now covers about 2,730 hectares and has a circumference of about twenty-eight kilometers. Although once connected with the Mediterranean, it is today separated from the sea by a one-kilometer stretch of sand. For centuries the freshwater Albufera lagoon has been silting up; much of the land

56. Interviews with Angel Molina, Alfonso Ensenat, and Jeronimo Angulo Arambura.
57. Interviews with local officials and Juan Omenaca, a local journalist who covered the Ford situation for Valencian papers, in Almusafes, Spain, June 19, 1980.
58. Ibid.

on the western side (where the Ford plant is located) was once part of the lake.[59]

In recent years eutrophication (resulting from siltation and increased nutrients from municipal and agricultural wastes) and chemical pollution (from pesticide residues and wastes from hundreds of small manufacturers on the western edge of the lake) have both increased. This has posed problems for local governments because the lake has been a source of fresh water and income from recreational facilities. In addition, conservationists and fish-and-wildlife authorities have expressed alarm because the lake has always been rich in fish and fowl. In fact, the Albufera lagoon is one of the major gathering points for migratory birds along the Mediterranean coast.[60]

The municipality of Valencia actually controls Lago Albufera, so Ford had to seek its permission to discharge water that would end up in the lake. With local newspapers focusing on the Albufera's serious pollution problems and groups organizing marches and protest campaigns against pollution in Valencia, Ford's proposal to discharge wastewater became a major political issue. Even though they had already certified Ford's wastewater as suitable for irrigation purposes, Valencian officials declined to permit Ford to discharge its wastewater, partly because they found it nearly impossible from a public-relations standpoint to endorse publicly a new proposal to put any kind of waste in the Albufera. But there were other, even more political reasons.

By a tradition that extends back to the reign of Jaime I in the thirteenth century, the network of drainage and irrigation ditches along the western fringes of the Albufera is actually owned and controlled by a private organization, Acequia Real de Jucar, which is composed of representatives of the local government and landowners served by the network. The "owners of the ditches" decided in the midst of great public turmoil to oppose Ford's discharge plans.[61] This decision was not necessarily binding on Valencian officials, who probably could have allowed Ford to discharge directly into the lake. That did not matter, however, since the Valencian authorities decided they did not want to take the political backlash that might come if they approved Ford's plans without the consent of the nominal owners of the canals.

In addition, both the owners of the ditches and the Valencian officials

59. The history of the Albufera is described in Altantica de Gragadas, "Dredging the Lago Albufera" (Valencia: Ilaco Iberica, 1970).
60. Ibid.
61. Ibid., and interviews with Juan Omenaca, Carl Levy, and local officials.

had strong reasons for refusing the Ford request that were not strictly related to the scientific question of the quality of the treated effluent. Valencian officials, wanting the national government to cover all the costs of the proposed drainage canal around the Albufera, figured that the Ford project was important enough to prompt the central government to act quickly to build the canal. Barring this, they held the hope that Ford itself would assume responsibility for the canal. The owners of the ditches, too, saw Ford as a potential means of cleaning up the trenches. Although the owners and local governments were reluctant to crack down on local polluters (especially the small chemical plants) and were unwilling to spend money themselves, they hoped to use the pipe or canal that Ford would build to clear away pollution from other local sources.[62]

Ford, with the construction of the factory running ahead of schedule, faced the prospect of having to delay opening simply because it had no place to discharge water. At one point, municipal officials in Valencia proposed that Ford build a pipe to pump its water to irrigate elevated arid lands about ten kilometers inland. However, Ford officials declined, claiming that the proposal was merely a ruse to get the lands irrigated. Besides, they contended, if the water could be used for irrigation in the mountains, why not in the Albufera vicinity?[63]

In the end, shortly before the factory began production, Ford constructed two large holding lagoons at the Almusafes site. When the plant opened, Ford used the water to irrigate over one hundred hectares of undeveloped land on its site and permitted local tenant farmers to plant and harvest crops of alfalfa and oranges in these fields.[64] In the meantime, Ford's request to discharge treated wastewater is still pending with Valencian officials, and plans to construct a canal around the Albufera have been all but shelved because of rising construction costs and severe fiscal difficulties.

The evolution of bargaining strength

Many studies of the general bargaining relationship between host countries and multinational corporations have noted that the initial bargaining advantage held by MNCs tends to lessen over time, as capital is sunk into the physical plant and as the host country gains more knowledge about the industry in general and about dealing with the specific company. In some respects, this is true of the bargaining relationship between local governments and multinationals with regard to pollution matters.

62. De Gragadas, "Dredging the Lago Albufera."
63. Interview with Carl Levy.
64. The site was visited by the author on June 19, 1980.

Pfizer, for example, might not have come to Ringaskiddy if it had known in 1970 that it would later be required to barge its nutrient-rich effluent out to sea rather than make use of the assimilative capacity of the bay. Yet, because it had built two large integrated plants in Ringaskiddy, its bargaining strength had diminished when the rules were changed. The local government had substantial leeway to change the rules without fear that Pfizer would abandon its multimillion-dollar plants.

On the other hand, companies continue to use the threat of closing the plant and moving elsewhere whenever they can. This has proven to be effective deterrence for Pfizer at Dungarvan. Local officials remain hesitant to crack down on Pfizer and risk the job loss, even though a recent report indicates that Pfizer's use of 89 percent of the Dungarvan Harbor's assimilative capacity has inhibited other industrial development.[65] Jim Shine, chief planning officer of county Waterford, says: "There must be a manual that U.S. industrialists use to deal when local authorities want to get the plant to clean up the muck. First, make some veiled threats to close. Then get the workers and unions involved. Then just sit back and let concern about jobs and the economy divide public opinion enough to immobilize local officials."[66]

In large measure, the difference in the evolving bargaining strength of Pfizer at Dungarvan and that of Pfizer at Ringaskiddy is related to three factors: the economic impact that a plant shutdown would have in each area, the relative efficiency and profitability of each plant, and the total capital invested in each plant. Pfizer at Ringaskiddy is a huge, integrated organic-chemicals complex. For Pfizer to rebuild the plant elsewhere would cost enormous sums today, and besides it is a profitable operation. Even though it employs close to a thousand workers, it is only one of many industrial plants in the Cork area. Its closing would hurt but not devastate the Cork economy. These circumstances gave local government more chance of changing the rules without pushing Pfizer out and gave Pfizer an incentive to comply unless the changes were drastic.

For Pfizer's Dungarvan operation, the situation was very different. The magnesite plant, though a large capital investment, is not nearly as sophisticated technologically as an organic-chemicals plant. Indeed, the plant has reportedly only been marginally profitable, and an Irish company, Cement Roadstone, recently opened up a more modern and efficient magnesite plant north of Dublin that has directly cut into Pfizer's markets. Although the plant employs fewer workers than Pfizer (about three hundred) it is one of the few large industrial operations in the Dungarvan area. For these reasons, local officials were in a more delicate position; the

65. Downey and Uid, *Coastal Pollution Assessment*, p. 207.
66. Interview with James Shine.

threshold for pushing Pfizer to close the operation was much lower than for Pfizer at Ringaskiddy, and the consequences of a closing would be more severe for Dungarvan's economy than for Cork's.

But political patronage also can affect the bargaining picture. Local officials in Dungarvan, for example, point out privately that the national government has sometimes exerted political pressure to force them to avoid confrontation over pollution at Pfizer's Dungarvan facility. John A. Mulcahy, a prominent Irish businessman and former president of the Quigley Company, the Pfizer subsidiary operating the Dungarvan plant, not only wields enormous political clout in Ireland, but was a major contributor to Richard Nixon's presidential campaign in 1972 and hosted Nixon when he visited Ireland in 1970. Thus, local officials say, representatives of the Irish government expressed concern on several occasions that nothing be done to antagonize Mulcahy, whose political and business connections on both sides of the Altantic were seen as important in fostering Ireland's image of favoring U.S. investment.[67]

The evolution of the relative bargaining strength between companies and host-country governments thus cannot be judged only on the basis of the investment cycle, the host-country learning curve, and the level of technology used by the company. By these measures Pfizer's bargaining strength for its Ringaskiddy plant should have been more solid and enduring than for its plant in Dungarvan.

In determining the balance of power in bargaining over pollution controls, several other variables seem to have been more important than the factors that predominate in most bargaining models of relations between multinational corporations and host countries. These variables are those that determine whether governmental officials have either the will or sense a political necessity to strike an uncompromising position on pollution control. The strength or weakness of the local economy influences how much local officials are willing to risk the possibility that the company will relocate. The relative profitability of the plant determines how far the local governments can actually push the company to make new, nonproductive capital investments. And local political factors are crucial in determining, on the one hand, how much political pressure the company can apply on local offficials, and, on the other, the degree to which pollution becomes an important political issue for the public.

Conclusions

As this chapter has illustrated, the bargaining relationship that develops between host countries and multinational corporations in the arena of

---

67. The allegation that local government came under pressure not to antagonize Mulcahy was made at a luncheon meeting between the author and local officials in Dungarvan, Ireland, April 1, 1980.

pollution control is often complex and erratic. Indeed, a consistent problem is that there generally is not one bargaining process and there often are more actors involved than national and company officials. Bargaining over pollution control tends to take place in stages, with each stage centering on a different level of government.

Broad questions of technology and product that have a bearing on pollution do frequently enter into the initial bargaining over crucial economic factors that determine whether a company decides to invest in a country. Sometimes, in fact, the constraints that countries have set on technology or products as a result of concern for pollution have caused negotiations to be canceled or substantial changes to be made by would-be foreign investors. But at other times, higher-priority economic considerations have overshadowed concern about pollution at this stage of bargaining, and government policies on other aspects of foreign investment, such as technology transfers, have inadvertently increased the potential pollution problems associated with an incoming company's industrial proposal.

Moreover, because pollution-control measures in most industrializing nations take into account the assimilative capacity of the environment, negotiations about precise amounts of effluents and emissions to be permitted tend to take place as part of local land-use planning. This means that a company that has already completed negotiations at the national level may still not know what pollution standards it will be assigned and what its costs for complying will be. It also means that pollution-control requirements for individual industrial plants may vary widely from time to time and locality to locality as a result of local politics and the degree of sophistication that local officials have acquired in pollution control.

Ireland, Spain, and Mexico have tried harder at the national level to coordinate and centralize responsibility for assessing the potential pollution problems associated with different industries. These efforts have lightened the burdens placed on local officials who must evaluate sophisticated industrial proposals. Even so, none of the countries studied has the domestic research capacity to assess the risks associated with some of the more subtle and long-term environmental and health problems that may develop in industries that do not create immediate and visible signs of pollution. This uncertainty about an industry such as pharmaceuticals has injected a great deal of concern into the public debate about industrial development in Ireland, and the Spanish have recently begun to express doubts. So far, though, little concern about so-called micropollution is visible in Mexico or Romania.

Generally, the lack of scientific research capabilities and the scantiness of the information that companies provide to host-country officials work to the advantage of incoming companies, because few local governments are willing to reject industrial proposals on the basis of hypothetical problems that may arise in the future. However, when local governments have poor information on potential environmental impacts associated with a foreign company's industrial proposal, the company sometimes suffers as well. Local officials may try to misapply environmental standards from more advanced countries to their situation, as when Eli Lilly sought to build a new plant in Córdoba. Or public suspicion about the lack of specific information may force local officials to articulate stringent criteria for supervising corporate productive practices, as has occurred in county Cork.

As a result of all these uncertainties, the balance of power between corporation and host country is not easily schematized according to the investment cycle and the host country's progression along the learning curve. Countries may have far more leeway than conventional models would suggest to bargain hard at the outset without upsetting the larger investment decisions. Companies, on the other hand, may be less willing to abide by more stringent pollution-control standards imposed shortly after new capital investment, an effect just the opposite of that predicted by bargaining models. In fact, many companies have made optimistic agreements on pollution-control targets in the preinvestment bargaining stage only to renegotiate for more liberal controls after the plant is completed.

7

The politics of pollution and multinational corporations in rapidly industrializing countries

Industrial-development officials in Ireland, Spain, Mexico, and other rapidly industrializing countries have become more active in bargaining over pollution with incoming multinational firms. When it suits their needs, they also make more vigorous attempts to renegotiate old rules after the plant has come on stream. While the bargaining process remains uncertain, subject to widely varying pollution restrictions from locality to locality and factory to factory, national and local governments have increasingly asserted themselves and built up their expertise in the arena of pollution-control negotiations.

One reason why governments in many industrializing countries have begun to bargain more assertively with foreign investors is that local citizens have become much more concerned about industrial pollution since the early 1970s. Such increased public activism has made it risky for governments, especially local governments, to be lax about pollution control. A public that perceives that it is considered expendable by a foreign company can conclude that its own representatives agree, especially if the officials have obviously turned a blind eye to the environmental problems associated with the company's operations. Some national and local governments therefore feel that they have a political mandate to be more stringent and to scrutinize more closely at the outset.

However, the mere fact that officials of host countries strike a tough bargaining posture does not necessarily mean that industrial-pollution problems caused by foreign investors are avoided or substantially reduced. And, perhaps more to the point, a balanced agreement on pollution control between government and foreign company is no assurance that controversy will be avoided in the future. The matter of industrial pollution and foreign investors is intensely political in the three countries studied – Ireland, Spain, and Mexico – where foreign firms actually operate factories.

The political dynamics of pollution and multinational corporations rarely are guided primarily by the optimal strategy for reducing pollution in host countries. In fact, the relative contribution that a multinational firm makes to the country's overall problems of water contamination, atmospheric pollution, solid-waste disposal, and workplace hazards is generally not the major focus of controversy. Governments often are most concerned with reducing political pressure on them. Consequently, they may strike a hard bargain even when they do not intend or do not have the capability to enforce the restrictions imposed on industrial facilities. Local groups or political organizations may be legitimately concerned about pollution, but often they have other political agendas or selfish interests as well.

Thus the question of how much pollution a foreign investor actually causes in a host country is not ultimately likely to be determined by what takes place at the bargaining table. Unlike the Ford case noted in Chapter 5, government officials at the national and local level may be in substantial agreement about the pollution controls necessary to prevent excessive pollution at a foreign investor's factory site. Yet an aroused public may reject such an agreement for political reasons. Or the vigilance of government officials in the bargaining process may simply transform a legal (and highly visible) right to pollute into an informal agreement to go easy on enforcement. And, because public outrage often focuses more on who is polluting (with foreign investors and large domestic companies generally the most vulnerable) governments and foreign investors are often content to deal with waste disposal problems by shifting the burden to small domestic entrepreneurs or local governments – in essence "laundering" pollution before its ultimate discharge.

This chapter examines the politicization of environmental issues in rapidly industrializing countries and outlines the implications that such a development may have for multinational companies and host countries. In particular, it illustrates that the uncertainties created by the volatility of pollution politics, and the increased vulnerability of multinationals when regulations are not enforced, may be far more detrimental for foreign companies, and for a host country's investment climate, than the stringency of the pollution regulations themselves.

Public opposition to industrial pollution

Concern about industrial pollution spread quickly from the most advanced industrialized nations to many rapidly industrializing countries in the 1970s.[1] Irish and Spanish antipollution groups organized demonstrations against industrial pollution and sought to arouse public opinion to demand more attention for environmental quality. This was particu-

1. For a discussion, see Leonard and Morell, "Emergence of Environmental Concern."

larly true in large urban areas of both Ireland and Spain during the late 1970s – Dublin, Cork, Madrid, Barcelona, Bilbao. Such large demonstrations, and the media coverage they captured, put local officials on notice that environmental quality could be an important issue in terms of local electoral politics. This was particularly important in Spain, it appears, because at the very time when such demonstrations were popular, the country was moving from the Francoist system, in which the central government appointed local officials, to a system of free local elections. And by the early 1980s, a growing number of large public demonstrations were occurring to oppose pollution in Mexico. Public consciousness has been rising, in part because several influential newspapers in Mexico City have focused intense coverage on pollution. Industrial pollution created by companies with foreign equity partners has often drawn particular scrutiny.

Ties with environmental groups in Europe and the United States, as well as a general tendency to follow whatever trends are current in Europe and the United States, contributed greatly to the increase in such general expressions of environmental concern in many industrializing countries. The former director general of energy in Spain's Ministry of Industry and Energy, for example, believes protests erupted in large Spanish cities as part of a "follow-the-leader" syndrome. "America is the leading country in the world," says Ramon Leonato Marsal. "If Americans like to sing and dance, everybody in Spain and in Africa and in Hong Kong is singing and dancing. The same is true with protest about nuclear power or pollution."[2]

In addition, awareness about pollution also spread as a result of increased political activity to oppose nuclear power, particularly in Europe. In both Ireland and Spain, groups that originally organized to combat proposed nuclear-power plants subsequently expanded to deal with industrial-pollution issues. The director of the Department of Nuclear Safety in Spain says he has observed antinuclear groups take up other environmental issues as well:

> It is very clear that people are starting to move toward opposition to industrial contamination. Five or six years ago, nuclear opposition was the only really organized opposition in Spain, but now other organizations are growing to protest industrial pollution [and] destruction of the natural environment as offshoots from nuclear protest. It is a natural thing, as the nuclear issue drags on, that people are moving into other environmental issues – they have learned about

2. Interview with Ramon Leanato Marsal, director general of energy, Ministry of Industry and Energy, Madrid, July 3, 1980.

ecological dangers and about how to get attention; you cannot expect them to go back to being docile.[3]

Perhaps even more important has been the long-term international spillover from highly publicized industrial disasters that have occurred in recent years: the explosion in 1976 at the Hoffman La Roche trichlorophenol plant in Seveso, Italy; the explosion and fire at the gas-storage facility in Mexico City in October 1984; and the December 1984 leak of deadly methyl isocyanate gas from the Union Carbide facility in Bhopal, India. These events appear to have aroused public fears about chemical plants in much the same way that the Three Mile Island accident spread worldwide concern about nuclear power.[4] And, as is illustrated below, groups and individuals have sometimes sought to play upon this increased public concern about industrial pollution and the dangers associated with large industrial plants to organize people for broader political agendas.

Pollution and partisan politics

In Europe the environmental movement has been closely identified with certain political parties and has generally had much broader political agendas than in the United States. This is especially true in Spain, where most ecological groups have strong biases against the national government and often are closely associated with the political forces pushing for regional autonomy. As a result, many environmental controversies in Spain have been played out in much broader political contexts. One Spanish government official says, in fact, that "in Spain, ecology is almost never just an issue by itself. It is almost always a means to political ends."[5]

In the Basque region of Spain, environmental protest has become an important way to express support for regional autonomy. Industrial pollution, particularly in Bilbao, is viewed as a result and a symbol of external control over the Basque economy. Throughout the Basque region, wall posters – supporting the separatist terrorist group ETA, the more moderate separatist political party Herri Batasuna, or other groups favoring some form of regional autonomy – often oppose nuclear power and decry pollution.[6] Quite frequently these posters single out U.S. business interests,

3. Interview with Augustin Alonso Santos, director of the Department of Nuclear Safety, Ministry of Atomic Energy, Madrid, June 16, 1980.
4. For a description and lengthy bibliography of the worldwide concern aroused by the Seveso accident, see Gladwin and Walter, "Environmental Conflict and Multinational Enterprise," pp. 899–911.
5. Interview with Fernando Barrientos, assistant to the director, National Institute for the Conservation of Nature, Ministry of Agriculture, Madrid, June 12, 1980.
6. Photographic examples are shown in H. Jeffrey Leonard, "Pollution Plagues Industrial Firms in Growing Nations," *Conservation Foundation Letter,* August 1982.

both for their contract work at Lemonitz, the nuclear power plant built by Westinghouse just outside of Bilbao, and for their contributions to industrial pollution in the Basque region. Though they generally are not the worst polluters in the area, which is one of the oldest and most heavily polluted industrial regions in Europe, nearly every American firm operating a production facility in the Basque region has had to face protests and efforts by local groups to block their expansion or new construction plans or to shut down existing operations. The protest against Dow Chemical's proposal to produce pesticides in one of its plants near Bilbao was so intense several years ago, for example, that the company eventually changed its plans and now produces the pesticides at one of its plants in the United Kingdom.[7]

In Trudella, Navarre, which is adjacent to the Basque region and located along the Ebro River, the Spanish subsidiary of Rohm and Haas has frequently been the target of several members of the municipal council, who have claimed since the 1970s that the plant is causing serious water pollution. The general manager of Rohm and Haas, España, Jorge Ramirez Rodriquez, admits that the plant – which produced soil fumigants, resins, and dispersants – did cause pollution after it was completed in 1968. The plant was originally designed to send its wastewater to a series of lagoons for settling and flocculation before final discharge. However, seepage from the lagoons was reaching the Ebro River and nearby wells providing water for Trudella residents. After lengthy negotiations, Trudella water authorities required that Rohm and Haas take steps to eliminate the problem and design a system of effluent discharge that could be monitored. The company did this by installing a $750,000 waste-treatment plant with a single outflow into the Ebro. By 1980, company officials, as well as Trudella water officials, were insisting that the plant was well within its assigned parameters and was meeting the same standards as its sister plant in France.[8]

However, whether or not the claims of company and governmental officials are true, Rohm and Hass's problems with the municipal council have always been highly political. In the early 1980s the Herri Batasuna party held two seats on the municipal council, and the mayor, as in many Spanish municipalities, was a member of the Socialist party. This, coupled with the fact that public opinion has been aroused about the pollution problems

7. Interview with Alfonso Ensenat, subdirector general for the industrial environment, Ministry of Industry and Energy, Madrid, June 11, 1980.
8. This summary is based on interviews with Jorge Ramirez Rodriguez, general manager, Rohm and Haas (España), in Barcelona, June 23, 1980; Jules Stewart, McGraw-Hill Business News Service, Madrid, July 3, 1980; Jeronimo Angulo, director general of the chemical and textile industries, Ministry of Industry and Energy, Madrid, June 17, 1980; and with local officials and citizens in Trudella, Spain, June 25, 1980.

in the Ebro, makes it nearly unavoidable that Rohm and Haas will continue to be caught up in local politics. Ramirez, a native Spaniard, says the political ferment in Navarre is today more of a problem for Rohm and Haas than the technical challenge of meeting the pollution standards:

> I believe that one of the problems we have is that we are a multinational firm in an area close to the Basque region which the Basque separatists would like to make part of an autonomous Basque nation. Even though we now have good treatment facilities for our waste, they [the Herri Batasuna council members] can always get a few votes and support for their cause by keeping the pressure on us. They probably would never shut us down, but they can make trouble and it would probably be very difficult in this climate for us to get permission to expand our plant or make new products.[9]

In Mexico, the organization of public concern about pollution is still in its formative stages, although Mexico City is now widely regarded as one of the most polluted cities in the world. However, officials in the administration of President Miguel de la Madrid, as well as political planners for the Partido Revolucionario Institucional (PRI), are increasingly worried that pollution may become a major political issue in the future.

One concern is that a prolonged temperature inversion in Mexico City during the dry (winter) season may cause "killer smog" such as occurred in London, Tokyo, and Donora, Pennsylvania. Mexicans fear that the government will be ill prepared to respond in the short term to such a disaster. In fact, during January and February 1986, a lingering inversion that pushed air pollution to record levels in Mexico City stimulated public demonstrations and intensified media pressure on the government to take action. In response, the government announced a new twenty-three-point plan to combat air pollution, and shortly thereafter a new secretary of urban development and ecology, Manuel Camacho Solis, was named.[10] A lingering political concern, expressed especially by PRI political strategists, is that when the Mexican economy picks up, quality-of-life issues – pollution, clean water, traffic congestion, and the like – may become important means by which Mexico's other political parties, especially the coalition of left parties and the right party Partido Accion National (PAN), seek to mobilize support.[11] Ever-pragmatic PRI officials have sought to align the party so it is prepared to integrate these concerns into its political platform. In fact, before the 1982 presidential campaign, PRI

---

9. Interview with Jorge Ramirez Rodriguez.
10. Interview with Juan Enriquez, coordinator, and Manuel Camacho, subsecretary for regional development, Secretariat of Programs and Budgets, Mexico City, May 17, 1983.
11. Interview with Socrates Rizzo, director of macroeconomic analysis, Secretariat of Programs and Budgets, Mexico City, July 15, 1982.

officials commissioned studies on the "Green party" movement in Europe to assess the likelihood that such a political force would emerge in Mexico. During his election campaign in 1982, Miguel de la Madrid tried to make concern about pollution an important campaign issue.[12] In December 1982, shortly after taking office, President de la Madrid announced a government reorganization that centralized responsibility for conservation and pollution control in a new Secretariat of Urban Development and Ecology (SDUE). Since then, SDUE officials have sought to review Mexican pollution-control laws and to show for President de la Madrid's administration a record of success on at least the most urgent and visible pollution problems.[13]

The risk of public backlash

On a number of occasions, local citizens have expressed outrage when they believe that foreign companies are unconcerned about what happens to the local environment. Once the public develops this impression, the foreign company is unlikely to avoid controversy, even when it is "cleaner" than most domestic firms, as is often the case. As a result, loss of credibility – whether deserved or not – has become a serious problem, not only for multinational firms operating in industrializing countries, but for government officials in these countries who have sought to insulate the companies from public scrutiny. The difficulties for government officials often lie in deciding how far to push foreign companies in response to public concerns about pollution and in distinguishing legitimate public concerns about public health and environmental quality from situations in which the perils of pollution are exaggerated or are being used for political purposes by particular groups.

The case of Raybestos Manhattan in Ireland, mentioned in Chapter 5, illustrates all these problems vividly. The company obviously was insensitive to and failed to address the public concerns raised about its use and disposal of asbestos. Representatives of the local government and of IDA felt compelled to support Raybestos in public, even while expressing misgivings in private. The resulting public backlash against both the company and the government – based somewhat upon the real dangers posed by waste asbestos but fanned by the interest of other groups and the exaggerated fears of uninformed citizens – culminated with the closing of the Raybestos plant.

12. Partido Revolucionario Institucional, "Medio Ambiente y Calidad de Vida," in *Consulta Popular* (Mexico City: Instituto de Estudios Politicos, Economicos y Sociales, 1982).

13. *Plan Nacional de Desarrollo: 1983–1988* (Mexico City: Secretariat of Programs and Budgets, 1983).

Raybestos, the largest U.S. manufacturer of frictional products, came to Ireland to manufacture brake pads, primarily for the European market, during the mid 1970s. At the time, the company appeared to fit perfectly into the IDA's evolving strategy of attracting smokeless, high value-added, export-oriented industries to Ireland. The original proposal for the $8 million plant, with a capacity to produce 10 million asbestos disk-brake pads per year, was eagerly accepted by both IDA and the Cork County Council. Local residents in the small town of Ovens, about fifteen miles from the city of Cork, and the Cork County Council showed little concern about the environment or workplace health, apparently for three reasons: (1) the plant was planned to provide 150–200 jobs; (2) it would have very low water use and effluent and little visible or odorous air emissions; (3) literature and scientific studies regarding the links between asbestos use and asbestosis, mesothelioma, and cancer had not been widely circulated in Ireland at that time.

However, at about the time that the Ovens factory was nearing completion, literature from British environmental groups and press clippings on the hazards of asbestos were widely circulated among the citizens of Ovens. Protests over the plant erupted, and a residents' committee issued a public report stating that the factory "constitutes a major health risk to the local population which we regard as totally unacceptable."[14] Nevertheless, local public opinion remained divided on the matter, with many people swayed by the jobs the plant was providing and by assurances from Raybestos that it was one of the cleanest of all manufacturing facilities in Ireland.

On the other hand, the community of Ovens was more united in opposing Raybestos's use of a dump site near the factory to dispose of waste asbestos and rejected brake pads; after all, the dump site brought no significant economic benefits or jobs to Ovens. Public protests at the dump finally forced Raybestos to close it down in 1977 and search for a new site outside of Ovens. In 1978, with the help of IDA, Raybestos located a new dump site at Ringaskiddy in county Cork. The site is part of the 1100-acre parcel owned by IDA for future industrial development.[15]

The people living near the Ringaskiddy dump site protested even more

14. The following description is based on a background report prepared for the author by Tom MacSweeney, journalist and public spokesman for NET, April 1980. In addition, the author visited the Raybestos Manhattan plant site in Ovens, and the dump site in Ringaskiddy, and conducted interviews concerning the Raybestos-Manhattan situation with Ted Dean, general manager, Raybestos Manhattan (Ireland), Ovens, April 2, 1980; Owen Patten, Murray Consultants (agents for Raybestos), Dublin, March 30, 1980; Liam Mullins, chief engineer, Cork County, Ringaskiddy, April 3, 1980; Ted Forde, chairman, Ringaskiddy Residents Association, Ringaskiddy, April 3, 1980; and Michael Lenihan, Ringaskiddy Residents Association, Ringaskiddy, April 3, 1980.
15. Ibid.

vigorously than in Ovens, clashing with police and company officials on several occasions when women and children prevented lorries laden with asbestos from entering the dump site. The residents called off their protests only when IDA officials promised that the dump would be temporary and Raybestos agreed to strict procedures for pelletizing and burying all asbestos-containing waste.[16]

Sporadically, between 1978 and 1980, new controversies over the Ringaskiddy dump site arose, generally centering around charges by local citizens that Raybestos was carelessly disregarding its agreements on dumping and was exposing residents and schoolchildren to asbestos dust stirred up in the wind. The smoldering controversy erupted once again in April 1980, when the local residents' association blocked access to the dump and invited reporters, photographers, and county officials to examine the site. Although Raybestos officials claimed that they were strictly observing all agreed-upon dumping procedures, on-site inspection provided clear evidence to the contrary. Asbestos pellets and waste brake pads were strewn about the site unburied, and a large waste bin left on the site was covered with substantial quantities of asbestos dust.[17]

After the eruption at Ringaskiddy, shipments of waste asbestos to the dump were once again halted, and Raybestos was forced to stockpile its wastes at the plant site. In May, the Ringaskiddy residents' association instructed lawyers to initiate proceedings against Raybestos under the provisions of the 1976 Local Government Planning and Development Act. Under these provisions any citizen or group may petition the high court to take enforcement action against a polluter alleged to be breaking the conditions attached to the planning permission.

After negotiations with the IDA and the Cork County Council, the residents later agreed to hold off on their legal proceedings and to permit the dump to reopen with the stipulation that the Cork County Council take legal action against Raybestos. As a result of the council's petition to the high court, Raybestos was found to have violated six conditions of its planning permission to dispose asbestos waste at the Ringaskiddy site.[18]

During the same period, Raybestos also was encountering problems with dust control inside the factory at Ovens. Twice in the summer of 1980, the company was forced to close a section of the factory after spillage of asbestos dust. Workers at the plant walked off the job at one point, because the asbestos in the air was so thick. Before the section could

16. Ibid.
17. These events are described in "County Council Encounters Difficulties in Search for Permanent Asbestos Dump," *International Environmental Reporter,* June 11, 1980. The author visited the waste dump site, speaking with local citizens, county officials and representatives of Raybestos on April 3, 1980.
18. "Raybestos Manhattan Waste Disposal Held in Violation of Permit Conditions," *International Environmental Reporter,* July 9, 1980, p. 285.

reopen, the Department of Labor, charged with overseeing the internal plant environment and ensuring that proper occupational health and safety precautions were taken, had to carry out a full investigation of the plant.[19]

Publicly, IDA and county Cork officials continued to defend Raybestos throughout the controversy, issuing statements denying that Raybestos had failed to live up to previous agreements or that it had arrogantly rejected any efforts to inform and reassure citizens and thereby exacerbated public protest. One official pointed out that several other companies in Ireland – including another American company, GAF in Mullingar – which were producing asbestos-containing products had managed to avoid controversy by dealing more carefully with alarmed citizens and following strict disposal procedures.[20]

Raybestos officials in Ireland denied that the company had suffered economically as a result of the prolonged controversies. But workers in the plant and a county official noted in April 1980 that the plant had frequently not operated at full capacity and that the company had lost key marketing opportunities in Europe owing to delays in production during the 1977 fight over the Ovens dump.[21]

Finally, in November 1980, Raybestos announced that it was closing the Ovens plant. At a press conference in Cork, Gabriel Flucci, the president and general manager of Raybestos International Division, denied that the public opposition had influenced his company's decision, saying that the immediate reason for the closing was the continuing recession in the U.S. auto market. But he did admit that production delays had hurt the company in Europe and forced it to send most of the Ovens brake pads to the United States.[22]

The Raybestos Manhattan controversy emphasizes a number of different points about the ways in which public opinion can affect the relationship between a foreign corporation and a host country. First, it clearly illustrates what can happen after (and often not so long after) an industry facing extreme regulatory and legal difficulties in the United States moves abroad to construct a new factory. Raybestos officials deny that the move to Ireland was in any way connected with the difficulties faced by producers of asbestos products in the United States.[23] But the former eco-

19. Ibid.
20. Interview with Matthew Lynch, manager, Environmental Department, Institute for Industrial Research and Standards, Dublin, March 27, 1980.
21. See n. 14.
22. Tom MacSweeney, "Controversial U.S. Asbestos Firm Pulls Out of Ireland," *World Environment Report,* November 17, 1980, p. 1.
23. Letter to the author from John H. Marsh, director of environmental and governmental affairs, Raybestos Manhattan, April 29, 1981.

nomic attaché for the U.S. Embassy in Ireland, Kenneth McGuire, says that while market factors may have been important considerations for Raybestos, the relocation factor probably cannot be entirely dismissed in the Raybestos case.[24] Either way, foreign companies like Raybestos are apt sooner or later to face serious problems as a result of public resentment.

The Raybestos case also illustrates the depth of general public concern and, at the same time, the enormous lack of knowledge that prevails among ordinary people, especially in small villages in Ireland. There is no question that the company did violate its dumping agreement and thus brought most of the trouble upon itself. Yet local people at Ringaskiddy, most of them poor farmers or laborers, exaggerated some of the perils that the Raybestos dump posed to them and their children. They had no concept of what asbestos was or how it could harm human beings. To many of them, asbestos was like a germ or a volatile chemical, contagious or corrosive upon inhalation or contact with the skin. One of Raybestos's biggest mistakes was to fail totally to deal with public perception as well as with the factual problem at hand.

But Raybestos worsened its own situation in a number of other ways. As the situation went from bad to worse, the company sent over a string of general managers from the United States to oversee its Irish operations. Even though the American managers were clearly in charge, they tended to deal through top Irish employees and to insulate themselves from the public. It is, of course, good business practice to permit domestic citizens to participate as much as possible in running the subsidiary and dealing with government officials and the public. However, the ranking Irishmen in Raybestos were largely cut out of policy deliberations and had no authority to deal with their fellow countrymen except in the capacity of public-relations spokesmen. This resulted in deteriorating credibility for Raybestos and increased the public's perception that company officials were arrogant and cared little for the welfare of the Irish people.[25]

Matters were further complicated when the Raybestos management responded to the concerns of the local public in Rangaskiddy and Ovens by accusing the leaders of the opposition of having links to radical and Communist elements.[26] The accusation was patently untrue, and, what is more, the general public in Cork knew it. In the end, public opinion in the Cork area was more or less uniformly against Raybestos. Three years

24. Interview with Kenneth McGuire, economic attaché, U.S. Embassy, Dublin, March, 25, 1980.
25. Interviews with Tom MacSweeney, Owen Patten, Ted Dean, and local citizens.
26. Interviews with Ted Dean and Owen Patten. The accusations were repeated by Raybestos officials in the United States in conversations with Gordon Binder, special assistant to the president, Conservation Foundation, Washington, D.C., April 1980.

of running controversy, in which the management was shown to have hidden information and ignored the legitimate concerns of local citizens, turned sympathy decidedly against Raybestos, even among the segment of the population that was little concerned with the details of the asbestos peril.

Finally, the Raybestos case points up several dilemmas confronting the IDA and any other similar agencies trying to attract foreign industry into an industrializing nation. When an industrial-development organization initially decides that a particular industry is a viable candidate to fit within its industrial-development strategy, it is faced with the difficulty of anticipating the future economic prospects of the industry. Similarly, some effort must be made to anticipate pollution or environmental hazards that may be discovered or confirmed in the future. In the case of Raybestos, IDA did not foresee the storm that the revelations about the hazards of exposure to asbestos would stir up. But IDA also faced a big problem about what to do once the storm had broken over Raybestos. Earlier IDA had made certain promises to Raybestos, including the commitment to find a new dumpsite when the original site in Ovens was vetoed. The success of an organization like IDA depends more than anything else on its reputation among international businesses for keeping its promises and helping to ease the siting and eventual operating process for foreign companies. In the Raybestos case, IDA felt obliged to stand by the company publicly, because it was concerned that any failure to support Raybestos would tarnish its reputation with other foreign companies.[27] On the other hand, in doing so IDA undoubtedly lost some degree of trust with the Irish public.

The politics of blockage

Some nongovernmental groups not only have protested pollution problems that arise after plant construction, but also have sought more often to participate directly in the local development process in order to oppose or seek modifications in specific industrial-development projects. Formal participation by environmental advocates has reached a much higher level in Ireland than in Spain or Mexico. An Taisca is one of six organizations with a statutory right to participate in the local development-planning process and to comment upon development proposals. An Taisce has local chapters throughout Ireland, and local volunteers scrutinize development proposals (commercial and residential as well as industrial) to ensure that they are consistent with conservation, historic preservation, and antipol-

27. Interview with Declan Murphy, special assistant, Industrial Development Authority, Dublin, March 24, 1980.

lution standards. Backed by a small staff of experts and a membership that includes a number of prominent Irish businessmen and aristocrats, An Taisce has so far maintained credibility as a responsible if somewhat persistent participant in the development process. It has strongly opposed some development projects when it appeared they would blatantly disregard the Irish environment. More often it has worked with local governments and incoming industries to alter industrial-plant proposals in ways that accommodate both economic and environmental interests.

In Spain, partly because of the deep political schisms along regional lines and partly because there is not an independent but establishment-oriented group similar to An Taisce, participation in the local process of approving industrial proposals has tended to be much more political and haphazard than in Ireland. But numerous spontaneous groups have also arisen in Ireland in recent years to oppose industrial proposals in local areas, a fact that has significantly complicated the siting process. The origins of these anomic groups in both Ireland and Spain are varied and almost always influenced by factors beyond a desire to see a particular pollution standard met.

One motivating factor for some of the local groups in both countries has been economic. Individuals such as farmers and fishermen who feel that an industrial proposal or an existing industrial facility threatens their livelihood have often come together to protest at the local level. Such groups have rarely functioned as more than a short-term coalition of individuals united by similar perceptions of their immediate economic interests; nor have they usually had an environmental focus or in-depth knowledge about ecological concepts.

A good example of such spontaneous protests arose several years ago when a large alumina plant was proposed by Alcan and a Spanish partner. The consortium originally chose to locate along the northwest Atlantic coast of Spain, near Pontevedra. However, Spanish fishermen – especially musselers and shrimpers – were already concerned about the damage to their livelihoods being caused by wastes from pulp and paper plants along the coast, and they put up an intense fight in opposition to the project. Eventually the entire alumina facility, almost identical to the one built by Alcan on the Shannon estuary in Ireland, was moved inland to San Ciprian in Lugo province. Alcan officials insist that the plant, like its Irish counterpart, would have segregated and dried all its red waste mud without permitting any runoff into the sea, but this did not reassure the fishermen.[28]

28. See H. Jeffrey Leonard, "Environmental Regulations, Multinational Corporations and Industrial Development in the 1980s," *Habitat International* 6, no. 3 (1982):332.

Though not tied into political parties or antisystem political movements as in Spain, a number of informal groups in Ireland managed in the mid- and late 1970s to arouse public concern and to use the local planning process to oppose new industrial projects in their area. Unlike An Taisce, though, these groups frequently have been spontaneously formed to oppose specific proposals and have not geared their participation toward compromise and modification of industrial proposals. Invariably, local groups in Ireland have become very adept in recent years at using "monkey-wrench" or obstructionist tactics to block or seriously delay industrial projects. Sometimes the concerns of these groups are well founded and at other times they are sincere but exaggerated, but they also sometimes appear to center around selfish considerations or to play upon a general aversion to any industrial development that persists in some parts of Ireland today. Mostly, though, the local protest has proven to be an amalgamation of all these interests. Quite often, the opposition groups have arisen so quickly that An Taisce has not even been aware of their existence. Indeed, many of the groups have raised their opposition even after An Taisce has indicated its tentative approval of a project.

Obstructionist tactics

In 1975 the American pharmaceutical company Schering Plough wanted to build a new pharmaceutical plant outside Clonmel in county Tipperary. The local veterinarian and a local-government employee joined together and gathered supporters to object to Schering's plans on grounds that the factory would pollute the local air and water. By fighting the Schering proposal at every opportunity, disrupting county council proceedings, and finally filing court challenges, the group helped to delay plant construction for close to a year. Finally, Schering decided not to build its plant in Ireland and instead located in Puerto Rico, where the siting process proceeded unencumbered.[29]

A similar case occurred a few years later. In 1977 a British firm, Beecham's, proposed to build a $24 million plant to produce semisynthetic penicillins and several bulk pharmaceutical compounds at Ballycaseymore, near Shannon International Airport. The company was granted planning permission by the Clare County Council, after inputs from An Taisce and other statutory participants, with the stipulation that the company make several alterations in the plant and abide by a number of pol-

29. Interviews with: Tommy Rice, county manager, Tipperary County, Clonmel, Ireland, April 1, 1980; Jim Keating, development officer, Tipperary County, Clonmel, April 1, 1980; and Joe Donahue, general manager, Merck, Sharp and Dohme (Ireland), Carrick-on-Suir, Ireland, April 1, 1980.

lution-related restrictions. However, the decision was appealed by the newly formed Wells Residents' Group, representing sixteen families living near the proposed site.

The objections of the Wells Residents' Group were that the factory, under any conditions, would create serious air, water, and noise pollution and would subsequently lead to drastic reductions in the market value of their homes. The residents' attitude was one of total opposition. They argued that they would support the plant only if they received assurance from Beecham's that there would be no detectable discharges from the plant into the air or the water and no noticeable noises beyond the perimeter of the plant site.[30]

The case was taken to An Bord Planala, the national board set up after the Schering debacle to hear appeals of local planning decisions. An Bord ruled that the planning permission was valid and listed thirty-nine planning conditions covering the appearance of the plant, public health, fire safety, and the control of effluents, emissions, and noise. Most of the conditions were identical or nearly identical to the ones originally set down by the Clare County Council. In spite of the positive ruling, the Beecham's plant was never built. Because the Wells Residents' Group was threatening to drag the case all the way through the High Court of Ireland, a process that could have taken another year or more, and because the plant had already encountered long delays, Beecham's canceled its plans to construct its new plant in Ireland.[31]

In Ireland in the mid- and late 1970s, then, small groups of people became quite skilled at strategically using the local planning process to draw out the siting process. Although these groups were nearly always in a distinct minority and did not win any significant planning appeals or court cases, they were able to create a situation under which the delay was too long for anxious corporate planners to endure.

Of course, the companies involved were not blameless in such cases, even where they were not seeking to "dump" on a locality in ways they would not be permitted to do at home. In retrospect, county Tipperary officials say, several of Schering's actions helped the cause of its opponents. First, they say, Schering did not tender a formal proposal for more than six months after it had been publicly announced that the company intended to locate near Clonmel. Under these circumstances, Tipperary county manager Tommy Rice says, the opponents of the factory had six months to gain support and spread fears among local people, while the

30. "Planning Board's Green Light to F24M. Beecham Plant," *Clare Champion,* November 18, 1977, p. A17.
31. Interviews with: Dermott Gleason; and John Gannon, An Bord Planola, in Dublin, Ireland, April 8, 1980.

county council had no concrete proposal to refer to and no clear idea of what kinds of environmental safeguards Schering would use.[32] Moreover, Schering never delegated a local representative in Ireland to negotiate with the council; instead, every issue and decision had to be referred to U.S. headquarters. This not only drew out the process, it created a serious credibility problem for Schering and the county council. The company also made no concerted efforts to deal directly with the opponents of the plant or to mollify the concern that was building among the general public.

Schering's failings were exacerbated by the physical surroundings and terrain around Clonmel. The area is in a lush, green, broad valley of rolling hillsides. It is almost entirely agricultural and the people traditionally are highly suspicious of any landscape that is not misty green and any smell that is not agricultural. By playing on people's fears of industrial development and portraying Schering as the "foot in the door" that would lead to the rapid overindustrialization of the area, plant opponents gathered public support.

Finally, Schering dragged its feet instead of acting quickly, it appears, because even after its initial agreement to locate in Ireland it continued to try to play the Irish government and the Puerto Rican government against one another. County Tipperary officials contend that had Schering dealt quickly and forthrightly with the council and tried to calm the fears of local citizens, it probably could have been sited.[33]

Some substantiation of the county officials' claims is provided by the fact that only a short time later the American company Merck, Sharpe, and Dohme received rapid approval with little opposition for its pharmaceutical plant a few miles from the Schering site. County officials say part of the reason was that there was a significant proindustrial backlash among local people eager for more jobs after the Schering controversy. But another reason was that Merck appointed a local Irish designate to negotiate with the council and went to great lengths to reassure the public about the safeguards the plant would employ. Once the company announced its decision to come to county Tipperary, it acted quickly to submit its proposals and worked with the county council to integrate additional measures designed to reduce its impact on the environment.[34]

The volatility of public opinion

Public participation in most industrializing countries is much more volatile, haphazard, and uninformed than in the United States. In Mexico vir-

32. Interview with Tommy Rice.
33. Interviews with Tommy Rice, Jim Keating, and Tom MacSweeney.
34. Interview with Joe Donahue.

tually all concern about industrial pollution at a specific plant is a result of some flare-up, since no organized sentiment has yet been expressed by independent public groups about the environmental impact of industrial development. Even in Ireland and Spain, long traditions of acquiescence (for political reasons in Spain, for social and economic reasons in Ireland) had to be transcended as environmentalists sought to bring concern about industrial pollution out into the open and to ensure that environmental factors were duly considered in negotiations with foreign companies. In Ireland the biggest barrier to speaking up to oppose an industrial development proposal or an operating industrial plant was the grave concern about creating jobs. To some extent, this remains an inhibiting factor for Ireland's silent majority, even when they express obvious concerns about Ireland's environment. In Spain, since environmental concern coincided with the recommencement of democracy and the right of individuals and parties to participate in the political process, standing barriers to environmental activism were more easily reduced. However, environmental concern has not yet widely emerged in Spain as an issue in its own right. Except for cases of economic hardship, as faced by the fishermen of Galicia, people in Spain rarely react spontaneously out of a pure desire to protect the environment. Environment is nearly always used as a rallying cry for some other political cause.

These circumstances make public reaction to issues involving industry and the environment very unpredictable. In Ireland environmental activism has tended to wax and wane with the economy, while in Spain it has been correlated with the agendas and political needs of various local political groups. This means that something that arouses great public concern in one place or at one time may not be an issue at all in another place or another time. A company that goes through the siting process may face an aroused public, as Schering did, whereas only a short time later a different company may find the public in the same area anxious to accommodate a new industrial plant, as Merck did. In Ireland, having the local government behind an industrial proposal may not be enough for a foreign investor if public opinion about pollution is aroused. In Spain, on the other hand, a firm that ingratiates itself with local political leaders (as Procter and Gamble did in Córdoba)[35] may face much smoother sailing, even when concern about pollution is high, than one that is not as well connected (as was the case with Eli Lilly when it sought to build in Córdoba).

35. Procter and Gamble, because it worked with the mayor of Córdoba and publicly supported the mayor's campaign to clean up the Guadalquivir River, encountered few difficulties in its pollution-control negotiations with local officials. Interviews with John Asher, general manager of Proctor and Gamble (España), Madrid, June 19, 1980; and Julio Anguita, mayor of Córdoba, Córdoba, July 1, 1980.

Public opinion is unpredictable in other ways that have very significant overtones for the industrial plans of both countries and companies. There is considerable concern in Ireland about what one official in the Department of the Environment calls the tendency toward an "overuse of democracy."[36] The theme is raised by members of An Taisce, numerous local government officials, central government officials, representatives of IDA, and virtually every foreign company interviewed in Ireland. Indeed, IDA officials issued a stern warning in late 1980 that extreme opposition by a small minority was liable to damage seriously Ireland's reputation as a hospitable country for foreign firms.[37] At a recent meeting, environmental officials for the U.S. pharmaceutical industry generally agreed that the IDA warning was valid. Dorothy Bauers of Merck, Sharp and Dohme contended that the recent completed Eli Lilly plant may be the last major international pharmaceutical plant to be built in Ireland.[38] A study by An Foras Forbatha advised IDA that because of public activism, a number of other nonpolluting industries would be preferable even over light chemicals and pharmaceuticals.[39]

The problem evidenced in Ireland is that heightened public awareness of industrial hazards can turn into blind opposition to industrial development. Opponents of the Syntex and Beecham's plants in western Ireland openly admit that they are suspicious of all industry. Spreading literature about the Seveso disaster and about Agent Orange, these opponents have warned unsophisticated Irish farmers and villagers that the only way to avoid such debacles in Ireland is to close all chemical plants. Dermott M. Gleason, the lawyer representing the opposition groups, says:

> It may well be that Syntex currently are [not] producing anything as dangerous as is mentioned in these two disasters situations [sic] but the fact remains that we have no guarantee that they will not do so in the future. Apart entirely from that you will note that in both of these instances and indeed in many other instances of Chemical Factories assurances were not only given by the Factory people themselves but the Scientists that certain chemicals and drugs were harmless but which, a short time afterwards, they had to admit were extremely harmful to health. Need I mention Thalidomide? My logical conclusion therefore is that all chemicals and drugs, and plants in

---

36. Interview with Daniel O'Connell, assistant principal, Department of the Environment, Dublin, March 24, 1980.
37. "Industrial Development Authority Warns Environmentalists Not to Scare Investors," *International Environment Reporter,* December 10, 1980, p. 538.
38. Interview with Dorothy Bauers, director of environmental affairs, Merck, Sharpe, and Dohme, Rahway, N.J., August 6, 1980.
39. An Foras Forbartha, "Proposed Industrial Development at Keenaghan, Carrick-on-Shannon, Co. Leitram" (Confidential background report, October 1978).

which they are produced are per se a danger and a hazard to be treated with extreme caution and suspicion.[40]

But the other side of the equation is that it is still often very difficult to obtain enough information from companies or from local officials so that responsible groups such as An Taisce and the general public can make an unbiased assessment of industrial proposals. In Ireland, Spain, and Mexico, the public has no clear entitlement to information about industrial facilities or even about the agreements made between governments and companies. Often this leads to the kind of problem that occurred in both the Schering and the Raybestos cases: the general public has no basis on which to evaluate claims made by opponents and proponents of the plant. Eventually, many highly technical issues are settled in an emotion-charged atmosphere in which corporate public-relations officers oversimplify and concerned citizens exaggerate potential problems. Local officials perpetuate the black-box syndrome for fear of stirring too much public involvement, and companies generally fail to provide enough information about their operations. Both therefore help to create a situation where small minorities can sway the general public and help to increase the incidence of social blockage in countries like Ireland and, to a lesser extent, Spain.[41] Yvonne Scannell, a law professor and environmental attorney in Ireland, says: "Irish environmentalists are largely uninformed. It isn't that surprising that they get hysterical over an issue that concerns them, since they haven't got access to the information that would answer their questions."[42]

In spite of the many barriers to public participation in industrial-development decisions in Ireland, Spain, and Mexico, citizens in these countries have a final recourse that appears to be very difficult to rely upon in Romania: they can hit the streets in spontaneous protest. As noted above, such shows of concern by a largely uninformed public have canceled, delayed, or altered the plans of U.S. companies on a number of occasions in both Ireland and Spain. Although public concern about pollution has not yet blocked the construction of industrial plants in Mexico, most observers now agree that it is only a matter of time before such siting controversy arises, and chances are that the protest will center on the plans of a foreign company.

Romanian officials, by contrast, assert with pride that the rapid buildup

40. Letter from Dermott Gleason, solicitor, May 5, 1980.
41. Philip Mullally, "Planning Problems and the Public," *Taisce Journal* 3, no. 1 (February–April 1979):15; and Yvonne Scannell, "Citizen Participation in Public Decision-Making" (Paper presented to the EEC Commission, Brussels, Spring 1978).
42. In an interview with Yvonne Scannell, Professor of Law, Trinity College in Dublin, Ireland (March 25, 1980).

of productive capacity for export in the areas of basic chemicals, dyestuffs, lacquers, and other products that are now heavily regulated in the West has aroused no public concern about industrial pollution. However, there are no indications that the Romanian public or workers have been informed of the potential pollution and health consequences of their government's strategy to produce and sell products that are extremely dangerous to manufacture. A spokesman at the Chemical Ministry says there is no need for private citizens to protest for stricter pollution regulations in the industrial-siting process, since the ministry, which controls all industries, represents the best interests of the people:

> All these [pollution-control] criteria and details are done on the basis of a great deal of analysis, in such a way that the public is never in a position to protest it. As compared to Ireland or Spain, we have considerable advantages generated by our Socialist system which enables us to resolve pollution problems without conflict.... we are better able to structure public opinion. The state represents the people's interest in reducing pollution from industrial plants, and since the state owns the factories, the people are assured that adequate pollution measures are always taken.[43]

Are environmental regulations enforced?

Both Ireland and Spain now have a patchwork of overlapping local and national environmental restrictions that are nearly up to the levels of those in the most advanced industrialized countries in the European Common Market. Of the four countries considered here, Romania publishes the most stringent standards for industrial pollution and workplace health; in some instances, the emission and effluent levels permissible for certain pollutants are substantially lower than those in the United States or those set by the EEC. Mexico, too, has strengthened its environmental laws in recent years and is now expanding the scope of regulatory instruments to cover a broader range of industrial pollutants.

Consequently, it is not sufficient to look only at the environmental legislation published by these countries and the additional restrictions placed upon industrial facilities as a result of the bargaining process between corporate officials and government officials. Of far greater importance is the question of whether these laws and stipulations are enforced on a regular basis. And it is also important to determine whether the willingness of local and national government officials to enforce regulations is different

---

43. Interview with Mariana Zugravesc, special assistant to the Ministry of the Chemical Industry, Bucharest, July 7, 1980.

for foreign companies than for domestic companies, and how this affects the calculation by foreign investors of the stability of the investment climate in the host country.

In all four countries there appears to be overwhelming evidence that pollution-control regulations are not enforced in a consistent and concerted manner. Government officials and multinational corporate executives openly acknowledge that. A recent report by the Irish Water Pollution Advisory Council, an intergovernmental task force set up to make recommendations to the minister of the environment, claimed that the country has made little progress toward controlling water pollution and that there was little evidence that the 1977 water-pollution legislation was being enforced.[44]

Yvonne Scannel says:

> Some people here say the problem is that there is not an adequate body of environmental law in Ireland. But that is not true. There are 55 or so laws that affect what private industry can do to the environment. They are just not enforced. You can take it for granted that every single law is not being adequately enforced. Local authorities and corporations, too, actually have a pretty good record for responding to citizen complaints about pollution, since by then it is a political matter. But what you very rarely find is a local authority playing watchdog, checking up to see if regulations are being followed.[45]

In Spain, too, the regulations are far more impressive than the record of enforcement. Rodrigo Mendez-Penalosa, Union Carbide's European manager for energy conservation and environmental affairs, says candidly:

> In Spain, we have beautiful laws to protect the environment, but nobody is really complying with them. Industry knows that the chances are not very great that the government is going to suddenly crack down and begin enforcing the laws. They say they will gradually get tougher, but in my opinion it would be better to have fewer and simpler regulations and get a better record of compliance from the very beginning.[46]

There are a number of reasons why pollution laws are not consistently enforced. External political pressures have dictated that these countries devote more attention to putting regulations and restrictions on the

---

44. Environment Council, *Towards an Environment Policy* (Dublin: Irish Stationery Office, 1979). Also "No Effort on Pollution Say An Taisce," *Irish Press*, March 25, 1980, p. 3; and "Lack of Pollution Code Criticised," *Irish Times*, April 3, 1980, p. 5.
45. Interview with Yvonne Scannell.
46. Interview with Rodrigo Mendez-Penalosa, European manager for energy conservation and environmental affairs, Madrid, July 2, 1980.

books, but such pressures rarely compel enforcement. For example, with Ireland already in the EEC and Spain on the verge of joining, both countries have been adjusting their legal codes on pollution to EEC-wide standards. It is easiest for them to upgrade their laws and then either seek a waiver on certain regulations or simply drag their feet in implementing them. In the context of European community politics, this is much more acceptable than openly flouting EEC standards.[47]

Romania, like other Eastern-bloc nations, appears to publish stringent standards for environmental and workplace health for international consumption more than for internal application. Frequently, Soviet and Eastern European representatives have brandished these standards at meetings of the World Health Organization, International Labor Organization, United Nations Environment Program, and other international groups as proof that the capitalist countries achieve progress at the expense of the workers and the environment and that the socialist systems are more humane and more closely attuned to preserving environmental quality.[48]

In Ireland and Spain, the burden of enforcement falls on the biggest polluters of all: municipal governments. It is difficult for municipal governments to muster the resolve to crack down on enforcement, because this would call attention to their own problems, particularly with regard to serious pollution caused by the almost total lack of treatment for domestic sewage.

In Ireland, a quirky loophole in the 1977 Water Act allowed local governments to go slowly in enforcing the act even into the 1980s. The legislation required all dischargers of foreign substances into the nation's waterways to apply for a permit from local authorities by October 1, 1978. The legislation then provided that once such an application had been made, the discharger could continue current practices (if legal under existing laws and planning permissions) until the local authority held hearings and acted on the permit application. However, since the legislation did not stipulate any time limit for local authorities to act on the permit appli-

47.   Indeed, nearly every country in the EEC is failing to comply with or seeking a waiver of at least one of the community-wide environmental standards. An overview of the international politics of pollution in Europe is provided in Peter Haas, "Coordinated Pollution Control in the Mediterranean: The Mediterranean Action Plan" (Paper presented at the International Studies Association Convention, Atlanta, March 29, 1984).

48.   See Richard L. Siegel and Leonard Weinberg, *Comparing Public Policies*, pp. 407–409; Donald Kelley, Kenneth Stunkel, and Richard Wescott, *The European Superpowers and the Environment* (San Francisco: Freeman, 1976); Marshall Goldman, *The Spoils of Progress: Environmental Pollution in the Soviet Union* (Cambridge, Mass.: MIT Press, 1972); Thane Gustafson, *Reform in Soviet Politics* (New York: Cambridge University Press, 1981).

cations, only a very small number of permits were actually issued after the applications were filed.[49] Local authorities were not eager to act on the permits and thereby to incur more statutory responsibilities.

Another barrier to enforcement is that the worst industrial polluters in all four countries are state-owned or quasi-public companies. In Ireland, where the public industrial sector is not large in comparison with that of many rapidly industrializing countries, the fertilizer plant operated by the government-run company NET still produces more pollution than any other industrial plant.[50] In both Spain and Mexico, as noted in Chapter 5, state-owned companies dominate in many of the heavy, pollution-intensive industrial sectors, especially steel, oil refining, basic chemicals, fertilizers, and mineral processing. The difficulties that one segment of the government (in this case, the regulatory bureaucracy) has in enforcing restrictions upon another (the productive industrial sectors) are numerous and in many cases insurmountable.[51] It is enough here to note that in neither Spain nor Mexico has the government taken strong action to force the public sector to comply with governmental pollution-control regulations.

The government's unwillingness or inability to crack down on its own polluters complicates the situation for regulators intent on reining in corporate polluters in the private sector. Representatives from both domestic and foreign corporations in Ireland, Spain, and Mexico all insist that they would be much more willing to stay abreast or ahead of the government's antipollution efforts if they felt that the government applied as much pressure on municipal governments and public industries as on the private sector.

Shortages of money and personnel

In Ireland, municipal engineers also delayed the enforcement of the 1977 Water Act. The provisions of the act significantly increased the workload of the engineers, whose duty it is to enforce the act, but provided neither additional pay nor additional personnel to compensate. The municipal engineers' union refused to take on the additional duties until the dispute was settled.[52] This dispute underlines one of the difficult problems encoun-

---

49. "Managing Our Waterways," *Business and Finance* (Ireland), January 3, 1980, pp. 26–27; and Sean McMorrow, "Water and Law," *Taisce Journal* 1, no. 4 (August–September 1977):6–8.
50. Leonard Doyle, "How Grey Is My Valley," *Irish Times*, March 13, 1980.
51. See Leonard and Morell, "The Emergence of Environmental Concern."
52. See n. 49.

tered even when governments are committed to enforcing regulations: regulators lack the money and the personnel to do so effectively. The national governments of both Ireland and Spain have vested substantial enforcement responsibilities in local governments but have not transferred funds for fulfilling these responsibilities. Tom Kilgarrif, the chief assistant county engineer for sanitary services in county Westmeath, says: "There is no question but that local governments are taking a softly, softly approach on enforcing the water pollution act. But you can't really blame the locals; the Irish government is going to have to come up with some money if it is really serious about stepping up enforcement."[53]

Another money-related issue that inhibits enforcement is the general economic situation, which makes officials of national governments reluctant to impose major nonproductive expenditures on industry and makes officials of local governments highly sensitive to any suggestion that increased regulatory enforcement may jeopardize jobs. Francisco J. A. Manrigue, the head of the American Chamber of Commerce in Spain, says:

> In today's climate, it is difficult to enforce regulations; too many of Spain's factories would be shut down. Generally, the worst of the worst polluters are fined. They have a choice: pay the fine or observe the rules, which would be very expensive. With the economic situation, the Spanish government has not been very tough on the fines, so from time to time a company will pay a fine but keep on doing what it is doing.[54]

And Daniel O'Brien, of Ford Motor Company's Spanish subsidiary, Foret, says:

> No blatant polluters are going to get into Spain anymore, but for the companies that are already here, the regulations are not going to be strictly enforced – at least not consistently – for quite a while. Nobody is going to shut anybody down for polluting because the major problem right now is unemployment. As long as that is the case, environment is going to be a secondary concern.[55]

Local governments and national environmental regulators in Ireland, Spain, and Mexico also face a serious shortage of trained specialists in pollution control and the environment. This problem affects multina-

53. Interview with Tom Kilgarrif, chief assistant county engineer for sanitary services, Westmeath County, Mullingar, Ireland, April 9, 1980.
54. Interview with Francisco J. A. Manrique, managing director, American Chamber of Commerce, Barcelona, June 24, 1980.
55. Interview with Daniel O'Brien, executive director, Foret, Barcelona, June 23, 1980.

tional companies operating in these countries as much as it affects the governments. There simply are not enough highly skilled domestic technicians with experience running waste-treatment plants for chemical manufacturing facilities. Joe Harford, a pollution-control expert for Squibb's Irish subsidiary, Linson, says: "Most of the multinational firms here in Ireland have the funds and the technology to build a good treatment plant. As much as anything, though, the problems that have arisen relate to the fact that it is difficult to get trained operators."[56] Harford says he has frequently been called upon by other foreign and domestic companies in Ireland when they have problems operating their effluent treatment plants.

The problem of old industry

The worst industrial-pollution problems in Ireland, Spain, and Mexico – for either domestic or multinational companies – are caused by old industrial facilities that were built when pollution-control technologies were less sophisticated, when concern for incorporating waste-control measures was less acute than it is now, and when governments were less capable of assessing potential environmental impacts. Just as in the United States, the rising vigilance and concern about pollution have caught many industrial companies operating in these three countries in the middle of their long-term plant-investment cycle.

The studies of industries in the United States referred to in Chapter 4 have generally shown that when regulatory and plant-investment cycles have been out of sync with each other, ill-timed pollution-control investment is often more onerous than the actual technical challenges posed by new antipollution requirements. Retrofitting an existing plant is expensive; replacement of the plant when it has served only a portion of its useful operating years is even more expensive. Besides, once environmental factors are plugged into the economics of location and operation, an entirely new location – either nearby or in another region – might be better for the company.

National and local governments face an obvious dilemma when old plants are operating with levels of air emissions and water effluent that are no longer acceptable to the public and under the law. More often than not, they apply double standards that are much more lenient toward old factories than new ones, as has often occurred in the United States. National pollution standards for emissions and effluents in Spain make a clear distinction between new and old plants. In both Ireland and Mexico,

56. Interview with Joe Harford, process manager, Linson, Dublin, March 28, 1980.

there is a defacto distinction simply because pollution-control conditions attached to planning permissions have become tighter, while old plants continue to operate, except in extreme cases, under the terms originally negotiated.

Thus, Ireland, Spain, and Mexico, like most industrialized and industrializing countries, continue to suffer pollution problems or industrial hazards as a result of decisions made in the past. The governments of all three countries have shown that in cases of extreme pollution they will shut down a plant regardless of the economic impact. But in many instances, little can be done to correct the pollution caused by old plants until the plants themselves are obsolete. The governments of these countries are not likely to allow stringent regulatory requirements to speed the obsolescence of such plants. Even more than in the United States, then, many industrial-pollution problems are likely to remain generational: they will be eased only with a new generation of industrial development, and then only if that new development takes place in locations designed to minimize the dangers of pollution and with adequate pollution-reduction techniques built into productive processes.

One example of a multinational corporation still operating a plant that was built with preecological technology is Pfizer, with its magnesite plant at Dungarvan. A new magnesite plant built in Dungarvan today would probably not be built in the same place and would have much stricter air-emission and water-effluent standards. But the problems at the Pfizer plant cannot be solved at this stage by adding pollution controls at the end of the process. Any substantial effort by authorities to end the pollution problem at Pfizer would require the company to more or less redesign and reequip the entire plant; rather than doing that, Pfizer would probably close the plant altogether. Although officials have required marginal adjustments to deal with the worst problems, they still permit much higher increments of pollution from the older plant than they would if a new plant were being built.

Two foreign firms producing titanium dioxide in Spain also illustrate the dilemma. Between them, Dow Chemical and Titanio account for all the titanium dioxide produced in Spain.[57] Until recently Titanio was jointly owned by a subsidiary of the British firm Imperial Chemical Industries, The Tioxide Group, and a Spanish company, Union Explosivos Rio Tinto. The entire operation has now apparently been sold to the Tioxide Group. The Titanio plant is located in Huelva and has a capacity to produce about fifty thousand metric tons annually. Dow's plant, located at

57. This overview of the titanium dioxide industry in Spain is based primarily on a background report prepared for the author by Jules Stewart, McGraw-Hill Business News Service, Madrid, April 19, 1981.

the Dow complex in Bilbao, can produce about twenty-four thousand metric tons per year. Both plants are old and use the sulfate process, which creates significantly more pollution than does the newer chloride process.

Throughout Europe, plants producing titanium dioxide pigment faced major disruptions and public outcries in the late 1970s and early 1980s because they caused pollution.[58] Although no major demonstrations have focused specifically on the operations of either Titanio or Dow, neither is meeting EEC standards on water effluent, which are now supposedly in force in Spain. And, in fact, the increasingly stringent standards for titanium dioxide wastes in the EEC were among the few EEC regulations that Spanish officials said they would have difficulty meeting when they entered the community.[59]

Titanio's Huelva plant, because it is larger and discharges directly into the harbor, has a more acute problem than Dow, but both plants are being forced to make substantial improvements. Presumably, since it has been converting its other European plants and did not buy total interest in the Huelva facility until 1981, ICI has plans to convert the Huelva plant to the chloride process at some point in the future. Dow, however, decided to sell its facility. Since it was built in the 1950s, was a small-scale operation, and was Dow's only titanium-dioxide plant in Europe, the company apparently concluded that the plant was not worth the new investment needed for conversion.[60]

In either case, though, Spanish officials and the Spanish public are probably going to have to continue living with the titanium dioxide waste problem caused by the old sulfate process until demand picks up (there is substantial overcapacity in Europe at the moment), the general economic situation improves, and pressures from EEC regulations become more imminent. Even in the mid-1980s, enforcement of strict effluent standards on titanium dioxide plants in Spain would force them to reduce or halt production and leave the country dependent upon imports.

But government regulators may not be the biggest threat when old plants are owned by multinationals. Sometimes the public-relations and liability risks of continuing to operate an old, polluting plant become too high for a foreign corporation, and the plant is either closed or sold to a domestic firm. Foret closed an old plant in Valencia several years ago, even though Spanish regulators had been reluctant to force the company to the wall. The plant was situated in an increasingly urbanized area, and local residents had complained about pollution. Because it was too expensive to

58. See Chap. 7, n. 53.
59. Background report of Jules Stewart.
60. Robert E. Davenport and F. Alan Ferguson, "Titanium Dioxide Pigments," in *Chemical Economics Handbook* (1978), international tables.

take the necessary steps to reduce the pollution, Foret decided to close the plant before a major public controversy arose. Foret's Daniel O'Brien says:

> The stacks of the plant were spewing smoke right into nearby apartments, and we were getting a lot of complaints. So we paid off the workers and shut down. We were lucky, it never even hit the papers. It didn't take a genius to see what we were doing to the people. Sooner or later people would have become upset enough and the newspapers would have begun to go at us, anyway, so we decided to get out of it clean.[61]

In Mexico, the fear of adverse reaction will probably push some foreign investors to move away from Mexico City before government officials force a showdown or the plants are ready for replacement. Camilio Gutierrez, head of operations for Dow Chemical Mexicana, says that Dow's Tlalnepantla plant will be able to comply with virtually any requirements that government regulators are likely to make in the foreseeable future. However, Gutierrez adds: "I think we might end up leaving here, since this is no longer a very appropriate site for a big gringo company like Dow. At some point I think somebody upstairs [in corporate headquarters] is going to want to get us out of here to a more typical Dow site; we are practically in the middle of town now."[62]

Sometimes multinational firms find themselves saddled with the old-industry problem when they buy out domestic companies or when they establish close relationships with domestic companies. In Mexico spokesmen for several multinational companies acknowledge that their domestic partners and suppliers often are unable to comply with worldwide environmental standards set out by corporate headquarters. These officials fear that the public, the media, and the government will eventually associate them with the pollution that is being caused by antiquated plants operated by domestic affiliates.[63] This is no longer a hypothetical problem, even in Mexico.

Infrastructure and transport

As noted in Chapter 2, a major dilemma for any country seeking to stimulate rapid industrial development is when and how to provide the mod-

---

61. Interview with Daniel O'Brien.
62. Interview with Camilio Gutierrez, head of operations, Dow de Mexico, in Tlalnepantla, Mexico, July 27, 1982.
63. This was a sentiment often voiced in interviews with officials from subsidiaries of thirteen U.S. chemical and mineral-processing companies, as well as in a breakfast meeting with six members of the permanent commission on the environment of the Mexican association of manufacturing industries (CANACINTRA), arranged by the commission's president, Raul Suarez Munoz Ledo, Mexico City, July 20, 1982.

ern infrastructure and services necessary to support manufacturing industries and to ensure the safe transport of industrial chemicals, fuels, and products. This is particularly true when – as is the case in Ireland, Spain, and Mexico – the country is attempting to encourage industry to locate in less-developed areas instead of selecting sites near already-industrialized areas. Many bottlenecks and problems have occurred in these three countries because industrial development has gone ahead in remote areas without adequate supporting infrastructure, because dangerous materials must be transported haphazardly, and because waste-disposal facilities are unavailable. And, in Mexico, the lack of sufficient infrastructure and amenities is one of the key constraints frustrating the government's efforts to encourage industry to locate outside of the Mexico Valley.[64]

In some cases the problems result from the failure of government planners and industry planners to anticipate each other's needs. For example, pumping enough water for both municipal and industrial use is a problem that many localities run into, since one new industrial facility may suddenly double the demand for potable water. This occurred in county Westmeath, Ireland, after the county successfully attracted a number of new industries with high demands for fresh water. One plant alone, operated by GAF Corporation, needs approximately a quarter of a million gallons per day; and another, General Tire, depends on a constant water pressure of sixty pounds per square inch in order to achieve the proper quality in its production process. In both cases, county Westmeath found it difficult to consistently meet the specifications of the companies.[65]

Both GAF and General Tire had major confrontations with local officials because of the water supply. GAF was accustomed to drawing its water in large amounts when needed, but at times of peak water demand the company was drawing water away from other users. Finally, the county installed a special valve to ensure that GAF could draw water only in incremental amounts. At the same time, General Tire frequently complained to local officials that because of fluctuating water pressure they had been forced to throw away incomplete product batches.

In both cases, county officials complained that the industries were not considering their plight, while company officials argued that the county was not meeting the obligations it had incurred as part of the bargain that brought the industries to Westmeath. In a sense, both parties had a legitimate complaint, but only after a long period of confrontation could they

64. Interviews with Edward Wyegard, Arthur D. Little (Mexico), Mexico City, July 28, 1972; Sally Mott, economist, BANAMEX, Mexico City, July 14, 1982; and Kevin Reger, economist, American Chamber of Commerce of Mexico, Mexico City, July 15, 1982.
65. Interview with Sean Lucy, Westmeath County Council, Mullingar, Ireland, April 9, 1980.

work out a means to satisfy all the demands for water. Now county officials say they are focusing on bringing in dry industries that will not put further strain on their capacity to supply water to existing industries and municipal users.[66]

Sometimes, though, the problems created by an initial lack of infrastructure are cumulative: they cannot easily be remedied later. For example, one of the most serious potential industrial-pollution problems in Ireland, Spain, and Mexico is that virtually no special provisions have been made and almost no facilities are available for the proper disposal of hazardous and toxic waste materials. Little effort is made to segregate potentially hazardous and toxic chemicals from normal effluent wastes. The public-health, economic, and political implications of this little-discussed situation are potentially of massive proportions, as the U.S. experience with toxic-waste dumps in the 1980s emphasizes.

Many officials of the approximately sixty American-owned factories visited for this study admit candidly that the problem of toxic-waste disposal is now largely ignored and acknowledge that better provisions will have to be made soon for the disposal of some of their wastes. But before the problem can be addressed, the governments of these countries will have to take responsibility for providing proper facilities, because the economics and logistics of toxic-waste disposal often demand centralized dumping, incinerator, or disposal facilities.

The most serious problem may be solid-waste disposal. American companies operating plants in Ireland today are extremely sensitive about the question of solid wastes, since they want to avoid a situation such as the one involving Raybestos, where the company had nowhere to send its solid waste. Although solid-waste disposal is also covered by local planning permissions, most of the time the planning condition states that the company must make suitable arrangements for the removal of its solid wastes. Where there are no toxic chemicals, no problems arise. Indeed, Squibb's subsidiary, Linson, sells its solid waste to a local golf course for use on greens.[67] Sometimes a planning permission outlines clear procedures that a company must follow to avoid problems arising from toxic metals or other compounds. For example, according to the terms of its planning permission granted in 1974 by the Clare County Council, Syntex must precipitate from its effluent the salts of magnesium, zinc, iron (in their insoluble hydrosides), and fluoride (as insoluble calcium fluoride). These salts, and all other sludges and solid wastes from the plant, are then

66.   Ibid. A general overview of the problem of water supply and sewer facilities is provided in L. Brassil, "The Provision of Water and Main Drainage" (Paper presented at a conference on Planning Industrial Development, Dublin, November 16, 1978).
67.   Interview with Joe Harford.

buried at a site approved and monitored by the county according to strict procedures to prevent seepage.[68] However, the Raybestos controversy emphasized to the Irish public that county authorities cannot always be relied upon to monitor waste-disposal procedures.

Other companies meet the terms of their planning permission by hiring a private contractor to haul away solid waste. But the Irish government and many companies are reluctant to account for the destination of the waste that contains toxic materials. Frequently, it appears, companies consider their responsibilities fulfilled once the waste is removed from their site. Irish officials claim that much of the country's toxic waste is now being sent to England for proper disposal, as there is a severe shortage of toxic-waste disposal facilities in the country.[69] However, there is strong evidence that more toxic solid waste than anyone will admit winds up being dumped at local public refuse dumps or being dumped illegally.[70]

The absence of a controlled waste-disposal facility in Ireland, particularly in the Dublin and Cork areas, has been the source of increasing public concern and a growing sore spot for both the Irish government and Irish and foreign companies in recent years.[71] Coming to Ireland at the height of the Raybestos-Manhattan controversy in county Cork, Eli Lilly's new plant in Kinsale probably never would have been granted planning permission if the company had not made explicit plans to dispose of all potentially toxic waste materials at the plant site. Lilly's plant therefore includes a thermal oxidizer that will incinerate the plant's solid waste and incorporates advanced activated-charcoal water treatment to deal with minute quantities of toxic chemicals that might be in the plant's effluent.[72]

Not every company can afford or justify the in-house measures being taken by Eli Lilly. Most other industrial spokesmen argue that toxic-waste dumping is as much the government's problem as it is the private companies', and spokesmen for the Irish, Spanish, and Mexican governments agree. In fact, all three governments have expressed concern about the need for procedures for dumping toxic wastes, yet fiscal limitations, public opposition to local sites, and numerous other factors have significantly slowed progress. Alfonso Ensenat, subdirector general for industrial environment, says the Spanish Ministry of Industry and Energy has been nego-

68. Clare County Council, "Local Government (Planning and Development) Act, 1963, Notification of a Grant of Permission (Subject to Conditions)," issued to Syntex Ireland Limited on January 21, 1974.
69. Interviews with Matthew Lynch, Tom MacSweeney, and Ken Gunn.
70. "Drive Accused of Dumping Chromium Waste, Environmentalists Urge Toxic Waste Sites," *International Environmental Reporter*, July 9, 1980, pp. 285–86.
71. Barry Collins, "Toxic Dumping Causes Alarm in Cork," *Hibernia*, August 2, 1979.
72. Letter from C. P. (Bert) Gorman, director of environmental affairs for Eli Lilly (USA), dated May 22, 1981. See also Chap. 6. nn. 41 and 42.

tiating with the World Bank for financing of at least one major waste-disposal plant and has plans eventually to build five hazardous-waste facilities in priority regions around the country. According to Ensenat, private Spanish entrepreneurs have expressed an interest in operating such facilities, which he says would be preferable to government or foreign direction. At present, he says, the dumps are most urgently needed near Bilbao, and near Barcelona and Tarragona. Until the government actually gets around to providing these facilities, however, Ensenat readily admits that both the government and industry prefer not to tackle the issue of hazardous-waste disposal. "Our regulations on air pollution are highly advanced," Ensenat says, "but on the disposal of toxic wastes we need more time, a few more years; we cannot ban the dumping of the wastes if we do not have a disposal plant to accept them."[73]

In Ireland the need for toxic-waste dumps in several areas of the country has become acute, both because of the number of chemical-using industries that have located in the country in recent years and because of the high level of public arousal after the Raybestos and other recent controversies. John Gannon, a former head of the IDA and a member of the Planning Appeals Board, says that Ireland "needs some new arrangement for the disposal of toxic and problem wastes. ... [Indeed,] unless improved disposal mechanisms are introduced, Ireland's industrial development will be adversely affected."[74] Irish government officials have outlined a national strategy for providing industries with access to toxic-waste facilities, but the plans have not yet been implemented.[75] One problem is identical to that encountered in the United States: each time the national government has designated a particular area for a toxic-waste dump, opposition at the local level has been overwhelming. In the meantime, a report to the IDA in 1981 warned that the absence of adequate provisions for disposing of toxic wastes could inhibit future industrial expansion in Ireland.[76]

In all of Mexico, there are apparently only two facilities that are adequate for incinerating toxic wastes. One is operated by the government in Monterrey, and another, built by a consortium of private (mostly U.S.) companies to serve a complex of industrial plants, is now operated by the Mexican government near Cuernavaca.[77] In most cases, companies that

73. Interview with Alfonso Ensenat.
74. John Gannon, "Ireland's Industrial Development and Waste Management," in J. Ryan, ed., *Today's and Tomorrow's Wastes* (Dublin: National Board for Science and Technology, 1980).
75. Patrick J. Lynch, "Towards a National Waste Management Strategy," in Ryan, *Today's and Tomorrow's Wastes.*
76. "County Council Encounters Difficulties."
77. Interviews with Camilio Gutierrez and Raul Suarez Munoz Ledo.

need to segregate certain toxic substances from their water effluents appear to be following the same practice that was followed for decades in the United States: the wastes are put in drums to be shipped away from the plant by waste-disposal companies. Most of the U.S. firms whose wastes are disposed of in this manner cannot account for the final destination of the drums. Some seem to be disposed of at municipal and private landfills, but a few officials from U.S. companies candidly admit that it is probable that toxic wastes from Mexico City firms are often dumped into the sewer system. Since much of Mexico City's wastewater is pumped untreated to Hidalgo for use as irrigation water in agricultural areas, some Mexican officials express alarm at the potential long-term implications.[78] There is evidence to support the fear that drums of toxic wastes are being wantonly dumped: many empty drums have turned up in Mexico City's squatter settlements, where they are cut in half and used as water barrels by people without indoor plumbing.[79]

It is difficult to know how much of Mexico's toxic-waste problems are caused by foreign companies. Moreover, most of the companies do not have a choice; Dow Chemical, for one, was denied permission to install an incinerator at its Tlalnepantla plant site.[80] Until the Mexican government decides to do something about this still largely hidden problem, foreign companies are going to have to rely on joint private solutions, as in Cuernavaca, or hope that because toxic wastes are laundered through domestic firms, they will remain insulated when a controversy arises. But, as Dean Woods, director of Cyanamid's Mexican operations, says, "All we need is for one of these empty drums to be stamped with our name on it for this thing to turn into a major scandal."[81]

Destabilizing the investment climate

Assessing the overall investment climate in countries around the world has become an extremely important task for international corporate planners in recent years, in large measure because of the political problems encountered by companies in some countries that have undergone major regime changes or ideological upheavals. But even when a country appears politically stable, it is important to be able to predict specific investment regulations in the long term because multinational companies must project corporate capital-investment and marketing strategies over a time horizon

78. Interviews with José Luis Calderon, subdirector for water contamination, Secretariat of Urban Development and Ecology, Mexico City, January 24, 1984.
79. Interview with Dean Woods, director, Cyanamid de Mexico, Mexico City, July 27, 1982.
80. Interview with Camilio Gutierrez.
81. Interview with Dean Woods.

that equals or exceeds the expected economic life of the production facilities they build. Consequently, country-risk analysis has become increasingly sophisticated, encompassing a widening array of measures ranging from the overall level of political stability to the specific actions to be expected from various regulatory bureaucracies.

Pollution-control regulations, because they affect the long-term cost calculations for companies, obviously contribute to the overall investment climate offered by various countries, and companies have a vested interest in obtaining information on them. Unanticipated changes in pollution-control requirements can significantly alter previous investment equations by forcing large new capital investments at a later date and increasing the operating costs for production facilities. Yet, assessments of present and future environmental regulations, as well as the rigidness of government bargaining over antipollution requirements, apparently have not yet become major components of country-risk analysis.

One reason for the general lack of attention to pollution regulations in many country-risk studies is that the most quantifiable expressions of host-country militancy – actual pollution-control regulations – have not been a major source of consternation for companies. By this measure, the United States has provided a far more inhospitable investment climate. U.S. environmental regulations changed suddenly in the late 1960s and early 1970s and often were phased in through the application of "moving" or interim targets. This caused major disruptions in long-range capital-investment planning in the United States during the 1970s.

Most major multinational companies in key high-pollution industries learned from this experience and now tend to construct new plants around the world with enough attention to antipollution technology and procedures to be able to accommodate expected changes in pollution-control standards for a decade or more. Virtually every major company interviewed for this study sets down international minimum standards on a wide range of pollutants that all their plants around the world must meet regardless of the current regulatory situation in a particular host country. Thus, the problem of moving regulatory targets that was so disruptive to the capital-investment process in the United States has not posed a major obstacle for foreign investors in Ireland, Spain, or Mexico – most multinational companies that have built new plants in recent years have anticipated such changes.

Another reason that this has not posed a significant problem in these countries is that corporate negotiators and industrial-development planners appear to have successfully called attention to the disruptions of the U.S. experience and used this as an argument to convince national government regulators and local officials to build in long (often very long) time lags for full implementation of new pollution standards. Government officials in all three countries made a point of citing their fears of disrupting the investment climate as a major reason for the necessity of going slower than they might otherwise like in implementing stricter antipollution standards. This is obviously a self-serving viewpoint, but it is one that they often have compellingly presented in their respective national regulatory debates.

Even though regulatory instability per se has not been a problem of major proportions for foreign companies, the corporate perception of the long-term hospitality in host countries has sometimes been affected by the political nature of pollution-control questions when they involve multinational firms. This situation is reflected more on a company-by-company and industry-by-industry basis because it is difficult to pinpoint in aggregate country-risk studies. Still, the politicization of pollution issues in some rapidly industrializing countries has caused enough instability to be of concern to certain companies and to prompt them to reevaluate their perception of the long-run investment outlook in those countries. As already noted, the militancy of the Irish public when it comes to industrial pollution has certainly had a dampening effect on the once-glowing view that many major pharmaceutical and light chemical companies held of Ireland.

But two other more or less invisible circumstances have increased uncertainties for foreign investors by making it more difficult to predict the antipollution standards they will be held to over the long run. First, multinationals have found themselves increasingly vulnerable, regardless of the degree to which they are complying with objective regulations, when governments come under public pressure to show that they are doing something about industrial pollution. In addition, although multinationals may not encounter difficulties when pollution regulations are simply not enforced, they often have major problems when government officials are seeking payoffs rather than compliance. In short, when a government needs scapegoats or officials want bribes, it is often multinationals that get squeezed.

The vulnerability of multinationals

As the Raybestos case illustrates, multinational corporations are especially vulnerable to adverse publicity and punitive action in many countries. For this reason, multinational firms frequently must be careful to institute pollution-control measures in countries where regulations and enforcement are not yet strict. In Mexico, for instance, many pollution laws are ineffective because the fines are negligible and enforcement is sporadic.

Although many multinationals involved in heavy industries claim that their pollution-control measures exceed Mexican standards, the Mexican subsidiary of a large German company, Bayer, recently found out how much more vulnerable foreign firms are than domestic ones – strict enforcement can be arbitrarily invoked when it suits a government's needs.

In 1978 the Mexican Health and Welfare Secretariat (SSA) summarily closed a Bayer plant, ostensibly because the plant lacked an operating permit, and issued a statement accusing the company of polluting the air and endangering the health of workers. Spokesmen for the company denied the accusations, saying that the plant was a modern facility, equipped with the latest pollution-control equipment. Indeed, the Bayer plant was permitted to reopen shortly thereafter, once it updated its operating permit.[82]

Apparently, one factor in the SSA's harsh reaction to Bayer's oversight was that the government needed a "pollution scapegoat" to hold up to the public because of pollution problems created by a domestic firm, Chromotos de Mexico, that did business with Bayer.[83] Government officials were at first reluctant to go after Chromotos, which was eventually forced to close, because it was owned by a group of prominent Mexican investors. Ironically, Bayer officials contend that they had been approached about purchasing Chromotos, but that a company team from West Germany had concluded that the company's plant was antiquated and could not be brought up to Bayer's international efficiency and pollution standards.[84]

The Bayer case may be extreme, and Bayer's explanations are difficult to corroborate. Mexican officials generally acknowledge that their major concern was with the pollution created by Chromotos and that any pollution caused by the Bayer plant itself was minor by comparison.[85] At any rate, Bayer's run-in with Mexican officials illustrates that a host government under public pressure to deal with an industrial-pollution problem is likely to clamp down first on foreign companies.

Problems with corruption

During the mid-1970s a great deal of attention was focused on the problem of bribery and extortion in world business. The United States Con-

82. Katherine Hatch, "Mexico Forces Plant Closure," *Business Latin America*, August 30, 1978, pp. 18–20.
83. Ibid. See Katherine Hatch, "Mexican Chromate Factory Closed for Third Time," *World Environment Report*, October 23, 1978, p. 4.
84. Interview with Hans Schurlein, technical director, Bayer de Mexico, Mexico City, July 23, 1982.
85. Miguel Angel Mendoza, "Declarar a Lecheria Zona de Desastre Ecologico, Pide el Doctor A. Baez," *Las Noticia*, October 26, 1978.

gress held hearings, and a number of companies and their executives were prosecuted for paying large bribes in order to do business in foreign countries. Since then, new regulations and disclosure laws set down by the U.S. government have made it much more difficult for U.S.-based companies to operate in countries where business transactions routinely require bribes.[86]

In Ireland bribery is probably not very common, but the research for this study uncovered examples of efforts by local officials or government inspectors to elicit bribes from big U.S. firms in lieu of enforcement of certain environmental regulations. In Spain the problem does not seem severe and generally has centered around particular local situations. Several years ago, Bectin Dickenson, a U.S. pharmaceutical and health-care company, decided to locate in Spain. The company settled on an area just north of Madrid for its manufacturing plant. With the help of local real-estate agents, the company found a developed site with a factory shell already constructed along the N-1 motorway to Burgos. As soon as Bectin Dickenson completed arrangements to purchase the site and factory, problems began. The plant had been built in an area zoned for agricultural use, and the local master plan did not permit industrial uses. Guy Newland, the director of Bectin's Spanish operations, says that it appears the Spanish businessman who built the plant had taken steps to persuade local officials to ignore the zoning designation. When ownership was transferred to a foreign firm, however, zoning authorities in Madrid stepped in to enforce the master plan. Newland says it took more than a year to secure operating permits and special zoning exceptions because the company insisted on doing everything legally despite suggestions that the process could be speeded through informal procedures.[87]

Despite Bectin Dickenson's problems, Newland and Martin Clapes Pons, Bectin's personnel director, both agree that corruption at the local level in Spain has not been a serious impediment for multinational firms. Politics or the opposition of Spanish national companies have often proved more daunting problems for U.S. firms than demands for bribes. Moreover, Newland and Pons, both of whom have served at Bectin facilities in Latin America, say bribery and extortion are much more widespread in many Latin American countries than in Spain.[88]

Thus, in Mexico virtually every foreign corporate official interviewed for this study indicated in the early 1980s that the company was routinely

---

86. See Neil H. Jacoby and Peter Nehemkis, *Bribery and Extortion in World Business* (New York: Macmillan, 1977).
87. Interview with Guy Newland, director, Bectin Dickenson de España, Madrid, July 4, 1980.
88. Ibid.

approached by government inspectors to pay bribes rather than face prolonged pollution-control inspections. Although a few officials privately
admit that in the past they made a practice of providing government
health and pollution inspectors with gifts and monetary rewards, all
emphatically insist that their companies now have a categorical policy
against such practices.

Dean Woods, director of operations for Cyanamid in Mexico, says the
practice of doing favors for government inspectors in Mexico is widespread and that refusal to do so often puts U.S. firms in a difficult situation.
One claim that is made by almost all U.S. firms abroad is that their counterparts from other advanced countries, especially West Germany and
Japan, are not nearly as concerned about pollution or ethics in other countries. Whether this is true is impossible to prove, but it is clear that, all
other things being equal, host countries tend to punish U.S. firms for
transgressions more harshly than they do firms from other advanced
developed nations. Woods says one reason for this is that the most pious
posturing about pollution and ethics tends to come from the United States,
so everyone expects U.S. firms to "practice abroad what is preached in the
United States."[89] As a result, Japanese and West German firms may be
more free to go along with existing customs of favors and bribes than U.S.
firms.

But some U.S. companies have found that refusing to pay government
inspectors the money they expect is not a one-time ordeal, and it frequently leads to a long-term test of wills between company officials and
the inspector. Camilio Gutierrez, Dow's plant manager in Tlalnepantla,
says that government inspectors from several agencies used to show up
frequently at Dow to conduct inspections. Sometimes, he says, "it is a pain
in the neck to have these guys around, because they don't really want to
do the inspection, they want us to pay them to go away." Gutierrez says
that one inspector came to Dow's plant daily for a prolonged period, each
time saying that the necessary inspections would be long and arduous for
the company to endure and suggesting that they agree on a settlement that
day. Each time, Dow officials insisted that the inspector should begin the
inspection. Gutierrez says the inspector finally stopped coming, but not
before making things as difficult as possible for Dow.[90]

In any case, the practice by government officials of satisfying pollution
standards by eliciting payments under the table instead of monitoring
plant emissions and effluents can create a number of problems for foreign
investors, particularly those from the United States. It increases the long-

89. Interview with Dean Woods.
90. Interview with Camilio Gutierrez.

term uncertainty already associated with pollution control, since it is extremely difficult to judge what will constitute compliance with environmental regulations at any given time. Companies that do not go along with the norms of corruption may find themselves at a competitive disadvantage in relation to domestic firms or foreign firms that do go along. Moreover, failure to pay up may result in petty harassment or enforcement of unreasonable pollution-control standards by government inspectors. All of these potential problems only make it more difficult for companies to predict with assurance what they will have to do to satisfy their pollution-control obligations in rapidly industrializing countries.

Conclusions

The politicization of pollution problems in rapidly industrializing countries has greatly increased the level of uncertainty in the relationship between host-country governments and multinational corporations. In contrast to the situation in the United States, the most destabilizing effects have not been those of regulatory targets that constantly move as a result of the phasing in of new pollution-control standards. The major problems in industrializing nations for multinational companies seeking to predict their pollution-control expenditures and obligations over the long term have generally arisen from the erratic and haphazard process by which pollution standards are imposed and enforced.

Concern about industrial pollution varies greatly in location and time in the countries examined. A foreign company may receive the blessing of a local government to emit certain wastes from its plant, only to face a strong public backlash at a later date. Or partisan politics may stir so much sentiment against foreign companies that overly stringent pollution restrictions are assigned without regard to technical merit. Past experiences with industrial pollution, hearsay about industrial-pollution disasters in other countries, or selfish motivations of a small minority may cause public groups to delay the siting for so long that a company cancels or moves its plant.

National pollution regulations, and assigned pollution standards for specific factories, are generally not consistently enforced, but enforcement can be fast and furious when a government sees the political necessity or opportunity. Antipollution requirements are often issued even when governments (and sometimes companies, too) do not have enough technical personnel and equipment to monitor them. These requirements may be predicated upon a government promise to provide certain infrastructural amenities for incoming industries – sewers, pipelines, water supply, waste-disposal facilities, and so forth – even though these promises may not be fulfilled by the time new industrial plants are on line. Multinational firms, in particular, may be caught between a rock and a hard place when the goal of government officials is not ultimately to reduce the level of industrial pollution, but rather to gain political mileage from tough actions against foreign companies or to extort money and favors in return for a promise of nonintervention.

The effect of all these circumstances has been to move the determination of how much pollution a particular industrial facility actually contributes to the local environment away from the formal legal arena of the legislative/bargaining process. Pollution-control requirements are rarely a matter of government regulators' determining optimal standards and corporate technicians' aiming to meet them. Governments may have model pollution standards and may bargain effectively with individual companies, but in reality corporations aware of that enforcement may still take advantage of them.

But the opportunity to pollute without regard to the legal situation is a mixed blessing for a large multinational corporation. Because public opinion about industrial pollution is volatile and the regulatory levers for enforcement already exist, legal action against polluters can come with little warning when governments believe it is expedient. Generally, it is the multinational polluters that bear the wrath of the public and the regulators first and hardest. The paradox for multinational corporations, especially those from the United States, is that not only stricter regulations but also more consistent and objective enforcement procedures may better serve their long-term interest in a stable, predictable regulatory situation than does the current situation of loose enforcement with erratic, politically motivated crackdowns.

8

Theoretical implications and policy recommendations

The costs and logistics of complying with environmental regulations are not a decisive factor in most industrial decisions about desirable plant locations or in the international competitive picture of most major industries. Industrial flight from regulations has not become a significant enough phenomenon to diminish the comparative advantage of the advanced industrial powers. There is no evidence that pollution havens are enhancing their comparative advantage in industrial production by luring whole industries away from the United States and other countries with strict environmental standards. Nor is there any reason to believe that the major trend in international industrial comparative advantage – the gradual shift of many heavy industries such as steel from the most industrialized to rapidly industrializing countries – is being significantly heightened by stringent environmental regulations in the most advanced countries.

Such conclusions do not necessarily prove that environmental factors never influence international industrial-siting decisions or the evolution of comparative advantage in certain industries. They do indicate that the differentials in the costs of complying with environmental regulations and in the levels of environmental concern in industrialized and industrializing countries have not been strong enough to offset larger political and economic forces shaping aggregate international comparative advantage. An interesting and important question is whether in "normal" times, if political and economic turmoil and barriers to trade were lessened, pollution-control expenses and other environmental factors would become more important in the choices made by countries about industrial specialization and the choices made by corporations about location. Would this encourage more U.S. companies to export on a selective basis pollution-intensive factors to less industrialized countries? In other words, it is possible that if the world were to move closer to the conditions postulated by the Heckscher-Ohlin model, in which other circumstances were more or less equal, environmental factor endowments would prove more decisive in the international evolution of comparative advantage.

231

For the present, there appears to be a relatively small number of U.S. industries whose international location patterns have been significantly affected by environmental regulations and concern in the United States. In some of these exceptional cases of conformance to the industrial-flight hypothesis, ongoing trends – such as backward integration for mineral-processing industries and worldwide sourcing of chemical intermediates – appear to have been speeded up by environmental factors. In such cases, the evolution of comparative advantage from industrialized to industrializing nations had already begun for reasons other than environmental ones, but the onset in the 1970s of stringent environmental regulations accelerated the trends. In a few cases, though, industries appear to have consciously adopted a pattern of flight directly in response to environmental regulations, as an alternative to modernizing technology, finding substitute products, or installing expensive new pollution controls. Inevitably, though, these industries are simultaneously experiencing static or reduced demand as a result of product obsolescence or hazards. They therefore find few incentives to upgrade production facilities and product quality. It is unlikely that comparative advantage in such industries will be particularly meaningful as major industries for industrializing nations in the future.

Still, even if not significantly boosted by environmental factors, the spread around the globe of American industry and technology continues in the 1980s. Particularly significant is the movement of U.S. industry into a small group of rapidly industrializing, free-enterprise-oriented countries; Ireland and Spain are two of the most advanced and highly developed of these countries, and, because of its location, Mexico is one of the most strategic. In addition, a smaller group of rapid industrializers, especially Romania and other Eastern European socialist countries, have relied heavily upon technology imports and agreements for the construction of turnkey industrial plants to build their industrial capacity in certain industries. Evidence presented in this study demonstrates that all these countries did attempt to increase their industrial comparative advantage by acting in accordance with the pollution-haven hypothesis during the mid- and late 1970s. But, as Chapters 5 and 6 showed, their success was mixed and attitudes about pollution have evolved in recent years.

In each of the countries studied, the government has begun to pay considerably more attention to environmental problems associated with industrial development. Public concern about the environment, although muffled in Romania, has been vehemently expressed in Ireland and Spain, both because pollution is increasing and because changing economic and political circumstances make people more willing to question the wisdom of public officials. In Mexico pollution is rapidly emerging as an important public issue, although it is still unclear whether this will provide a means of mobilizing support for government policies or for opposition political interests. Quite often American firms operating in these changing contexts have taken elaborate measures to comply with and even exceed evolving environmental regulations. In most cases these companies are not the sources of the country's worst domestic pollution problems and, almost without exception, are better equipped to minimize pollution and other environmental disruptions than are domestic firms in the same industry.

Yet serious environmental problems remain in Ireland, Spain, and Mexico, and in a few instances American firms are making substantial contributions. Of even greater significance, the political situation in all three countries makes it highly unlikely that U.S. companies will be judged solely on the basis of their relative contributions to pollution. The expectations of government officials and the local public will invariably be much higher for foreign, especially American, companies than for domestic firms. This is a reality that cannot be overlooked.

In Romania multinational corporations have not been affected by the whims of public opinion and by conflicts with local governments. In the first place, the political system is much more autocratic and centralized than in Mexico, Spain, and Ireland. In the second place, foreign companies have merely been government contractors and sellers of technology. It is clear that Romania's efforts to establish itself as a major exporter of certain chemicals – benzidine-based dyes, polyvinyl chloride, and other dangerous substances – may be accompanied by serious environmental side effects and public-health dangers. There are strong indications that, even when the Romanian government is using modern Western productive technologies, environmental and workplace safeguards are ignored, and workers and the Romanian public are not adequately informed about the dangers they may face.

Still, there is no evidence that the Romanian public has protested the government's tacit endorsement of pollution-intensive industrial development. In Romania, in contrast to the other three countries, public opinion has not limited the government's efforts to use its environmental assimilative capacity to enhance its comparative advantage in international trade. What has reduced Romania's ability to reap the benefits of trade in some of these products has been the waning of detente and the restrictive nature of product standards in many Western nations.

In short, the impact on international comparative advantage of differential national environmental factor endowments (embodied in pollution regulations, levels of environmental quality, and attitudes about industrial pollution) has been considerably more complex and subtle than was predicted by extending the Hechscher-Ohlin model of relative factor endowments.

Pollution and theories of comparative advantage

Shortly before his death in 1979, Bertil Ohlin wrote a brief essay on insufficiencies in theories of international economic relations. He concluded that "highly simplified models, which may be useful as pedagogic aids, can seldom reflect reality unless, as a second stage, modifications are made in unrealistic assumptions." Ohlin noted in particular that economists had not developed enough tools to explain international factor movements; to do so they needed to focus on problems that "may not lend themselves to simple, rigid, and precise models." Included in his list were the international effects of internal national policies, more emphasis on location theory, the influence of nonfactor payments (internal tax subsidies, internal protection, and the like), the role of risk in international production and location decisions, and the factors that are important to multinational corporations themselves as they actually make investment decisions.[1]

This study underlines Ohlin's point. It has not been particularly useful to stretch the simple factor-proportions model to hold other factors equal and to examine international comparative advantage in light of theoretical assessments of relative environmental factor endowments. International economists first predicted the theoretical effects that the growing importance of pollution would have on international trade and investment patterns, and eventually these predictions were translated into policy analyses at the national and international levels. The effects have not materialized.

At the macrotheoretical level, this study has found that there is not enough evidence to confirm the expectation that the relative abundance of environmental factor endowments among nations would become a significant determinant of international comparative advantage in so-called pollution-intensive industrial sectors. Therefore, differences in the stringency of environmental regulations, the abundance of natural environmental assimilative capacity, or social attitudes toward pollution will probably not correlate clearly with the comparative advantage or disadvantage that different countries hold in pollution-intensive industries.

The theoretical framework for this study has sought to overcome the rigid limitations of simple models by explaining the international trends that determine comparative advantage in the real world. These explana-

1. Bertil Ohlin, "Some Insufficiencies in the Theories of International Economic Relations," *Essays in International Finance*, no. 134 (Princeton, N.J.: Princeton University, Department of Economics, September 1979).

tions account for patterns of international trade and investment (product cycle, foreign direct investment, and industrial location). They also help to account for the efforts of industrializing countries to manipulate and capitalize on these patterns (industrial-development planning and bargaining between host countries and multinational corporations). We have examined the impact of new pollution regulations in the United States in light of other factors that influence the product cycle, foreign direct investments, and industrial location decisions. We have also evaluated the role of pollution factors in the industrial policies pursued by industrializing countries and in the relationship between these countries and multinational corporations. This study has thereby underlined some of the complex political and economic circumstances that now complicate the theoretical notion of comparative advantage. In essence, examination of the less quantifiable factors described by Ohlin helps explain why real-world political and economic factors have frustrated expectations based upon the simple factor-proportions account.

Nevertheless, this study also has positive theoretical utility, because the particulars concerning environmental factors shed some light on current thinking about international trade and location, as well as industrial development and multinational corporations.

International trade and location

The studies of different pollution-intensive industries emphasize the increasing role of external factors in disrupting or speeding up the product cycle. Some products may be produced overseas sooner than the natural dynamics of the product cycle would lead one to expect. Others may wither before making it through all the stages as a result of such externalities as pollution-control regulations, product standards in major consumer countries, or replacement by safer, less polluting products.

Pollution regulations – both because of their costs and because of difficulties in meeting technological requirements – seem to have compressed the sequence of international dispersion for some chemical intermediates that U.S. companies might have preferred to continue producing in the United States. U.S. and worldwide consumption of these products has remained strong, but the environmental damage caused by their production has erased the advantages of producing them in the United States. On the other hand, it appears that the U.S. markets for products such as asbestos and benzidine dyes are disappearing almost as fast as production facilities because of regulations to control environmental hazards caused not only by production but also by consumption of the final product. In these cases, the ability of foreign producers to take advantage of the workings of the product cycle and to grab increasing shares of the U.S. market by imitating and undercutting U.S. producers is obviously diminished. Before the product cycle has run its natural course, such products may have been replaced by safer, cleaner, higher-technology products that will start the cycle over.

The ability of external factors to speed up or short-circuit the product cycle raises the possibility that pollution regulations could in some instances induce U.S. firms to initiate production of newly developed products at overseas facilities, skipping the home-country production phase entirely, if they suspected that production in the United States would involve difficulties that could be avoided at overseas production locations. This, in effect, is what some critics say several U.S. pharmaceutical companies are doing in Ireland: producing for U.S. markets high-technology, research-intensive, high-value drugs that they have been reluctant to begin producing in the United States, where regulatory requirements are more stringent.

Some of the examples cited in this study also add another dimension to the "appropriability" explanation of foreign-direct-investment patterns, summarized in Chapter 1. Industries are more likely to be dominated by multinational firms when the technology is complex and difficult to imitate. Likewise, companies using modern technologies in which pollution control is also a technological challenge are more apt to pursue a strategy of foreign direct investment to supply home and foreign markets. By contrast, in industries where pollution control is difficult because of the low technology used in production or the pervasiveness of the problem, companies are more likely to allow firms in foreign countries to manufacture the products; the U.S. firms simply purchase the products for shipment back to the United States.

This study underlines the very large role that governments now play in influencing the locations of many industries through the provision of infrastructure and amenities. Pollution-intensive industries need more governmental services and assistance – not only direct services such as sewer lines, but also guaranteed access to offsite dumping facilities. Because proper waste-disposal facilities, particularly for industries using toxic substances, are often economical only on a large scale, governments must construct or facilitate centralized solutions. The role of government services in industrial location is likely to become even more vital when an industrializing country reaches a point where its natural environmental assimilative capacity diminishes, or when public concern about the haphazard disposal of industrial waste grows.

Location theorists have not yet paid enough attention to the increased role that the public and nongovernmental organizations play in the industrial-location process in many countries. Finding a hospitable country and region, and most of all a specific site, is no longer a matter between companies and governments only. In many countries the public has become involved in ways that inject more uncertainty and delays, and can subject the process to the whims of partisan politics. Concern about pollution, in particular, has rallied the public to scrutinize the industrial-development plans of their governments and to object to many proposed industries or potential locations. While difficult to quantify, the phenomenon of social blockage, as well as more constructive public oversight, has significantly altered the industrial-location process in many countries. It has reduced not only the range of available sites but the degree to which industrial locations can be selected by least-cost, market-oriented, or other empirical formulas.

Industrial development and multinational corporations

The world has not been divided into core countries that export industrial polluters and peripheral countries that are forced to accept these rejected industries, as some observers apparently had anticipated in the 1970s. Nevertheless, environmental factors have had an increasing effect on the industrial strategies pursued by different countries and have become a more central factor in the negotiations and ongoing relationships between host countries and multinational corporations.

Some rapidly industrializing countries did attempt to offer pollution-haven status as a negative incentive to attract multinational corporations during the 1970s. That strategy generally failed to stimulate new investment: the savings realized from the absence of pollution controls are not substantial enough to alter fundamentally the locational preferences of multinational firms. At a more general level, the failure also shows that even though governments exert great influence in creating a hospitable investment climate, the most important contributions must be positive – that is, governments must provide services, trained labor pools, political and economic stability, and the like.

Negative incentives – forced low wages, permission to pollute, short-term tax exemptions – may be valuable to firms that do not need to make large capital investments and can therefore sell out or close down on short notice (for example, producers of asbestos textiles). But the more capital intensive an industry, the greater is its need to be assured of long-term positive support from host-country governments. Without that support, firms are reluctant to consider large investments in the form of immobile capital stock. This is a major reason why most large multinational chemical companies have not generally found permission to pollute a compelling location incentive by itself.

Several factors complicate the task of industrial-development planners who must select industries that will prove to be "winners" in international trade. It is difficult to predict the potential environmental problems associated with different industries, and pollution hazards are often discovered long after a country has accepted an industry. Industries that seem quite promising for rapidly industrializing countries can turn out to be failures because international demand is dampened by external factors associated with environmental hazards. Industrial-development planners may assume that an industry is relatively nonpolluting only to find out later that serious invisible environmental hazards are associated with the industry.

Many analysts have identified the bargaining process as the focal point of the relationship between host countries and multinational corporations. A close look at that relationship from the perspective of pollution control indicates that the bargaining process may not be nearly as important in determining the actual terms of business as they sometimes suggest. Negotiations take place at many different levels, not just between national government officials and companies; and officials of local and national government in the host country are often at odds with each other and sometimes make different promises to multinational companies. Added to this is the growing role of nongovernmental actors in rejecting or insisting on changes in agreements already made between government officials and companies.

The increased divergence of interest between levels of government and the importance of nongovernmental participants obviously are more influential in pollution control, where the results of ineffective government bargaining may be highly visible and may directly affect the public, than less visible aspects of corporate bargaining such as control of profit repatriation. Still, these factors emphasize that the relationship between host countries and foreign companies is more free-wheeling, and subject to greater fluctuation, than can be explained by the investment cycle of the company and the learning curve of national officials. Moreover, because the host countries' governments cannot closely monitor multinational corporations and enforce pollution regulations, the official bargain that is struck between country and company does not always determine the amount of pollution a firm contributes. This is probably true in other areas of the relationship between the host country and the multinational companies; the formal bargaining outcomes by themselves may not reflect the actual balance of the relationship.

Reconciling pollution and industrial policies

At the level of practical policy, this study has shown considerable room for improvement in the ways that government and private companies have responded to greatly increased concern about industrial pollution throughout the world. Consequently, this final section outlines some recommendations for the U.S. government and governments of rapidly industrializing countries, as well as for multinational corporations that produce and trade in these countries. Ultimately, each of these actors can take specific steps to reduce the various problems associated with industrial pollution identified in this study. These steps could minimize not only environmental hazards but political controversies and economic disruptions as well.

The United States government

On the whole, the argument that U.S. environmental regulations should be relaxed because they are helping to drain the country's industrial base cannot be substantiated. It is not true that a higher percentage of overall productive capacity has been shipped abroad as a result of environmental regulations, and neither Congress nor the executive branch can legitimately use that argument to support weakening the environmental regulations affecting American-based industries. Similarly, numerous debates about the need for preempting public debates and the prerogatives of local governments in certain types of industrial-siting decisions should not be influenced by the argument that social blockage has sent more American industries scurrying abroad to search for industrial sites.

For the United States, across-the-board policy approaches to pollution-related industrial relocations – either restrictions on relocations or sweeping regulatory relief – are unnecessary, unwise, and unfeasible. It is necessary, on the other hand, to ensure that environmental regulations do not work at cross-purposes with government policies designed to bring about long-term technological progress and structural change in certain industries. It is important that environmental policies be viewed much more integrally, as part of the whole bundle of governmental policies that seek to enhance and reward the growth industries of the future and to cushion the hardships wrought when old industrial sectors begin to decline.

U.S. policymakers should be *more* concerned if environmental regulations drive otherwise healthy industries abroad or increase foreign dependence within essential sectors of the industrial economy – neither of which appears to be occurring. But rolling back environmental regulations where they speed up the decline of obsolescent industries may be counterproductive for the long-term goal of reindustrialization.

Rapidly industrializing countries

Although no atrocious examples of negligence by American companies have been chronicled in this study – deaths in factories from chemical poisonings or local villages overwhelmed by toxic fumes, for example – U.S. firms have clearly been implicated in such events in other parts of the world. One recent report described, for example, how subsidiaries of American firms were creating serious problems in several countries: a Pennwalt affiliate in Nicaragua has been discharging mercury into a lake; in a Johns Manville affiliate in India, workers observe no precautions around asbestos fibers; a Kaiser cement operation in Indonesia is grossly polluting its surrounding area; in a battery factory operated by Union Carbide in Indonesia, almost half of the workers have liver damage from mercury exposure.

The most important point of the research presented here, however, is that industrializing countries do not have to tolerate such negligence by foreign firms. There are companies – whether American, German, or Japanese – that will operate modern facilities with far more concern for the workers' safety and the surrounding environment. A government that outlines frankly and forthrightly its minimum conditions for foreign investors will find that fewer and fewer multinational firms will withdraw from negotiations for this reason alone.

A tough bargain on pollution. Of course, not every country can be as selective in screening foreign-capital, export-oriented industry as Ireland has been. Any country that includes bulk chemical production, mineral processing and smelting, and such products as automobile batteries and pesticides in its plans to integrate into worldwide production networks is obviously going to have to accept more pollution and take more health risks for its population than a country that produces athletic shoes, computer parts, or even fine chemicals. But there is no reason why, from the outset, industrializing countries should not strike a very tough posture with foreign firms about pollution controls and workplace standards, requiring incoming companies to match standards and technologies they meet elsewhere.

All of the research presented here indicates that rapidly industrializing countries have a great deal of leeway to control industrial pollution and hazards without inhibiting the flows of foreign direct investment. Only a very small number of multinational firms in select industries – none of which are likely to contribute substantially to a nation's overall development – appear to be fleeing the advanced nations in search of pollution havens. For the vast majority of multinational industries, environmental-control costs are not a large enough part of overall capital investment to override the key elements that affect a decision about where a firm will locate: labor costs, tax incentives, market factors, political stability, and availability of transportation and infrastructure.

Including pollution-control technologies on the list of import-tax exemptions or reductions and in the overall package of grants and incentives can minimize the added costs of complying with regulations and requirements. Thus, at little or no direct cost to its treasury and no sacrifice in the amount of investment by multinational firms, a rapidly industrializing country could ensure that most incoming industries take essentially the same precautionary measures to safeguard the environment and public health as they do in their home countries.

This is an important finding, since many international economists and international organizations concerned with industrial development continue to accept the conventional view that environmental controls on industry must be carefully geared to coincide with the level of development and affluence in the country. There is no evidence that a country can get ahead in the international investment game by keeping its environmental regulations at a minimum; nor is there any evidence that an industrializing country intent on attracting multinational corporations will lose any business by maintaining environmental codes that require incoming companies to make adaptations similar to those they have been required to make back home.

The pitfalls of a dustbin strategy. Indeed, there is strong evidence that consciously maintaining low environmental restrictions in the hope of attracting more foreign industry is an extremely risky strategy. One problem is that the few industries that are likely to find such a strategy attractive are involved in producing goods that are hazardous not only to manufacture but to use. Thus, product- and consumer-safety standards or public concern in developing countries is likely sooner or later to cut off the key markets for the product. This certainly has been the case in Romania, where exports to the United States of benzidine dyes and polyvinyl chloride have been disrupted by U.S. standards, which apply to imports as well as home-produced goods.

In addition to the problem of trade barriers, there is a very real danger that a country, if not careful, will end up taking on declining or stagnant industries that are trying to perpetuate themselves through international flight or resisting the technological advancements that will be necessary in the long term. Production of asbestos products, for example, may seem an attractive export industry at present, because demand in the advanced countries is not yet falling off sharply even though producers in the United States and Europe are facing intense regulatory pressures and court battles. But the attraction may be relatively temporary, because the use of asbestos is likely to decline rapidly as safer substitutes are commercialized.

But the research here also indicates that industrializing countries do more than assess the obvious forms of pollutions: they must consider carefully the unseen or unanticipated hazards of certain industries. To Irish officials in the early 1970s, the production of asbestos brake pads seemed a fairly innocuous industry. Had they more carefully evaluated the literature on the perils of asbestos, they might have exercised a great deal more caution when they accepted the Raybestos Manhattan proposal for the plant at Ovens.

There is another danger for a government using loose environmental constraints as an enticement for foreign industry: the strategy risks a strong public reaction against the government and foreign enterprise. As many examples presented in Chapter 7 demonstrate, pollution has frequently become a volatile issue at the local level, among people who are far less affluent than the stereotypical environmentalist in the advanced countries. For economic or political reasons, or because they distrust foreigners, people have frequently taken matters into their own hands when they think their government is colluding with foreign firms to despoil their environment. Thus, a strategy of consciously attracting pollution-creating industries and permitting them to pollute at will may not be tenable in the long term anyway.

Minimizing blockage. Although industrializing nations have a great deal of leeway to ensure that most incoming multinational corporations do not cause serious environmental problems, they must be careful to devote attention to a number of possible problems. First, there is such a thing as overreaction. The danger is not so much that regulations will be too stringent, since countries are unlikely to go beyond the regulatory restrictions already prevailing in the advanced countries. Rather, the problem is that they may create an unstable, irrational, or slow-moving investment climate for international corporations. For example, allowing companies to build factories under lax pollution-control terms, only to crack down once the major portion of the capital investment has been committed, may be far more deleterious for a country trying to attract long-term capital than laying out elaborate controls from the outset. Indeed, many companies, anticipating a plant life of twenty-five to forty years, are leery of any regime that promises not to enforce significant pollution-control regulations over the long term.

Even more problematic, though, is the rise in the incidence of social blockage in countries all over the world. New plants proposed by foreign corporations have been opposed on environmental grounds in Ireland, Spain, and many other rapidly industrializing countries. In some cases, the issues have been more politically than environmentally motivated; in others, there were strong reasons to suspect the project would cause severe environmental disruptions. But in many instances the opposition has rallied support against a new plant proposal by exaggerating potential impacts and playing upon the fears of uninformed local people.

The important point is that in many rapidly industrializing countries, not least Ireland and Spain, the problem of social blockage is exacerbated when the general public and responsible groups concerned with improving industrial-development proposals cannot obtain complete information. By making it hard for these groups to offer constructive criticisms, the system often leaves the way open for extreme antiindustrial opponents to create widespread fears and mobilize opposition. Thus, the opening of channels for responsible groups to participate in industrial siting, in addition to improving the quality of development, may help a great deal to reduce extreme social blockage by groups pursuing political or selfish goals.

Differential treatment for foreign firms? One question often raised in policy debates in rapidly industrializing countries is whether foreign and domestic companies should be treated differently. In many industries, multinational companies setting up facilities around the globe model the plants after those they have built in their home countries. Especially in industries where the new plant will be part of an integrated world system of production, the biggest difference between a new plant built in a rapidly industrializing country and the one in the home country tends to be scope of production and size. Plants operated by American firms in Spain and Ireland tend to be more highly specialized and much smaller than their counterparts in the United States. But technologically they are at least as advanced as the older plants back home.

The problems arise in trying to apply the same stringent standards to fledgling domestic industries without multinational technological, technical, and capital resources. Tailoring environmental regulations to the country's level of development seems more logical in the case of domestic firms than of foreign companies. Applying stringent pollution-control regulations to domestic firms might simply give an edge to foreign firms more capable of complying. Yet it is difficult for a number of reasons to promulgate separate regulatory codes for foreign and domestic industries. One problem lies in the fact that unequal treatment goes against the rules of GATT and many other international treaties and precedents. Particularly since developing countries frequently complain that multinational firms resist being treated under the same rules that apply to domestic firms, it would be difficult to justify dual sets of pollution-control regulations.

However, as the case studies in Chapter 6 indicate, regulations vary quite a bit in many rapidly industrializing countries, because incoming firms and local governments often bargain about particular antipollution measures during the process of obtaining local land-use permits. A national government may concentrate on setting a floor for health, safety, and esthetic concerns by means of national standards. This is essentially the approach of the Irish and Spanish governments, although EEC membership may alter it. Individual planning permissions can require greater or lesser safeguards, as the situation warrants. Obviously, the process at the local level is so easily influenced by politics that a foreign firm's proposal almost always creates more opposition than the proposal of a domestic firm with less technological know-how and capital-raising ability.

The problem of old industries. Old industries, whether multinational or domestic, are the biggest industrial sources of environmental problems. At the same time, they are the least capable of coping with their pollution, as has been shown in the United States as well as in industrializing nations. Regulatory systems in most countries tend to be much tougher on new industries than on old ones. Unless rapidly industrializing countries muster the will to close old, polluting plants – which is unlikely in times of high unemployment – they are going to have to live with some of the mistakes of the past. Yet, as the contrast between the two Pfizer operations in Ireland illustrates, local circumstances and the economics of different types of factories do give governments more leverage to require improvements in some multinational operations than in others.

In applying different standards to new and old industries, rapidly industrializing countries must be careful not to give foreign companies more incentive to buy or expand existing plants than to build new ones, a problem that has quite often arisen in the United States. This appears to have been a factor in Eli Lilly's decision to purchase an existing plant owned by a Spanish company instead of constructing its proposed plant in Córdoba, as described in Chapter 6.

Multinational corporations

Firms in pollution-intensive industrial sectors in the United States have long complained that strict environmental laws and elaborate technical requirements are overly costly and often lead to long delays in the construction of new industrial facilities. But the most trenchant criticism of U.S. regulations is that they disrupt long-term investment planning by increasing uncertainty and requiring new investments for pollution control at the wrong time in the plant-investment cycle.

Concern about the damage that industry may cause to the environment has greatly increased the difficulty of long-term planning in many other countries as well. This is true even in countries in which the fiscal and technical burdens of the actual regulatory requirements may seem quite minor in comparison with those in the United States. In fact, as some of the case studies in Ireland, Spain, and Mexico have demonstrated, multinational firms operating on foreign soil generally are much more threatened by the politics of pollution than by the technical measurements taken by regulatory inspectors. In rapidly industrializing countries, the question of whether a foreign company is causing undue pollution is rarely decided in the halls of regulatory agencies or in courtrooms. For foreign firms, the most significant threat is often whether the public, government officials, and politically motivated groups *perceive* that the firm is causing pollution and, more important, whether there is some political advantage to be derived from making an issue of the firm's pollution.

This fact has two major implications for multinational corporations. First of all, it is difficult to know with any assurance what the real pollution-control standards for an industrial plant will be over the long term. Indeed, because regulations are sporadically enforced and pollution is a highly charged political issue, the standards to which a firm is held may vary greatly from year to year. This means that it is prudent for multinational corporations to overestimate standards when they construct new factories overseas. It is much easier to fit a new industrial plant with pollution-control technology beyond what is necessary to meet assigned standards than to risk having to retrofit as regulations change rapidly or to face the political fallout if the public decides that the firm is causing pollution.

The second consequence is more difficult for firms to deal with. Public awareness of industrial pollution has grown quickly in all rapidly industrializing countries in recent years. Most of the countries that have attracted investors from the United States have also been successful in attracting investors from other nations. They have also stimulated an expansion of domestic industrial firms, which generally contribute more than foreign firms to increasing industrial pollution. In Ireland, Spain, and Mexico, however, foreign investors (especially those from the United States) have always been the first to be scrutinized when industrial pollution becomes an important consideration for the public and for government officials. Even firms that are meeting all reasonable environmental standards are therefore not always secure from the wrath of an aroused public. They are also subject to the whims of governmental regulators under political pressure to demonstrate they are doing something about industrial pollution.

Ford Motor Company's experience in Spain illustrates what can happen when discussions between a company and local officials must be carried out in a charged political atmosphere, amid intense intergovernmental conflict, and in overlapping jurisdictions. The problems may arise long after a country and a company have reached a formal agreement, and even after negotiations at the local level have supposedly resulted in agreements on pollution standards and antipollution measures. One reason is that pollution-control issues are always subject to renegotiation as circumstances change. Another reason is that, whereas standards must be outlined long before a plant is built, final permits and certifications cannot be issued until the plant is ready to operate. Meanwhile, the atmosphere at the local level may have changed radically, and local governments may have to enforce different standards from those they originally outlined. Often, as in the Ford case, renegotiations about pollution controls may deal only peripherally with the actual quality of the wastewater to be discharged or the question of what effect it will have on the receiving waters.

Government officials and the public often want the foreign firm to do more than reduce its pollution; they want it to assist with the overall antipollution efforts needed in a particular area. In Spain, local officials, as well as industrial and agricultural interests, wanted Ford to construct a wastewater canal that would help them get rid of the pollution that local municipalities, small chemical companies, and farmers were creating.

For multinational companies, the challenge, then, is not only to over-comply with regulations, but to make some positive contribution to the country's efforts to reduce industrial pollution. Sometimes, as in the Ford case, the demands are unreasonable and difficult to meet without large expenditures. But foreign companies can take, at little additional cost, many steps that will help to improve their position when pollution becomes highly politicized in rapidly industrializing countries.

For example, companies can help local officials and responsible local groups to obtain information about pollution and industrial pollution-control measures. The inability to obtain information that is readily available in the United States has often increased suspicion of foreign companies and given groups with ideologically motivated biases against industrialization or foreign businesses an opportunity to exaggerate the dangers of industrial pollution. Companies also should give more consideration to constructing waste-treatment facilities jointly with local governments or with other private firms. In these and other ways multinational corporations can ensure that officials of the host country continue to focus on minimizing pollution and resist the temptation to confront foreign firms for political gain or to use them as convenient scapegoats.

Index